CO-ORDINATION IN CONTEXT

For my son, Konstantin

Co-ordination in Context

Institutional choices to promote exports

G.P.E. WALZENBACH
Nuffield College, Oxford

Routledge
Taylor & Francis Group

LONDON AND NEW YORK

First published 1998 by Ashgate Publishing

Reissued 2018 by Routledge
2 Park Square, Milton Park, Abingdon, Oxon OX14 4RN
711 Third Avenue, New York, NY 10017, USA

Routledge is an imprint of the Taylor & Francis Group, an informa business

A Library of Congress record exists under LC control number: 97077555

ISBN 13: 978-1-138-61113-9 (hbk)
ISBN 13: 978-1-138-61115-3 (pbk)
ISBN 13: 978-0-429-46363-1 (ebk)

Contents

List of Figures

List of Tables

Acknowledgements

In the course of working on this book I have benefited from the advice and comments of many individuals. My thanks go to Alan Cafruny, Helge Hveem, Christian Joerges, Giandomenico Majone, Patrick Messerlin, Roger Morgan, Fabrizio Onida, Volker Rittberger, Susan Strange and Daniel Verdier. Among the many representatives of official insurance agencies, financial institutions, interest groups and international organisations, who helped me to understand the intricacies of export promotion policies, I must single out Peter Kraneveldt, Bernd Meyer, Harald Müller, and Akira Yamamoto. I am also indebted to Laurence Cole, Sabine Hofmann, Tom Lawton and Alistair McMillan for stimulating discussions, editorial assistance and for improvements in the readability of the book. Finally I have to record my appreciation of the financial support given by the German Academic Exchange Service (DAAD) and the European University Institute in Florence.

Abbreviations

AEG	Allgemeine Elektricitäts-Gesellschaft
AKA	Ausfuhrkredit-Gesellschaft
ATP	Aid and Trade Provision
BDB	Bundesverband Deutscher Banken
BDGA	Bundesverband des Deutschen Groß- und Außenhandels
BDI	Bund der Deutschen Industrie
BFCE	Banque Française du Commerce Extérieur
BIS	Bank for International Settlements
BNP	Banque Nationale de Paris
BOTB	British Overseas Trade Board
Casa	Construcciones Aeronauticas
CBI	Confederation of British Industry
CCCE	Caisse Centrale de Coopération Economique
CFCE	Centre Français du Commerce Exterieur
CFSP	Common Foreign and Security Policy
CGCE	Commission des Garanties et du Crédit au Commerce Extérieur
CIRR	commercial interest reference rate
CIS	Community of Independent States
COCOM	Co-ordinating Committee for Multilateral Export Controls
COFACE	Compagnie Française du Commerce Extérieur
COREPER	Committee of Permanent Representatives
DAC	Development Assistance Committee
Dasa	Daimler-Benz Aerospace
DESO	Defence Service Organisation
DG	Directorate General
DIHT	Deutscher Industrie- und Handelstag
DIW	Deutsches Institut für Wirtschaftsforschung
DREE	Direction des Crédit au Commerce Extérieur
DRS	differentiated rate system

DTI	Department of Trade and Industry
EBRD	European Bank for Reconstruction and Development
EC	European Community
ECA	Export Credit Agency
ECE	Economic Commission for Europe
ECG	High Level Group for Export Credits and Export Credit Guarantees
ECGD	Export Credits Guarantee Department
ECU	European Currency Unit
EEB	European Export Bank
EEC	European Economic Community
EECIF	European Export Credit Insurance Facility
EGAC	Export Guarantee Advisory Council
EIB	European Investment Bank
EMU	European Economic and Monetary Union
ENA	École Nationale d'Administration
EPC	European Political Co-operation
ERP	Euroepan Recovery Programme
EU	European Union
G-7	Group of Seven
G-24	Group of Twenty-Four
GATT	General Agreement on Tarriffs and Trade
GDR	German Democratic Republic
GEC	General Electric Company
GNP	gross national product
ICC	International Chamber of Commerce
ICIA	International Credit Insurance Association
ICSID	International Centre for Settlement of Investment Disputes
IDA	International Development Agency
IMA	Interministerieller Ausschuß
IMF	International Monetary Fund
JAPC	Joint Aid Policy Committee
KfW	Kreditanstalt für Wiederaufbau

LDC	less developed country
LLDC	least developed country
MIGA	Multilateral Invesment Guarantee Agency
NATO	North Atlantic Treaty Organisation
NCM	Nederlandsche Credietverzekering Maatschappij
NEI	Northern Engineering Industries
ODA	Official Development Assistance
ODA	Overseas Development Administration
OECD	Organisation for Economic Co-operation and Development
OEEC	Organisation for European Economic Co-operation
OPEC	Organisation of Petroleum Exporting Countries
PG	Participants Group
PHARE	Poland-Hungary: Assistance for Restructuring of the Economy
PMS	Portfolio Management System
SCAT	Sub-Committee on Aid and Trade
SCOR	Société Commerciale de Réassurance
SDR	special drawing rights
SFAC	Société Française d'Assurance Crédit
SITC	Standard International Trade Classification
TEU	Treaty on European Union
UAP	Union des Assurances de Paris
UMM	uniform moving matrix
UN	United Nations
UNICE	Union des Confédérations de l'Industries et des Employeurs d'Europe
US	United States
VAT	value added tax
WEU	West European Union

Introduction

The central aim of this book is to combine the normative and empirical elements of policy analysis in a national, European and international context. For this reason the argument presented on the following pages will be of little interest to those political scientists, economists and lawyers who want to stay within the immediate boundaries of their disciplines. Some of them will even be displeased with the study's central finding that international institutions have the potential to complicate co-ordination problems in situations of economic interdependence. Nevertheless, because of the book's interdisciplinary flavour, each of their specialised subject areas has shaped the structure and content of its chapters. The concern with institutional variation both at the national and international level, for example, is the domain of political science, while regulations that stand on the output side of international and supranational organisations have been for a long time the main focus for the elaboration of legal doctrine. Similarly, in economics the discussion of policy co-ordination has concentrated on the realisation of quantitative targets and the definition of what precisely constitutes a subsidy. To arrive at a comprehensive view of a policy problem and to suggest solutions that take real world constraints seriously, however, the combination of these three perspectives into one framework is indispensable.

Co-ordination as a theoretical concept fits well into such a framework, since it does not only carry meaning in a national and international context but also allows one to arrive at some prescriptive conclusions from a normative point of view. I significantly depart from a large body of literature that confines co-ordination to interactions among individuals and their choice of actions. Instead I concur with Heyman (1973, p. 804) who argues that it is highly plausible that similar problems occur with regard to the choice of rules and, more generally, with the selection of institutions to facilitate co-ordination.

Substantially, my empirical analysis is based on the observation that in the decade between 1980 and 1990 the export promotion policies of Britain, France and Germany show an extremely uneven distribution of official support measures to industry and a steady increase in the spending of budget resources. How does the use of export credits, export credit insurance and development aid in three leading European countries match with repeated and long-standing efforts undertaken by the European Community (EC) and the Organisation for Economic Co-operation and Development (OECD) to control state aids to industry? Why have both organisations failed to keep national support measures to exporting firms competitively neutral? Which direction did institutionalised expert advice take before it became influential at the various levels of the co-ordination process, and what influence had institutional reforms on the co-ordination capacity of the control system for subsidies as a whole?

My answer to these questions rests with the fundamental difference between the co-ordination mechanisms which are applied at the three levels under study and the often contradictory aims that are manifest in the regulations of international and supranational organisations. By setting these mechanisms into context I first compare the promotion systems of three important trading states and, secondly, compare in this particular policy area the genesis of a set of rules that has been formulated in the organisational settings of the EC and the OECD. While it would be 'absurd to study everything simultaneously' this research design allows to include the international level in a more traditional form of comparative analysis (Rose, 1991, p. 462). Since the argument is developed in stages, it can proceed in the second and third part of the book *as if* outcomes are mainly determined by interactions within a particular sub-system, i.e. nation states or international institutions, rather than by interactions between these systems. However, in the conclusion the separation of institutional contexts is given up, so that the comparative method can show its full potential for the analysis of co-ordination problems across levels.

At the same time one must be clear about the limitations of a research design that decomposes the international level into two different organisations and selects only three of their respective member states as units of analysis. In so far this work can only provide reasons why policy failures should also be expected in other areas where similar co-ordination problems exist.

Despite these limits export promotion policy is an intriguing example with broader implications because of its historical background as an instrument in the pursuit of national power politics. In particular, German trade policy had given rise to demands in the early post-war period that the institutional framework of foreign trade should be drafted on supranational lines. In the words of Hirschman (1969, p. 72):

> (an) international authority should be not only the ultimate supervisor of the machinery of international trade, but should also provide several of the most essential mechanisms of this machinery.

Then during the 1970s it seemed that such strict limits on national sovereignty had become obsolete and that the resistance to protectionism was by far more important. Now the argument was made that international agreements among major economic powers - or trading states - are effective even during periods of crisis (Rosecrance, 1986, p. 59).

By contrast this book argues that the effectiveness of institutional mechanisms must be evaluated with regard to different sectors of trade policy which are further disaggregated into the instruments at hand to the policy-maker. Since neither the EC nor the OECD does have the regulatory powers to control all instruments available to governments in the promotion of export industries, their partial intervention can aggravate the policy problem at the domestic level. In this respect Britain, France and Germany constitute 'most similar cases' where each national setting allows for a direct or indirect linkage between export credit, insurance and aid policy. The selection of countries, thus, serves the purpose of isolating the effects of institutional differences more precisely, and giving sufficient consideration to their relationship with the quantitative results of policies. In the next step this output of national systems - interpreted as target values for the convergence of policies - is used to supplement the assessment of international co-ordination mechanisms on the basis of qualitative data extracted from interviews and primary source documents (Steinherr, 1985, p. 296). Finally this analysis suggests which form an institutional solution to the problem of selective subsidisation should take.

For these historical and methodological reasons the study concentrates on three countries. However, this should by no means exclude the applicability of a similar framework to other member states of the EC and the OECD. The puzzle of negative effects generated by an interaction between the domestic and European policy level, for example, also occurred in the Republic of Ireland. Here, an independent inquiry revealed substantial abuses of the EC's beef intervention system in connection with the Irish government's export credit insurance scheme in the period between 1987 and 1988 (Irish Times, 1994). It was just one company that achieved a virtual monopoly of export credit insurance cover for its beef exports to Iraq; and these exports had already benefited from EC subsidies because they had been purchased from intervention stocks held by the Irish intervention agency and the Ministry of Agriculture. Similar to the country studies of this book the domestic co-ordination process for policy formulation did not entail an investigation of the costs and benefits for the economy as a whole. Moreover, when the Ministry of Industry and Commerce decided to grant cover in the 'national interest' it could do so without consulting the Ministry of Agriculture. Thus this brief episode indicates that the type of co-ordination problems observed in this book can be equally important to some of the smaller EC member states.

Likewise an investigation into the detrimental effects of international institutions could focus on numerous other international organisations which created rules that overlap with those of the EC. Accordingly, the wider implications of the proposition put forward in this book can be examined by revisiting some of the issue-areas analysed in the framework of regime theory. Since this study presents a first move towards a more realistic analysis of international policy-making, it has to start off with some largely destructive exercises. In contrast to conventional objections against the assumptions of regime theory the argument presented in Chapter 1 follows a soft rational choice approach to provide an internal critique of that theory.

Although traditionally the task of welfare-improving policy co-ordination was conceived within the boundaries of nation-states the same problem can be formulated within the context of international institutions. This leads to a second order co-ordination problem as rule-making at this level has to be compatible with those rules already in place within domestic settings. In addition, because of variations in the degree of institutionalisation of international regimes, any analysis has to include the interaction between them, thus posing a co-ordination problem of a third type.

Within this framework the activities of international institutions as third parties and political entrepreneurs can produce detrimental effects. Because they possess their own mixture of conflicting and common interests in how a dispute between their constituencies is settled, they will not be able to perform the role of an impartial arbiter. Moreover, analogous to Williamson's notion of opportunism, their different organisational characteristics will allow for strategic behaviour among them in expectation of higher individual benefits. The traditional analysis of institutions as active mediators, passive instruments or guarantors of a particular order has not adequately taken account of all these elements. In particular, liberal and (neo-) realist accounts favour incrementalism as an approach to institutional reform and policy-making. However, with regard to its outcomes this type of strategy is seriously flawed. Likewise, regime analysis has overlooked this fact because at the level of abstraction on which it works, the necessary long-term evaluation in terms of efficiency and effectiveness is not possible.

In Chapter 2 I argue that, as a corollary, standard scholarship in the field has not paid sufficient attention to contextual factors, i.e. how co-ordination mechanisms are tied down to concrete organisational settings. On the one hand, the European Community provides a context for improving this situation. Since integration is to be achieved 'through law', few facets of the overall co-ordination process can maintain their voluntary character in the long run. As a consequence, the Commission can exploit the indeterminacy of the co-ordination concept in Treaty provisions. In the case of the OECD, on the other hand, the overall organisational features are those of a think-tank that draws heavily on co-ordination procedures as a never-ending cycle with no final consensus. Here, international rules with minor safeguards are implemented due to the interest constellation and political-economic influence of single members.

In both cases, the welfare potential is exaggerated for the following reasons: (1) transferring rule-making powers to more distant institutions can diminish the effectiveness of monitoring because of the information deficits of the above-mentioned institutions relating to the behaviour of national actors; (2) the bureaucratic capture of international institutions, where the regulatory practice increasingly reflects the individual aims of the staff, can in certain organisational contexts also involve political aims beyond the mere correction of regulatory failure at the unit level; and (3) international institutions only become selectively active in the control of limited policy areas, rather than addressing the entire policy space and, therefore, cannot take some of the consequences of policy choices sufficiently into account.

In the second part of the book I begin each chapter with a description of the domestic system of export promotion. Instruments of foreign economic policy such as export credits, export credit insurance and official development assistance have been widely used during periods of recession to safeguard national economies. In this respect, Britain, France and

Germany have developed distinct modes of foreign economic policy that were adequately summarised under the headings of *levelling the playing field*, *libéralisme organisé* and *Ordnungspolitik*. From the 1980s onwards these conceptions became increasingly challenged by the EC and the OECD, who were pursuing their particular organisational goals through various demands for market liberalisation and the reduction of state aids.

Throughout Chapter 3, 4 and 5 I apply a comparative perspective, to point to divergent and convergent trends in government policies reacting to these pressures. The main features of interministerial co-ordination processes and ongoing reform discussions underline the political nature of a seemingly purely technical policy area. My analysis provides for a dynamic picture of national interests and how they evolve around country specific variables. In particular, changes in export markets have exercised a strong influence on the relationship between government agencies and interest groups. In each of these chapters I present data on the performance of national promotion schemes in order to show how official agencies have rewarded business with special concessions. Ultimately, three different sets of institutional responses emerge by which states maintain their room for manoeuvre.

In the third part, I investigate why the non-neutrality of the EC and OECD co-ordination mechanisms can be expected to aggravate rather than ameliorate the original policy problem at the national level. In Chapter 6 I show that according to the EC Treaty, common institutions have the obligation to co-ordinate and harmonise regulations concerning national export promotion measures. However, even if a proper implementation of these tasks is assumed they could only avoid distortion of competition within the common market itself. As a consequence, firms in the member states are put at a disadvantage relative to competitors from countries outside the European Community. As a result of such concerns, expert knowledge becomes influential in the policy process when it is directed towards the creation of an independent agency rather than to the mediation between diverging interests of the member states. Yet this European agency could only distribute additional resources to reinforce the highly fragmented industrial systems of the member states with regard to firm size and foreign markets.

In Chapter 7, I evaluate the consequences of the particular institutional choice in the OECD. Through the Arrangement on Guidelines for Officially Supported Export Credits, the OECD has established several co-ordination mechanisms to deal with the problem of competitive subsidisation among a broader membership. This less formal institutional arrangement creates bias effects that favour some countries more than others. The analysis then shows how the influence of expert knowledge has led to incremental changes, but without establishing uniform regulations concerning the whole policy space of export-support measures. As a consequence, member states continued to give support to particular industries by shifting official subsidies between export finance, export insurance and development aid.

In the last part of the book I review the major findings of my case studies to assess the possibility of reform. Each country follows a model of negative co-ordination where specific interests influence government policies, and where the costs are diffuse while the benefits are concentrated. Concrete attempts at problem-solving by international institutions would require this pattern to be reversed. The comparative study of the EC and the OECD revealed that the working of their co-ordination mechanisms cannot fulfil this task. Microeconomic institutions in Britain, France and Germany have shown their resilience to demands for reform coming from the international level. In Chapter 8 I conclude therefore that the answer to deficiencies in international policy-making lies in the domestic sphere. In practical terms, this means allowing for symmetrical co-ordination by giving non-business interests an equal standing in governmental committees and advisory councils; although the delegation of certain tasks to international institutions has only served to limit the possibility of reform steps in this direction.

The goal of this book is not to discredit international institutions in general, but to provide a systematic method of analysing their failures in policy-making. Filling this gap by reassessing international and supranational institutions is, I believe, an important alternative to the current orthodoxy in international relations as well as a challenge for all social scientists.

PART I
THEORETICAL
FOUNDATIONS

1 Welfare and Institutional Design

Whatever the specific context in which they occur, problems of co-ordination are a basic feature of social life, because they reflect the need to sequence several different actions in order to arrive at certain goals. Far from providing definite solutions to these problems, the development of institutions over time will be interpreted here as an attempt to increase the capabilities of actors to structure their own behaviour in a way consistent with their aims. As Dahl and Lindblom (1976, p. 38) have put it:

> An action is rational to the extent that it is 'correctly' designed to maximize goal achievement, given the goal in question and the real world as it exists. Given more than one goal (the usual human situation), an action is rational to the extent that it is correctly designed to maximize net goal achievement. When several actions are required to attain goals, rationality requires coordination; that is, the actions must be scheduled and dovetailed so that net goal achievement is not diminished by avoidable conflicts among the actions.

Traditionally this task was conceived of as taking place within the boundaries of the nation-state, but has increasingly been reformulated within the context of international institutions. This leads to second order co-ordination problems, since rule-making at this level also has to be compatible with those rules already in place at 'lower' levels, i.e. within the jurisdictions of individual states. In addition, the variations in the degree of institutionalisation of international negotiation systems means that the analysis should include the interaction between them as well, thus producing a co-ordination problem of a third type. Before discussing the latter in Chapter 2 we can look first of all at problems of co-ordination occurring on levels one and two.

1.1 First and Second Order Co-ordination

First order, or domestic, co-ordination frequently implies negative co-ordination, a term coined by Scharpf (1991) to describe conflict avoidance rather than consensus formation in national policy-making. In terms of strategy, this involves the minimisation of potential conflicts through a process of sequential decision-making, whereby issues are divided into smaller segments to reach agreement more easily. The process has the advantage of reducing the complexity of policy issues by keeping functionally related policy decisions separate and accommodating only those new initiatives which are compatible with the already existing, fixed positions of the participating government agencies. Established interests are recognised in return for enduring exchange relationships. By focusing on governments, the approach rejects the unitary actor assumption concerning states, which are instead seen to provide formal structures within which interests can be articulated. The nature of the domestic co-ordination process, however, will not always produce coherently fixed state objectives and negotiating capacities; nor will they be without changes over time, across issue areas and among states. This suggests that we first need to investigate empirically exactly how government policies are formulated within a domestic context. Here, we can expect to show that differences in domestic structure lead to political choices that nevertheless display recognisable patterns across issue areas and countries.

Second order co-ordination refers to the increasing number of multiple and functionally overlapping negotiation systems which are usually examined under the heading of regime analysis, but which are better and more comprehensively characterised as belonging to the domain of international institutions. Keohane (1993, pp. 28-9) offers a definition that describes them as:

> persistent and connected sets of rules (formal and informal) that prescribe behavioral roles, constrain activity, and shape expectations. International institutions include formal intergovernmental or transnational organizations, international regimes, and conventions. International organizations are purposive entities, with bureaucratic structures and leadership, permitting them to respond to events. International regimes are institutions with explicit rules, agreed upon by governments, that pertain to particular sets of issues in international relations. Conventions are informal institutions, with implicit rules and understandings, that shape the expectations of actors.

Common to nearly all international institutions is a non-hierarchical, network-type organisational structure, which inevitably leads to questions of effectiveness and efficiency relating to the management of policy interdependence. While these multiple and overlapping systems have a welfare potential residing in the reduction of transaction costs, it is by no means clear that use will always be made of it. Again, this ultimately represents an empirical question that necessitates a thorough analysis of the relationship between the national and the international, rather than simply assuming the whole issue is one of the erosion of state power. At the same time, it is possible to put forward some theoretical arguments concerning second order co-ordination in support of a critical analysis of international institutions.

One of the major shortcomings of regime analysis stems from an overly optimistic expectation as to what happens when institutions over time take on a life of their own and only incompletely express the interests and objectives of a hegemonic state. By maintaining an essentially top-down perspective, this kind of analysis suggests that the rules established by a regime would result in a redefinition of state interests, at least in the long run. However, whereas in most cases it will be impossible to clarify unambiguously the extent to which policy was driven by national interests or international norms, a more plausible approach would be to assume the existence of a dialectical relationship, putting more emphasis on the way state actors actually define their interests. In the words of Katzenstein (1990, p. 18), 'tracing the policy process makes it possible instead to uncover how interests are defined and redefined'. In doing this it makes more sense to start from the bottom up, thus leaving more room for the contextual factors that determine policy-making during crisis situations and over longer periods of time. This approach enables us to investigate more precisely to what extent the interest structures of state actors who do participate in different, but linked, negotiation systems correlate to their institutional choice. In the final analysis, if a relationship of this type can be established, it then has some instrumental value, in so far as it can be used as a prescription for reform. Once changes in the interest definition of states have occurred, it becomes possible to rethink institutional arrangements and probably reshape them in the light of new policy goals, which is undoubtedly relevant for all those policy areas where the interdependence of markets requires some kind of regulation. At the same time, the complexity of international policy issues makes it necessary to concentrate the study on a single policy area.

Using game theory as their major analytical tool Putnam (1988) and Tsebelis (1990) have both examined two or more co-ordination levels in combination. For our purposes the importance of the Putnam model lies in its incorporation of domestic interests, in order to explain the strength and weakness of international institutions. International rules that are supported by stable domestic coalitions are likely to be characterised by a higher degree of compliance, whilst governments are assumed to act sequentially at the domestic and international levels. In the national context, domestic groups pursue their interests by pressurising government agencies to adopt favourable policies, and politicians seek power by constructing coalitions among those groups. At the international level governmental actors attempt to maximise their own ability to satisfy these domestic pressures, while minimising the adverse consequences of foreign influence on their own policy conduct.

By way of contrast, analysing co-ordination using the nested game perspective of Tsebelis allows for the simultaneous combination of multiple arenas. Starting with a game situation in the domestic setting as the principal arena, the other arenas at the international level are considered as contextual factors that influence the payoffs to be gained by each relevant player at the national level. For example, a game at the national level taking on the form of a Prisoner's Dilemma between firms and governments is at the same time nested inside a bigger game at the international level, such as a Battle of the Sexes between European governments about which co-ordinated solution to choose. The size of the payoffs (not the order) in each of these games is variable, but the final outcome in the primary domestic game is determined by events in the other arena. Consequently, the payoffs (not the nature) of this end game can change, depending on the amount of benefits available in the other setting. Moreover, other contextual factors - i.e. whether or not the actors can communicate effectively with one another, and whether or not the game is repeated over time - can have a similar effect. This line of reasoning has its identical expression in the concept of externalities (Tsebelis, 1990, pp. 58-60): rather than viewing the interaction between two actors in isolation, the consequences to third parties are usually not insignificant either, as they in turn react to the initial game.

International institutions can constitute such a third party. As the Coase theorem suggests, however, it has to be noted that the presence of externalities alone does not necessarily prevent effective co-ordination between independent actors. Welfare enhancing results are still possible, as long as negotiations are allowed for and compensation payments made possible. This assumes that national governments are willing and able to consider the international repercussions of their policy choices, that they have perfect information as to one another's intentions; and that the costs of organising and monitoring policy co-ordination were negligible. Market failures would then be managed in a co-operative fashion, without the need to delegate powers to an authority at the international level. Although this would at best ascribe a minimal role to institutions, the observable diversity in reality of both hierarchical systems such as the state and also negotiation systems (as embodied in various different international organisations) point to a more balanced analysis of the exact role of the latter.

Institutions can have detrimental effects, a hypothesis which is also to be found in co-operative game theory. Co-ordination problems can exist whenever the pay-off to a single actor is partially determined by the action taken by another. Furthermore, it is assumed that specific actions are not taken simultaneously, but in reaction to each other. The outcome of such interdependent but uncoordinated action will in general be suboptimal, that is to say both parties gain less than in a situation where they try and pre-arrange some sort of mechanism to bring their individual behaviour closer into line. Sometimes, basic communication can be sufficient to make participants aware of the potential for realising gains (Kydd and Snidal, 1993). More often, however, it will require co-ordination schemes in the form of institutional arrangements to provide a means of enforcement and arbitration. The former allows for either the imposition of sanctions on those who ignore, or the offering of incentives to those who respect, certain agreed rules. The latter involves the interaction of an intermediary between the parties facing a co-ordination problem. Ideally, this neutral arbiter combines the two functions of selecting a co-ordinated solution and of enforcing that particular choice (Calvert, 1992). The notion of an impartial arbiter, however, will only be applicable in the unusual circumstances of some third party having an interest in their dispute being resolved, but no interest in how it is actually settled. More frequently, the intervention of a third party with its own mixture of conflicting and common interests will make matters more complicated (Goodin, 1976, p. 48; Schelling, 1980, p. 14).

In consequence, where the role of an institution is limited to that of an external mediator, the resulting strategy is to rely on the services of (ideally) competent and impartial actors, such as teams of independent experts acting as honest brokers, who provide information on various co-operative options, and evaluate and compare them with regard to a commonly acceptable solution. These improvements in the information base of international negotiations are in themselves nonetheless insufficient, because there is a second aspect to ensuring the co-operation of an institution. The communication mechanism which provides the information is also the precondition for knowing when the policing and the punishment of non-co-operation is required, but although this resort to coercion should in theory benefit the community as a whole, its actual implementation brings with it a potential for misuse. The alternative is a purely voluntary institutional system which, notwithstanding the advantages of lowering the information cost about other parties, can be rejected, because it would entail rapidly increasing transaction costs (North, 1990). Section 1.2 will discuss this argument in more detail, which North presents in a national context for international institutions. Here, I will put forward some further theoretical arguments as to why institutional neutrality cannot be expected.

It should be noted that even if mediators are by definition only in a position to give suggestive rather than authoritative instructions, they already gain an influential role through their control over communication. Or as Schelling puts it (1980, p. 301):

> If we give a third player power to send messages to the original two tacit players, he is in a good position to help them; he is even in a good position to help himself if he gets a payoff that depends on the pair of strategies that the original two players choose.

While this still falls short of manipulation, the activities of a potential mediator do not just comprise putting a constraint on communications. There might be an extension to the limitation on the order of offers and counter-offers, for instance, by simply inventing 'contextual material' to support certain suggestions. In fact the mediator's position opens up ample possibilities to 'influence the other player's expectations on his own initiative, in a manner that both parties cannot help mutually recognizing' (Schelling, 1980, p. 144). Nothing other than outright manipulation occurs if part of the information is suppressed. This, however, can be done in very subtle ways such as inconsistently activating the institutional memory. Obviously, it is not necessary to convert mediators into arbitrators by an irrevocable surrender of authority for these effects to be produced; less severe actions can still satisfactorily achieve the desired result. Goodin (1980, p. 214) argues that in circumstances where there is a conflict about which co-ordinated solution should be chosen, the information need not be biased in favour of the desired alternative, nor even be on balance favourable. It is sufficient that 'everybody be talking about it' for an alternative to emerge as the obvious solution. Goodin's emphasis is on established elites, who alone are able to systematically work this politics-of-the-obvious strategy to their advantage.

In theory, the case of third-party enforcement - the second aspect of institutions - likewise involves a neutral party with the ability to measure the attributes of a contract-like arrangement and to enforce its content. Although in principle it makes no difference whether institutions mediate or arbitrate in the latter, as North (1990, p. 58) argues, it is more recognisable that:

> the enforcer is an agent and has his or her own utility function, which will dictate his or her perception about the issues and therefore will be affected by his or her own interests.

This issue of interpretation is superseded, and its consequences further aggravated, once sufficient attention is paid to the impact of ambiguity and unanticipated contingencies in the implementation of substantive rules. With these kinds of 'incomplete contracting problems' disputes between the parties are not directly covered by the mandate of institutions, but if they nevertheless claim (or actually possess) autonomy to make the final decision, 'there is nothing to stop them from abusing their positions' (Weingast and Garrett, 1993, p. 185). Potential correctives in the form of simple non-compliance, legislative action or new constitutional safeguards can be expected to face the resistance of actors pursuing their own institutional self-interest.

Another form of criticism as regards the role of international institutions deals with the third party problem from the viewpoint of the originally participating parties. Wassenberg (1991, p. 261) uses a 'triad power approach' according to which actors are not involved in exchange transactions, but in decisions as to whether or not to invest in the (re)-production of mutual power relationships. The availability of a third party, (i.e. the international institution) is just a potential substitute for an existing coalition, in order to maintain the capacity to enlarge or restrict the room for strategic choices, for oneself or for others. Following the argument of the seminal work by Tversky and Kahneman (1986), institutions can be understood to be a deliberate choice by the parties seeking co-ordination to frame a problem in a particular way, including some factors for the assessment of gains and losses while excluding others. The respective institutional setting to which preference is given *a priori* partly determines how the consequences of a co-ordinated policy are going to be evaluated. Gygi (1991, pp. 114-8) addresses the issue in terms of a principal-agent framework. The principal delegates certain tasks which are of benefit to him or her to someone else - an agent. In the case of international institutions, a threefold principal-agent relationship exists. Citizens delegate to their governments, governments to diplomats or representatives within an international organisation, and finally these in turn delegate to the managers of the international institution. This *delegation* causes transaction costs because of asymmetrical information on the part of the agents. Agents are assumed to use those comparative advantages for their own purposes, with the consequence that the more the levels of delegation, the greater will be the cumulative negative effects. Although the principal-agent model can still provide a rationale for delegation if information and credibility gains outweigh the costs of political control (Ordeshook, 1992, p. 122), it requires some important qualifications in the context of international institutions.

Firstly, over time governments try to change the original agreements which led to the creation of an international institution to their own advantage. As Section 1.4 discusses in greater detail, regimes for example aim at a long-term binding of governments instead of giving way to short-term preferences. Likewise international organisations frequently try to stabilise contracts between governments against the immediate interests of the contracting parties. Under these circumstances the problem is to distinguish between the flexibility of international institutions that is actually desired and that which serves only particular interests. Secondly, doubts exist as to whether national representatives in international organisations exercise the control function as demanded by their home governments (Vaubel, 1986, p. 51). Due to the particular position they maintain in the decision-making process there will be strong incentives to exploit information asymmetries to their own advantage. Thirdly, given difficulties in evaluating the output of international organisations, governments focus more on their individual contributions rather than on an organisation's management capacity.

What is more, in technical issue areas there are important obstacles for political control measures to become effective. The principal cannot observe all actions of the agent because of rapidly increasing control costs (Laver, 1997, p.76). Judgements as to whether the agents have indeed selected a course of action that best serves the goals of the principal require detailed knowledge of the policy area (March and Olsen, 1989, p. 27). There will always remain a problem of identification: since the impact of international institutions is likely to be evaluated at a highly aggregated level, it rests with the principal to sort out to what extent the agents have influenced the output or whether external factors have played a decisive role. In the final analysis positive effects from control measures depend on an improved information base as well as on possibilities for action. In case deficiencies are detected but no appropriate steps can be taken, there is no or only little reason to start with the control process in the first place. In other words, the use of incentives and safeguards will largely remain internal to the political process (Dixit, 1996, p. 93).

A third and final perspective on the role of institutions seems to challenge the other two interpretations. Precisely because international institutions are not neutral but act as *political entrepreneurs,* they can organise groups of states using a variety of incentives, supply public goods, make a profit and yet leave every participant better off. In relation to concrete European policy-making, for example, Majone and Dehousse (1993, p. 27) define institutional actors as:

advocates who are willing to invest their resources - time, energy, reputation, money - to promote a position in return for anticipated future gain in the form of material, purposive, or solidary benefits.

However, as this statement indicates, there is an ambiguity inherent in the role of political organisers. It is far from certain that their own rewards will actually ensure an incentive system that is beneficial to everyone. Why should that be the case? There are basically three points to note:

In the first place, the very possibility of gaining rewards for themselves potentially encourages purely instrumental leadership. Dahl and Lindblom (1976), when examining co-ordination problems, pointed to the danger that actors only behave as if there is a real need for the service they provide, simply to enter into positions of a high status. In addition, the specific context is here particularly relevant as to how entrepreneurs rationally pursue their dual concern of increasing the chance of staying in office, whilst also increasing the rewards from office. The extent to which political organisations are to a greater or lesser degree based upon the realisation of community benefits, rather than the realisation of rewards for their leadership, can thus vary considerably (Frohlich, Oppenheimer and Young, 1971). Secondly, Frohlich and Oppenheimer (1978, p. 88) have suggested the possibility that,

> the political entrepreneur (is) capable of protecting his resource stream, which is likely to be based on positive and negative 'private good' rewards. The protection of the resource stream usually involves the establishment of a monopoly and/or a coercive organization for taxation. Both situations lead to morally reprehensible interactions with others. Both situations require the same sort of guile and willingness to coerce as Macchiavelli discussed with reference to the role of princes.

Finally, once an organisation has established itself as the single supplier of a public good, one important characteristic comes to the fore. If the good is supplied to one member of a group, it is supplied to all of them, but at the same time - and unlike the dissatisfied consumer who just goes shopping in another store - any type of choice is now foreclosed. However, the existence of strong alternative preferences among a sufficiently large subgroup can motivate another aspiring entrepreneur to try and supply substitute collective goods. Thus, while competition between institutions is ruled out, it is still initiated internally through the struggle for control over the organisations' programmes.

To sum up, this introductory section has presented arguments of a methodological and theoretical nature. The implications for the structure of the thesis are twofold. Firstly, it is organised in such a way that the presentation of the empirical material in Chapters 3, 4 and 5 adopts a bottom-up approach to analysing policy-making within national contexts, before moving on to the supra-national and international levels. Secondly, Chapter 2 and the remainder of Chapter 1 are devoted to a more extensive discussion of the role of international institutions, intending to provide a differentiated examination of their activities.

1.2   Ideal Designs

In the preceding section, an attempt was made to lay the ground for a critical view of international institutions. The next stage is to examine three design perspectives on institutions, in order to asses their relevance in dealing with problems of second and third order co-ordination. Can respective design criteria - as implicit in the nested games approach, the transaction cost approach and the approach of institutional evolution - form the basis for successful reforms?

Most writings on international institutions argue that their policies are a reflection of interests that are located within states rather than within their own organisational structure. Therefore, as Haas (1990, p. 178) suggests, 'we have to look at the way in which states experience their interdependence before we can address matters of organizational design'. This interdependence is variable, not uniform, and some states are more interdependent than others, a fact of basic importance in understanding why certain forms of multilateral co-operation are not equally as attractive to everybody. Two practical limitations make choices especially difficult under these circumstances. Central decision-makers must choose between different conceptions of the territorial space to which choices are to be applied, and they have to weigh the short-term against various longer-term perspectives. At the same time, preferences (in the sense of being synonymous with interests) may also change in two different ways as a result of increasing levels of interdependence. First, even if states were in fact unitary decision-makers, their capacity to achieve their objectives would be increasingly affected by the actions of others in a situation of greater interdependence including those taken by the international institution. Second, even if with the rise of interdependence the opportunity costs of not co-ordinating policy increase, the making of binding agreements at the international level is likewise liable to affect domestic political institutions and coalitions over time.

Is it possible to deliberately design institutions that will be conducive to the solution of specific interdependence problems? In analysis given by Tsebelis (1990, p. 248) 'institutional design refers to the choice of rules as opposed to the choice of strategies inside existing rules'. In comparison to the two approaches to be mentioned in the following, namely those of the transaction cost type and those of the institutional evolution type, this can be considered to be a more realistic explanation. Yet in defining institutions as constraints, Tsebelis still adheres to the notion of 'ideal design' thus providing the same justification for his argument as do the others. But if we assume that institutions systematically produce certain kinds of outcomes, then institutions can be modified to alter policy outcomes. Given sufficient knowledge of the kinds of outcomes different institutions produce, preferences relating to policies can transform into preferences regarding institutions. Consequently, the various interested parties will try to select different institutions, thus initiating a game of institutional selection and creating a new equilibrium.

However, the transition from preferences about policies to preferences about institutions is neither automatic nor straightforward, because the expected life of institutions is so much longer than the expected life of policies. Therefore, both the consequences of an institutional choice and the uncertainty surrounding it are much more important elements in the calculation. The choice between two institutions can be considered as a risk-laden decision, which will generate two different streams of income because the situation is repeated over time. In other words, political actors invest their resources in the creation of institutions. The subsequent dilemma for different players is whether they should try to make a short-term, high-return investment or a long-term one with lower rates of return. In addition to the games taking place in multiple arenas as described in the first section, the game in the principal arena is now nested inside a bigger game, where the rules of the game are themselves variable. The set of available options is considerably larger than in the original one. Institutional change becomes a problem of intertemporal maximisation, where complications arise because future events cannot be clearly anticipated. The available information about future events is of crucial importance to the choice between two ideal-types of institutions. On the one hand, if the transition from one institutional structure to another is achieved with the agreement of the actors, who consider it to be in their common interest, this change produces an efficient institution. On the other hand, redistributive institutions can serve two distinct purposes. In the case of a consolidating institution, they preserve the interests of the dominant coalition; in that of a new deal institution, a new majority is created which is composed of the previous losers and some of the previous winners. The latter example will change policies in a significant way.

In the transaction cost approach efficient resource allocation is the main aim to be achieved through the design of international bodies (Ruggie, 1972; Sandler and Cauley, 1977, pp. 259-60). The distribution of export subsidies, for example, can be seen as an allocative problem. A purely national solution can be expected to undersupply the collective good since the individual government will fail to include the effects on other nations when spending decisions are made. In theory an institutional link between nations that share the good's benefits can induce a common solution which fosters efficient resource allocation.

In contrast to the standard, regime-type explanation, the approach explicitly asks whether this institutional structure is likely to require complete political and economic integration, or whether it will merely provide a means for co-operation and co-ordination. When analysed, both transaction costs *and* benefits are the crucial consideration in fulfilling the condition of Pareto-optimality. In determining the transaction benefits from the creation of a supranational structure, benefits must consist of gains superior to those benefits that are associated with the best available private or non-supranational means of allocation. Advantages and disadvantages resulting from the creation and the operation of the structure must be identified and evaluated. Costs and benefits that are associated with the mode of allocation, e.g. office space and communication networks, must be distinguished from the production costs of the good which is provided by the transaction. Because of this dual concern, the equally important (but usually neglected) possibility of transaction cost increase enters into the analytical framework from the very beginning.

Those primary transaction costs which are associated with the formal linkage of governments fall under three headings: decision-making, interdependence and enforcement costs (Sandler and Cauley, 1977, p. 266). In order to provide, finance and time decisions effectively, efforts at collaboration involve both the provision of information and administrative and planning costs. Neither participation expenditures to reproduce constituency desires in the choice of representatives for the international body, nor permanent bargaining by the participating parties to reach agreement under the unanimity rule, would occur under the national provision of the good. There is, in the words of Ruggie (1972, p. 878), 'a more general loss of independence or loss of control over one's own activities, resulting from the accumulation of collective constraints'. One particularly good example is the qualified decision rule, where a loss of autonomy and flexibility may be experienced since some states may have to go along with the decision of the majority, even though the national interest coincides with the minority position. Moreover, over and above the imposition of costs on the operation of national policy, any subsequently resulting conflicts inevitably lead to the question as to who is in favour of imposing sanctions.

Transaction benefits, on the other hand, accrue from the expected rise in efficiency gains, because a larger subset of individuals who are affected by the public good may have their marginal benefits taken into account when production decisions are reached. Along with the growing information and communication possibilities triggered off by the increase in exchange relations, economies of scale can lower per unit costs of policy activities whenever these are carried out on a larger output level.

Obviously, each of the transaction costs and benefits are dependent upon the 'tightness' of the international body in question. A loose relationship, for example, allows for a significant amount of autonomy and flexibility on behalf of the participants. In contrast, a completely tight relationship fuses together two or more component governments to the extent that they are forced to act as one. If we define the factors determining tightness to be the legal status of decisions, the number of participants, the decision rule and the size of the communication network, institutional tightness can be assumed to be positively related to each of the transaction benefits. As regards the transaction cost aspect, an increase in tightness, e.g. switching from the unanimity rule to majority voting, is negatively related to decision-making expenditure. In such instances, therefore, total transaction costs will rise with increased tightness only if the growth in enforcement and interdependency costs offsets the decrease in decision-making costs. Even so, the correlation between a highly structured institution and all three cost factors will usually be positive. Sandler and Cauley (1977) thus arrive at the following ideal assumption: as tightness increases, transaction benefits increase as well, but with diminishing returns. Similarly, the transaction cost function is assumed to exhibit increasing marginal cost, i.e. transaction costs are increasing at a growing rate as the institutional structure is strengthened. They then propose a two step procedure for finding the optimal institutional form: firstly, if an institutional connection between states is to be viable, then the expected net transaction benefits must be positive within all possible international institutional solutions; secondly, the form of the connection is determined by the degree of tightness that maximises net transaction benefits. In other words, 'tightness should be adjusted until the sum of the component marginal transaction benefits is equated to the sum of the component marginal transaction costs'.

Haas' notion of learning to manage interdependence can complete our presentation of ideal designs (Haas, 1990, pp. 177-212). Haas' approach stresses the time dimension in the activities of organisations facing substantive policy problems. For him possibilities of reform rest with the leadership of international organisations rather than with their state constituencies. When it comes to defining what interdependence actually means and what measures of co-ordination are appropriate for producing effective *programmes*, the administrators of international organisations remain the crucial actors. Hence the empirical research into concrete organisations has to start with a description of a particular interdependence problem before analysing the particular strategy that is chosen in response.

Once the objects of change have been clearly identified, the overriding design principle becomes the continuous initiation of learning processes. In a perfect world, this will find its expression in the choice of strategies which simultaneously use the three time scales of incremental, conjunctural, and secular time. Incremental time refers to activities of short duration and the socio-economic nexus in which they are embedded is shallow; organisational concerns are limited to how specific economic sectors will fare. But if the institutional leadership makes efforts to link these activities to the future of the social structure and military potential of the participating countries then their operations take place within conjunctural time. The socio-economic nexus is now much broader, deeper, and more abstract. Finally, secular time refers to when the socio-economic nexus includes all of the above plus a serious concern for society's relationship to nature, i.e. resource depletion and environmental limits. The main point Haas stresses is that various measures can simultaneously proceed without any co-ordination, or carefully sequencing and proper adjustment of the steps taken in different time scales, according to their net consequences in social time. There is no doubt that learning to recognise success and failure in most programmes requires a sensitivity to different time dimensions, which also implies different sensitivities to normative consequences and empirical linkages between causal factors. However, to recognise that 'single or related measures work out differently depending on the time frame we choose' is one thing, but to conjecture that this might lead to a 'new vision of what we mean by organizations' quite another altogether (Haas, 1990, p. 206). The unmistakable overtones of idealism are nowhere more clear than in the concept of 'timeliness by discretionary institutions' (Hayden in Haas, 1990, p. 206):

> More and more, it is understood that local, regional, national, and supranational processes must be coordinated and controlled if humans are to solve problems. This will lead to system real time and beyond that to social time, where the events are not just sequenced by the system but the socio-technical-

environmental system is determined by the conscious temporal concept of timeliness through discretionary social institutions.

Despite the significant differences between all these approaches, especially with regard to their status within social theory, they have in common an essentially reformist approach to international institutions. Although I have described them as ideal designs, they actually contribute to a more realistic understanding of what institutions are and what they could be. The (ultimately empirical) test for this claim is whether or not they have anything to offer in terms of practical policy-making. Even the transaction cost approach, when couched in conventional economic terms, demands that any viable international system of institutional structures must be subjected to periodic scrutiny and regular review, in order to ascertain when linkages between national policies should be added to or discarded from the system. In short, advances in technology - in exclusion mechanisms and monitoring devices, as well as ever increasing information and communication channels - might easily create pressure for the termination of relationships that have outlived their usefulness.

It is also necessary to remember the key point in the rational choice approach to institutional design (Tsebelis, 1990, p. 117):

the discriminating factor between efficient and redistributive institutions is not how long they last (their time horizon), but the uncertainty of the outcomes they produce. Indeed, if the actors who design the institutions can foresee their consequences for different political or social groups, then they can systematically favour some of these groups. If, however, they cannot foresee the redistributive consequences, then their only guide will be the increase in the efficiency of the institution.

This last argument proves particularly relevant, since the existing endowment enters into efficiency consideration on the basis of Pareto-optimality as the unquestioned starting point. The relative distribution of wealth is not assumed to challenge the status quo. Tsebelis links his argument on the design of efficient institutions with that of Rawls' 'veil of ignorance', as presented in the latter's 'A Theory of Justice' (Rawls, 1972, p. 378):

Now at this point one may extend the interpretation of the original position and think of the parties as representatives of different nations who must choose together the fundamental principles to adjudicate conflicting claims among states. Following out the conception of the initial situation, I assume that these representatives are deprived of various kinds of information. While they know that they represent different nations each living under the normal circumstances of human life, they know nothing about the particular circumstances of their own society, its power and strength in comparison with other nations, nor do they know their place in their own society. Once again the contracting parties, in this case representatives of states, are allowed only enough knowledge to make a rational choice to protect their interests but not so much that the more fortunate among them can take advantage of their special situation. This original position is fair between nations; it nullifies the contingencies and biases of historical fate. Justice between states is determined by the principles that would be chosen in the original position so interpreted. These principles are political principles, for they govern public policies toward other nations.

As becomes clear from this statement, the two are not actually congruent arguments because the 'original position' in the institutional design account is already one of imbalance, i.e. an interstate context of strong and weak states. Yet if we assume for a moment that the actors of institutional change in the rational choice account are identical with those in Haas' analysis, both approaches would in practical terms subscribe to a view which reduces uncertainty through the production of accurate rather than consensual knowledge. In order to operationalise such a scheme, reformist designers would have to insist on various innovative modes of decision-making, like multiple advocacy, planning and analysis by temporary teams, and rotating devil's advocates. The systematic participation of such units in decision-making would help prevent the survival of practices that defeat an organisation's purpose; they could be established as institutional safeguards, thereby encouraging the practice of arguing the most systematic case for a particular option within the policy-making confines of a bureaucracy through having to oppose an equally systematic case put forward by someone else from the same unit (Haas, 1990, p. 210).

Nonetheless each of these models remains vulnerable to criticism from the findings of more policy oriented research. All clearly assume in a general way that institutions can be important determinants in policy-performance, but that it is within the power of a government or administration to manipulate institutional conditions within a design perspective. However, even when the policy environment is the same, similar outcomes can be obtained by different policies, similar policies may be produced by different institutional structures, or a given institutional structure might be capable of producing a series of different policy responses. It should instead be assumed as Scharpf (1986, p. 180) has stated, that 'the empirical relationship between structure, policy and outcome is likely to be highly contingent in general'. In other words, there will be no direct relationship between institutional conditions and policy output, or output and outcomes. Due to the 'structural selectivity' of policy-making institutions, they will have independent effects upon the definition and articulation of societal interests and problems, and consequently at the international level, upon the differing chances of state interests being 'converted' into international public policy. In fact, policy-making institutions are not only the agents of economic and social interests, they also have institutional self-interests to pursue. Hence, policy designers need to recognise the importance of the self-interest of the institutions which they wish to redesign.

Again, it is little more than wishful thinking to argue that by and large the private interests of individual actors in terms of their career, status and income are both utilised and at the same time neutralised by organisations, who try and balance inducements and contributions in such a way that individuals are sufficiently motivated to pursue organisational goals. Moreover, this imperfect neutralising mechanism will not be available in times of crisis or fast changing circumstances, when the fate of the organisations themselves is at stake. Under these conditions the relationship between institutional choice and policy performance turns out to be highly confused, because organisational issues are frequently decided in the same process of settling conflicts over policy. In comparison to state interests, which are dependent for their articulation on mechanisms of formal representation, institutional interests have the advantage of privileged access when it comes to questions of design: they are directly involved in any decision-making about reforms which might alter their fate. The objective of improving policy performance is seemingly more constrained by institutional interests than substantive policy interests (Scharpf, 1986, p. 183). From this point of view, Haas - with his first design principle not to 'seek to rationalize organizations that suffer from turbulent nongrowth or net decline by fundamental constitutional revision' - is obviously in agreement with Scharpf's criticism. Rather than pushing for comprehensive constitutional reform, both consider the idea of a 'self-designing' organisation to be more appropriate. Modest internal co-ordination that eschews core constitutional change is assumed to be the preferred way for member states, non-governmental groups, and secretariat units to rearrange their mode of operation relating to a redefined task, once they have concluded that previous methods are no longer adequate. Both Haas and Scharpf share the view that it is necessary to resist an overt reordering and centralisation of authority; as Scharpf (1986, p. 187) concludes:

> Even though institutions, and even formal organizations in the narrow sense, do matter as a serious constraint on policy-making, institutional reform may not be a very promising strategy for the improvement of public policy. It is difficult to

achieve, its outcomes are hard to predict and its benefits are likely to be realized only in the longer term while the short-term costs are not negligible. Instead would-be policy designers might do well to try to working with (or if need be, working around) existing institutions. That would require a careful analysis of institutional self-interests and a creative search for policy options which could advance the public interest without violating the institutional self-interest of necessary participants.

To summarise the argument of this section, I have presented three approaches which at an analytical level allow for inclusion of international institutions. On the basis of the nested games framework, the transaction cost account and the concept of institutional evolution, it would be possible to present more or less explicit suggestions for reform. However, the close discussion of their respective implications has suggested the need for a very cautious understanding of institutional change. Instead of moving straight to a conclusion, I think it is worth briefly confronting this finding with Williamson's position regarding the organisational design issue. In essence, Williamson argues for organising transactions in such a way as to economise on bounded rationality, whilst simultaneously safe-guarding those transactions against the hazards of opportunism (Williamson, 1975). By giving an actor capacity to international institutions and allowing for the actually observable diversity in institutional forms (Le Prestre, 1986, p. 128), the end result is a far more increased potential for opportunism, i.e. strategic behaviour in expectation of higher benefits for one's own organisation.

This is not to be confused with free competition among 'institutional alternatives', since that would imply a free demand and supply for institutional substitutes. As a matter of fact, there is neither complete transparency of the (dis-) advantages associated with each alternative, nor negligible information costs for acquiring insights into those defects. Similarly, it is not possible to simply assume perfect mobility and prompt delivery of the substitute (once decided upon) nor a ready affirmation to proposed reorganisations of existing institutional arrangements. Hence it is safe to conclude that a switch from one arrangement to the other will be far too difficult - if not impossible - in practice. It should therefore be asked at a theoretical level whether interactions between entities should be included when designing different types of institutional forum. Equally, the same complications arise at the policy level. Insofar as transnational public goods may be complements or substitutes for one another, cross-effects between the activities of international institutions would be the rule rather than the exception. Moreover, the existence of overlapping sets of participants would indicate the likelihood of cross-effects (Sandler and Cauley, 1977, p. 271).

Where cross-effects occur, the influence of tightening any co-operative structure must be calculated with respect to the effects imposed upon the entire system. For example, the adjustment of a supranational solution to one policy problem may yield cross-effects relating to a less dense arrangement in the same policy area. These cross-effects may then cause an increase in the decision-making cost and a decrease in the efficiency gain for, say, the intergovernmental solution, when the initial policy problem is approached within a more tightly integrated structure. As mentioned above, optimal tightness is formally reached for each institutional link when the sum of the marginal transaction benefits derived by the system is equated to the sum of the marginal transaction costs imposed upon the system. Each of the sums is aggregated across the n links of the system. Thus, tightness for each of the n links must be determined simultaneously, in order to ensure that interlinkage and intralinkage costs and benefits are included when designing a whole network of international institutions.

To move from the abstract to the concrete, one useful general implication of the above would be to stress boundary spanning roles. Part of the environment within institutional work involves other institutions: the task of third order co-ordination is to minimise the importance of the boundaries between organisations and their environment, thus facilitating the flow of resources and information to and from the particular entity (Metcalfe, 1994, p. 55). In terms of organisational programmes and institutional mechanisms, this necessitates reacting to the lack of effectiveness or even non-existence of international policies by means of interorganisational co-ordination, (principally through the application of the principle of subsidiarity at the international level, i.e. the use of interactions between different institutional arrangements). This represents a proposal that is logically consistent with the nature of supranational organisations, because they include institutional features that are otherwise only found within individual international organisations. Indeed, interorganisational co-ordination has the potential to achieve similar and comparable results within policy areas, by giving preference to subsidiarial issues over the pursuit of comprehensive integration.

1.3   Incrementalism

Whereas Sections 1.1 and 1.2 looked at the problem of design by focusing on interests and institutions, in this section I consider ideas and knowledge as important variables in the international policy-making process. In particular, I will discuss the classical international relations paradigms in relation to the way they interpret institutions and what they suggest in terms of strategy. This makes it possible to evaluate the importance of incrementalism, and ultimately to propose a synthesis of several theoretical strands rather than treating them separately or as being mutually exclusive of one another.

According to the liberal, realist and structuralist theories of international relations, there are different ways of interpreting institutions, though each favours different sets of prescriptions for producing change. An awareness of the theoretical underpinning to the various proposals for reform brings with it the perhaps unexpected advantage of demonstrating their striking similarities. In principle, the conventional liberal model is the most sympathetic to the efficacy of institutional mediation, but as was suggested in Section 1.1, characterising institutions as mediators does not necessarily imply neutral arbitration. The crucial factor is the way in which such mediation is organised. Consequently, when studying institutional mechanisms, certain improvements can be suggested which might in turn modify state interests (reflected in public policy). More importantly, the potential of institutions to become actors has to be strengthened, which requires resources that are under the control of an international bureaucracy. At this point, most liberal accounts tend to emphasise the provision of highly valuable information. Because some international institutions occupy linchpin positions within a transnational and transgovernmental decision-making system, they immediately appear as the natural location for communities of knowledge (Haas, 1993, p. 189). How decision-makers define state interests and formulate policies to deal with complex and technical issues can be a function of the manner in which the issues are represented by specialists to whom they turn for advice in the face of uncertainty (Haas, 1992, p. 2). As networks of knowledge based experts, epistemic communities help states to identify their interests.

Thanks to improved information coming from the component parts of the system, the formal rights of institutions in the organisation of diplomatic exchange patterns and agenda-setting can be justified. In addition, processes of transnational coalition-building and a common commitment to a particular ideology, goal or doctrine, only serve to reinforce their capacity to modify governments' interests by changing the way in which they work. The influence of experts depends on their ability to avoid internal disagreement and to gain strategic positions in national administrations. From such positions they may influence political actors in the co-ordination of specific policies or even control their decision-making process (Haas, 1993, p. 179).

The realist position holds that states are the basic units in the international system. As rational actors, they have to protect their interests in order not to endanger their own existence in an anarchical environment; international institutions thus have at best a residual meaning but quite often can be considered as redundant. For such an organisation to be effective, it has to limit the room for manoeuvre of its members and the degree to which member states are able to maintain their independence severely limits the effectiveness of the international institution. In the zero sum game between nation-state and institution, the latter will always lose. Should there be a coincidence of interests, this would primarily and predominantly be a question of individual recognition by the states themselves. As Taylor (1986) puts it, 'if reform is possible, and in this view it is not necessarily accepted that it is, then it can only result from change in the interests, values and attitudes of the member states'. Strictly speaking, institutional changes are irrelevant in this respect. For Waltz (1979, p. 105), there is one other question worth asking:

> When faced with the possibility of cooperating for mutual gain, states that feel insecure must ask how the gain will be divided. They are compelled to ask not 'Will both of us gain?' but 'Who will gain more?' If an expected gain is to be divided, say in the ratio of two to one, one state may use its disproportionate gain to implement a policy intended to damage or destroy the other. Even the prospect of large absolute gains for both parties does not elicit their cooperation so long as each fears how the other will use its increased capabilities.

The proponents of neo-realism, such as Grieco (1990), modify this argument by suggesting that international institutions can become instruments in the hands of the participating states precisely in order to prevent changes in the relative gain structure of co-operation. A prescriptive element is now attached to institutional re-arrangements. 'Defensive state positionalism' describes a strategy whereby constitutional safeguards guarantee that the distribution of power among states remains stable, via a clear delineation of the limits of co-operation. Both through periodical revisions of agreements and the use of side-payments, international institutions can on occasion lead to greater efficiency in the pursuit of the originally chosen goals but essentially remain passive in character.

By contrast, the structuralist paradigm assumes that order can be sustained by the creation of international institutions that can take decisions which are binding even upon recalcitrant groups within states, either because of the existence of formal rules or because the way in which they work generates irresistible pressure to obey. On this view, there are already quasi-state structures at the international level which function in similar fashion to those of national governments (Pijl, 1984). If they succeed in managing areas of joint interests on the basis of a grant of power given to them by governments, organisations can then gain in vital importance as independent controllers. International agencies may even be associated with a form of 'supranationalism' in cases where they are themselves able to lay down rules, set new objectives or create new instruments, rather than merely executing already agreed tasks (Taylor, 1986). In contrast to the liberal model, however, the relationship between ideas and institutions is a dialectic one (Cox, 1981, pp. 136-7):

> Institutionalisation is a means of stabilising and perpetuating a particular order. Institutions reflect the power relations prevailing at their point of origin and tend, at least initially, to encourage collective images consistent with these power relations. Eventually, institutions take on their own life; they can become either a battleground of opposing tendencies, or stimulate the creation of rival institutions reflecting different tendencies. Institutions are particular amalgams of ideas and material power which in turn influence the development of ideas and material capabilities.

By interpreting ideas as 'ideology', structuralists are in a position to specify international institutions as guarantors of a particular order. The process that builds up this capacity can be described as follows (Adler in Katzenstein, 1990, pp. 19-20):

> Ideology thus ceases to be a mental phenomenon and becomes a collective product of the mind ... that can have real consequences. These consequences often take institutional form. Consciousness cannot help but become integrated into institutional designs ... institutions are but 'carriers' for a particular collective understanding that has consequences of its own.

For this reason, the main institutional activity of recognising and promoting a general interest in certain policy areas by exploiting technical and intellectual resources has to undergo a critical reassessment. Co-operative forms at international level help foster interaction between elites, thus contributing to the formation of something close to ideology. Anything that is presented as the realisation of a common interest, such as the making of concessions to less powerful members, thus appear as part of a class-based hegemonic strategy. An allocation or extension of institutional power is only welcomed to the extent that it serves groups other than capital to counteract these tendencies.

The structuralists are generally a bit rash in their judgements about the other two main theories, largely because of their ahistorical approach to problem-solving. Liberals and neo-realists, however share the belief that incremental institutional changes take place over a period of time. Consider, for example, the way Keohane (1991, pp. 37-8) argues:

> In seeking to account for the increase in the number of international regimes, the contractual theorist will not ignore the structure of world power or domestic politics. But she should also expect to find an incremental pattern of change, promoted by officials of international organizations as well as by those of central governments: we should observe responses of regimes to problems involving externalities, uncertainty, and high costs of transactions. Increased interdependence should lead to intergovernmental attempts to promote cooperation.

Now compare Grieco's four competing hypotheses challenging liberal institutionalism: firstly, realists prefer less dense and durable arrangements because of lower exit costs in case there is a change in the relative gain situation; secondly, a growing number of partners is an advantage in cases of potential co-operation with less powerful partners in order to weaken an increasingly strong partner; thirdly, short time scales are desirable because long-term arrangements run the risk that lengthy negotiations can alter relative gain situations; fourthly, linkages between different issues can have negative consequences should another participating state gain significantly more in the newly added policy areas. In terms of outcomes, all four points imply fairly small moves away from the status quo precisely because 'defensive state positionalism requires that a balance has to be struck between rigidity and flexibility of obligations within a cooperative arrangement'(Grieco, 1990, p. 232).

Yet, the concrete policy-making measures that Keohane (1988) proposes are very much the same, at least in terms of policy outcomes, if not in strategy: specific reciprocity in the form of tit-for-tat moves counteracts the incentives to free-ride on international arrangements (cf. the first point); the reduction of the large game to bilateral obligations prevents the partners from cheating in their co-operative behaviour (cf. point 2 above); the heterogeneous interests existing among the original participants can be narrowed down by the formation of smaller clubs possessing similar interests (cf. point 2 above); finally, already truncated negotiation sets can be expanded again by changing dichotomised topics into incremental ones (cf. point 3 above). Reciprocity is of course institutionally less demanding than redistribution, whilst an increasing number of participants in arrangements will at the same time always entail a greater potential for internal coalition-building. At the same time, certain topics never end up on the negotiating table anyway, precisely because actors have already evaluated their stakes in terms of a much longer time scale. Finally, to take Grieco's fourth point, which constitutes a firm opposition to the neo-liberal statement as to the propensity of issue linkages to encourage international co-operation, the argument relies upon the capacity to split policy decisions between different levels. However, the well-known experiences of fully developed federal systems strongly suggests that their consequences are negative, particularly in relation to incrementalism, failing reform efforts and immobility. The same would only be the more true for international co-operation in multi-level systems of a pre-federal type.

In the end, therefore, it comes as no surprise that in the liberal approach - just as in the realist - the primary design question is to find arrangements which also meet a dual requirement. In the words of Keohane (1988, p. 36): 'The exercise of reciprocity plays a role, but is constrained by an overall set of norms and institutions that emphasize non-discrimination and liberalization'. Though institutional mechanisms should be capable of deterring actors from defecting, they have at the same time to provide incentives or at least opportunities for sub-sets of actors to develop their relationship further, through an exchange of reciprocal favours or concessions. In terms of theory, the dilemma remains the same: how best to achieve the combination of preventing deterioration and encouraging the incremental evolution of co-operative arrangements.

In general, the design of substantive solutions is not simply a one-off application of the product of formal decision theory, but seems instead to be much more of an incremental process of trial-and-error. The significance of incrementalism within the two paradigms varies according to the strategic moves within power constellations or the value systems of the major actors. Realism favours statism in both cases, whereas for liberalism, statism is preferred as a long-term strategy for achieving an increasing similarity in the respective value judgements of states. However, in a 'realistic' scenario (and contrary to tit for tat assumptions) several strategic moves can simultaneously made in any direction and of varying extent, so that the received rules make the outcome of incompatible moves much more problematic for either side. And in the games that real actors play, things can and do happen abruptly; as Schelling (1980, p. 171) states:

> There seems to be less chance to develop a modus vivendi, or tradition of trust, or dominant and submissive roles for the two players, because the pace of the game brings things to a head before much experience has been gained or much of an understanding reached.

What is more, an incremental game does not necessarily make collaboration any easier since it can encourage a riskier mode of playing, especially if the underlying value system requires the actors to strive for far-reaching changes. In my view, the only real possibility for making the incrementalism of the moves in the game commensurate with the evaluation standards of the participants is to identify a set of empirical benchmarks.

The structuralist objection that other approaches do not in themselves adequately take into consideration historical forces is misplaced, once we acknowledge how one important economic historian has analysed the topic of institutional change. According to North (1990), incremental changes in informal constraints will alter the game, either increasing or *decreasing* co-operative outcomes. Small changes to both formal rules and informal constraints will over a period of time gradually alter the institutional framework, such that it evolves into a different set of choices from that with which it began. North describes organisations as purposive entities designed by their creators to maximise wealth, income, or other objectives that are defined by the opportunities afforded by the institutional structure of society. In the course of pursuing those objectives, organisations incrementally alter the institutional structure, but the central point is that they are not necessarily socially productive because the institutional framework often creates perverse incentives. The ambiguous role of political entrepreneurs, as agents of change responding to the incentives embodied in the institutional framework, has already been mentioned in Section 1.1; here, it is relevant to note that organisations will be designed to further the objectives of their creators. Still more vital for our line of investigation is North's claim regarding the role of knowledge (North, 1990, p. 78):

> In all tasks institutions fulfil there is uncertainty and in which investment in information must be undertaken. The institutional framework will shape the direction of the acquisition of knowledge and skills. One way by which maximizing behaviour of economic organizations shapes institutional change is incremental alteration of the informal constraints as a by-product of maximizing activities of organizations.

The original goal of aiming for new objectives when 'the payoff from maximizing in that direction exceeds the payoff from investing within the existing constraints' is thus mirrored by attempts to improve the knowledge base. The historical development of institutions is path dependent - a combination of small events and chance circumstances encourages the success of certain solutions, which then set a particular direction - and so too are the learning process and the subjective modelling of their policy issues (North, 1990, p. 99). My criticism of the two traditional approaches to international institutions can therefore be summarised as follows: although they both equally as much rely on incremental changes, in the long term realism remains largely indifferent to the outcome, whereas liberalism almost forgets altogether that unproductive paths may in fact persist. Either way, neither paradigm takes institutions seriously.

Unfortunately, it is in the nature of incremental reform efforts that they tend to be highly deceptive (Goodin, 1982, pp. 19-38). In the first place, 'muddling through' will always run the risk of inducing non-incremental reactions in response to the originally chosen step-by-step measures. Favouring only small improvements can still prove irresponsible because of so-called 'sleeper' and 'threshold' effects, assignment problems relating to cause and effects, or the resulting difficulties in adequately assessing feedbacks. Inevitably, there will be a bias in policy-making stemming from the fact that within institutions, be they domestic or international, 'ideas and theories are used not only to discover new solutions, but also to make sense of what has already happened' (Majone, 1992, p. 9). Secondly, for 'piecemeal engineering' to become possible, a theoretically-informed hypothesis is necessary, but these will in general only insufficiently take up information about the broader environment surrounding the immediate policy arena. In terms of substantive policies, greater consideration should instead be given to the *policy space* - a whole set of policies 'that are so closely interrelated that it is not possible to make useful descriptions of or analytic statements about one of them without taking the other element of the set into account' (Majone, 1989, pp. 158-9). Otherwise it is impossible to anticipate distorting influences on the intended policy measures, with the result that the constant need to reformulate working hypotheses will lead to increasingly erroneous assumptions about reality. Thirdly, Dahl and Lindblom (1976, pp. 82-5) have argued in defence of incrementalism, as being a form of safeguard against the failure of ambitious and far-reaching reforms, the rationale behind this being not to foreclose future options from the very start but to allow for later adaptation. As a side-effect this would also permit the survival and continued alteration of the operating organisation. Yet as indicated above, the option to reverse a given course of action whenever it might be appropriate becomes more limited when the crossing of (natural) thresholds is involved, to the extent that irreversibility could even be positively desirable in certain cases.

What conclusions can be drawn from this part of the discussion? First of all, it has become clear that policy-making requires a comprehensive theoretical understanding of the broader system and this should be the starting point for any decisions on interventions and the scope of reform in particular. Accordingly, any *a priori* strategy can be assumed to be bound to fail. This kind of conclusion should nevertheless not be confused with the notion of 'institutional learning' as put forward by Haas (1990), for example. In contrast to patterns of change characterised by organisational adaptation through non-growth or incremental growth, the 'management of interdependence' stands out in the latter's work as a clear model for organisational development, and is marked by a reassessment of the 'basic beliefs underlying the selection of ends' and a different 'theory of causation defining the organization's task'. For such learning to occur 'there must be sufficient consensual knowledge available to provide the rationale for the novel nesting of problems and solutions' (Haas, 1990, p. 161). In highlighting the role of epistemic communities (groups of professionals who share both a system of causal beliefs and a set of political values) not only as forces in the emergence of consensual knowledge but also as agents of change, Haas' argument overlooks the importance of many other more influential actors. In addition, the allocation of that role to experts means that they too must become equally susceptible to the existing institutional incentive structure. In any case, at the level of individual actors it is only possible to speculate as to which lessons will to be learned from which experiences and what precisely will be memorised. There is, therefore, a clear-cut limitation to institutional arguments of this type. Rather than focusing on 'consensual knowledge' as the 'flip-side' of institutions, we should try and search for a better theoretical understanding how ideas and interests interact.

Although liberalism has made the most recent attempt at refining the role of 'ideational factors' in its approach, it is of limited help in understanding this problem. As was shown at the beginning of this section, liberalism tends to take a top-down view in which institutions change state interests. Nor does the realist hypothesis offer a conclusive answer, pushing as it does too far in the opposite direction and being seemingly unable to give sufficient room to cognitive factors. Implicitly, realists would in fact feel most comfortable with an argument exclusively rooted in state interests, where the process through which (instrumental) knowledge is produced and articulated is located in national systems. Lastly, the structuralist argument also fails to fulfil the purpose of our dual requirement; whilst it tries to encapsulate the mutual dependence of ideas and interests, it ultimately overestimates the actual power of institutions.

Given the different strengths and weaknesses of the various approaches, I would argue that the most plausible means of understanding the general problem is to carefully employ a combination of all three. Normatively speaking, and for the reasons presented in Section 1.1, institutional mechanisms should provide for *neutral* arbitration and this constitutes the major difference to (neo-) liberal accounts. With respect to policy-making, the domestic setting is the main arena where state interests are (re-) defined and thus forms the logical starting point for our empirical investigation. Yet at the same time, the state is not a monolithic entity but an arena where government agencies and interest groups interact, which represents a different emphasis to realist interpretations. Structuralism recognises that within institutions there is a danger that specific group interests can be presented as the common interest, but - contrary to what will be argued here - underestimates the possibility of institutional reform.

To recapitulate: the three traditional paradigms in international relations interpret international institutions either as active mediators, passive instruments or as guarantors of a particular order. For two of them, namely the liberal and structuralist approaches, ideational factors, either in the form of knowledge or ideology, play an important role; another two - the liberal and (neo-) realist hypotheses - basically favour incrementalism as an approach to institutional reform and policy-making. However, as has been indicated already, incrementalism is seriously flawed both as a strategy and in terms of its outcomes. Most theories of international relations have too often overlooked this fact, due to their respective deficiencies in adequately accounting for the interplay between ideas, interests and institutions. I would argue that the best solution to these difficulties is to think of these theories as complementary, rather than as being mutually exclusive.

1.4   Evaluation Problems

The remaining part of this chapter tries to anticipate some of the problems of empirical evaluation, in relation to the theoretical framework as it has been outlined so far. The initial methodological difficulty is in making use of criteria such as 'efficiency' and 'effectiveness' while at the same time attempting to control for institutional variation. In addition, since international policy-making essentially has to be conceived of as a process rather than as the attainment of some final status, the appraisal of outcomes is only one element within a dynamic overall scenario. To begin with, therefore, I will discuss some of the findings and unanswered questions of regime theory, before moving on to an examination of different gain situations, and conclude by stressing that evaluative criteria should refer to the main stages of the policy cycle.

It has been shown in Sections 1.2 and 1.3 that most conceptions of ideal designs disregard the potentially strategic use of *several* institutional structures by states, governments or societal groups in order to achieve higher individual gains. The deficits stemming from overlapping and contradictory organisational activities might thus be a crucial motivation behind the formal membership of concrete institutions. So rather than striving for ideal designs our first aim should be to clarify to what extent institutional variation over longer time periods influences the efficiency and efficacy of certain policies. There is scarcely any doubt that 'international institutions do matter' but there remains a limited understanding of the extents and ways in which they actually are of consequence (Young, 1994).

As regards policy-making in international organisations there are essentially two types of evaluation possible, both of which are part of the analysis in Chapters 6 and 7. One, focusing on *results*, asking questions that concern the distribution of costs and benefits between states. Here evaluation has some normative implications, in other words, has positive co-ordination at the international level led to problem-solving or were common interests, goals and values neglected because of 'separate, individual self-interest and distributional conflicts' (Scharpf, 1986, p. 187; 1994a, pp. 38-40). A second, more *process* oriented type of evaluation, redirects our attention to the constitutional provisions to be found in the statutes of international organisations.

In its more radical version, this approach basically employs three criteria to judge whether the rules of international organisations can be considered as efficient (Gygi, 1991, p. 120): (1) governments are the only source of value judgements and express their preferences accordingly; (2) all parties are in agreement as regards the organisation's founding treaty; and (3) all parties concerned by these rules have participated in respective negotiations. The last criterion, as will be shown in the final sections of Chapter 6 and 7, is particular problematic in the EC and OECD case. Therefore a more moderate way of evaluating these organisations suggests itself. By comparing rules which have been considered as efficient in one organisation with those in place in another the impact of different rules can be identified. However, since the management of international organisations has an interest in emphasising the uniqueness of their own achievements, there still remains a large potential for distortions in observing the output of an organisation's internal co-ordination process.

Similarly, the problem of effectiveness is not properly resolved by regime analysis. Nonetheless, there are good reasons for making some of these unsolved problems a central part of the discussion on co-ordination problems. Although the theoretical debate mainly involves 'liberal institutionalists' and 'neo-realists', the need to establish some kind of evaluative criteria cuts both ways - whether the aim is to pin-point the efficiencies or (as is the case here) to stress the deficiencies in international institutions. The fundamental difficulty in assessing the impact of regimes lies in the fact that there is no hypothetical institution-free baseline from which to measure the impact of actual institutions upon the interests and capabilities of states. As Keohane (1993, p. 27) recognises, causal statements about regimes are difficult to make, since the concept refers both to international agreements and rules, and to the behaviour that such rules were designed to regulate. It is therefore tempting to simply view them as just an important constraint on the interests pursued by states, which ensures that states co-operate with one another by following international rules. However, this does not rule out the 'null-hypothesis': regimes may have no effect whatsoever, since co-operation might be a reflection of some set of third forces such as complementary interests in certain issue-areas, the underlying distribution of power, or the asymmetrical influence of non-state actors.

Keohane (1993, pp. 32-3) has put forward at least five proposals as to how empirical research might be able to solve this dilemma: (1) compare behaviour before and after the installation of a regime; (2) see whether governments routinely obey the rules in situations which require co-ordination and where various courses of action would be possible; (3) examine the 'resilience' of regimes when faced with a deterioration in overall relations among the participants; (4) study whether the rules continue to apply even when the conditions under which one would expect states to follow such practices have disappeared; (5) find instances where compliance with international rules is inconvenient - that is to say, in which the regime disagrees with governments' perceptions of what their self-interest would be if there were no such institution. All five proposals have in common that they interpret the regime concept rather restrictively: it is measured by the stringency with which *rules* regulate the behaviour of countries and the extent to which states actually adhere to a package of injunctions.

The first of these proposals is as problematic as the others. Even if the operation of a regime causes state agencies to alter their behaviour, a particular response can still have detrimental effects with regard to the original policy problem. Likewise, under conditions of interdependence it must be expected that the behavioural changes solving one problem instantly create a new one (Young, 1994, p. 146). With problem-solving as the main objective leading to the creation of a regime there are two notions of effectiveness: on the one hand, there is the possibility of conceiving of it in terms of relative improvement and asking what might have happened without the presence of the regime as the intervening variable (Biersteker, 1993); on the other hand, it could constitute a normative reference point in the form of a collective optimum and a comparison with the actual results. But contrary to what the second proposal recommends, behaving differently does not necessarily imply that each state will behave in the same way: routine rule observation invariably has an interpretative dimension that allows for various kinds of conduct to still qualify as compliance. The two main objections raised so far are also relevant to the third proposal: a resilient regime might in practice be nothing more than an empty shell left in place because of its links to an organisational structure with its own interests. The fourth proposal is simply a generalisation of the previous one: if rules continue to apply they can indeed have an impact, yet one which is neither automatically effective nor efficient.

Before turning to the fifth and final suggestion, which includes the domestic setting, it is worth remembering how regimes affect both the capabilities and the interests of states. In the case of the former, they are a source of considerable influence for states whose policies are already consistent with international rules, or who are favoured by the internal decision-making procedures of an international organisation; regimes can also alter the underlying power capabilities of states, either by reinforcing the dominance of rich powerful states or by dissipating their resources. Viewed in this way, there is a striking similarity with the Tsebelis typology of efficient and redistributive institutions, with the regime concept equally covering efficient, consolidating and new deal arrangements.

In terms of evaluation, each type of institution then induces different gain situations. An efficient institution refers to a situation where no further increase in benefits to one party can be obtained without thereby leaving one or more partners in the arrangement worse off; in the case of redistributive institutions, one state or a coalition of states gains more than the other(s). If we now take 'problem-solving' as the baseline measuring the success or failure of a 'regime', it is evident that no *a priori* statement is possible as to which of the three types is actually the appropriate one. Depending on the type of problem at hand the redistribution of gains as well as an overall increase in benefits can be desirable, yet the level of abstraction at which regime theory has usually worked does not make that differentiation and hence, this type of evaluation, possible. Even Young (1994, pp. 143-50), who separates in his analysis 'problem solving' from a normative and result oriented notion of 'evaluative effectiveness', accepts the difficulty in specifying the relationship between various dimensions of effectiveness.

According to the second component, international institutional structures affect positively the calculation of state interests by providing information and altering patterns of transaction costs, and in the long-run they also change conceptions of self-interest through mutual persuasion and the accumulation of scientific knowledge. Consequently, this suggests approaching the measurement of success or failure from another angle, by asking what situation would have existed had the previous rules of the game been left unchanged; in short, by giving an evaluation in terms of incremental change. Section 1.3 has demonstrated that this is not a very promising alternative, partly because the information about the state of affairs is likely to be biased, and independent expert advice - if available - limited. So as stressed earlier, this makes it even more necessary to explicitly acknowledge the long-term character of changes in interests by understanding international policy-making essentially as a process.

The last of the above suggestions, in asking about the degree of compliance in critical situations, switches the analytical perspective from the systemic to the unit level. The realist perspective, therefore, loses much of its relevance, because it assumes that compliance with institutional rules to avoid gaps in gains is achieved through mutual control by states. Since the fundamental goal in co-operative efforts is not to attain the highest possible individual gain but to prevent others from achieving larger net benefits, all sides will suspiciously watch the behaviour of others. As soon as states realise that their partners gain more from the co-operative arrangement, they will abstain from participation. By contrast, it is a central tenet of the (neo-) liberal approach that costs and benefits will often be unevenly distributed among (and within) nations, leading inevitably to a measure of international and domestic conflict between winners and losers. This also introduces another gain category, namely that of group gains, a type to which structuralists would generally subscribe as well. Where the two approaches are most likely differ is over the question as to whether or not there are some groups which benefit with a certain regularity and to what extent intergovernmental bargaining and rule-making interferes in that instance with the domestic distribution of gains (Moravcsik, 1993b, p. 24).

In terms of empirical research this implies a need to identify more precisely the domestic societal interests in specific issue-areas, as well as the ways in which those interests influence government. This is by no means a trivial task because of the existence of three factors which might potentially distort a clear-cut identification of those interests:

- at the level of domestic interest groups. These groups calculate their interests in terms of the expected gains and losses from specific policies, but the estimation of the magnitude of benefits involves a degree of uncertainty and involves risk-laden decisions if particular outcomes are to occur. If the distribution of benefits from a policy deriving from an international agreement are clearly foreseeable, those groups most affected have a strong incentive for articulating their support or opposition. But if the costs and benefits of alternative courses of action are difficult to identify, then it is unlikely that interest groups will mobilise politically. Any *ex post* evaluation working with hard data has to take into account if, and how, accurate information on policy outcomes was initially distributed among the interested parties.

- at the level of governmental decision-makers. In situations of uncertainty governmental decision-makers do not know in which institution to invest or disinvest in order to achieve the highest possible return, so they will attempt to obtain better information. International institutions provide advice in the form of cost-benefit analysis and offer general guidelines according to which beneficial policy choices could be made. But - as has been constantly stressed throughout this chapter - in doing so, institutions can distort the actual interest structure of the participants. For example, if central decision-makers accept the specific advice offered by an international bureaucracy, they will assess a potential gain structure in a different way from that in which such information had not been available. As long as the (international) policy is credible political actors will be prepared to accept short-term losses in return for higher long-term benefits. However, there are usually several institutions fulfilling this function, weighing costs and benefits according to their own organisational goals and suggesting different reference points. The consequences of such a situation are twofold: Firstly, the calculation of national interests changes depending on the institution within which the policy is formulated; and secondly, for reasons of prestige politicians will attempt to justify and stick to their institutional choice, and hence their original evaluation, even in the light of new evidence to the contrary.

- at the level of international bargaining. In general, the institutional setting where bargaining takes place will be a mixture of the two ideal types of efficient and redistributive institutions, which is also reflected in the motivational basis of the participants: though they all have an interest in gaining as much as possible, at the same time they believe that the distribution of the gains from co-operation should be fair. Thus the description of the bargaining problem will not simply be expressed in neutral, strictly interest-oriented terms but will already include some aspects of what the parties consider to be their legitimate claims in each context. It can be expected, for example, that economic interests will be couched in discussions about principles of distribution, i.e. whether potential benefits should be assigned according to the contribution of the participants (*juste retour*), according to their actual need or in exactly equal shares. Therefore, evaluation at this level can only trace back interest structures in an interpretative way, based on the problem descriptions as originally put forward by the individual states.

In any case, evaluative criteria cannot simply refer to the formal compliance of states with international rules. As Young (1994, p. 147) points out in his notion of 'process effectiveness', the implementation of regime provisions entails a political process at the domestic level that leads to the passing of legislation in different member states. Therefore, as Section 1.3 has indicated, a long-term perspective which examines interest structures and institutional and ideational factors in relation to distinct phases of the policy process is much more important, in other words, analysing policy-making in international issue-areas with a clear concept of time. Though the identification and definition of an interdependence problem already constitutes an important step in the selection of potential paths to its solution, this can only be considered as the starting point of the co-ordination process. The subsequent agenda-setting by institutional fora represents a preliminary step, which does not exclude the fact that rival institutions with similar interests will take up the same issues or closely related ones. The respective negotiation agendas are not planned in detail, and will only imperfectly define the roles, norms and values of the participants. As long as the rules of the game are not fixed, the evaluation of gains and losses, as well as the description of the issues at stake, may shift significantly during this second phase of the policy cycle.

Just as effectiveness is not simply equivalent to compliance, so the formulation of the aims, strategies and instruments for a co-ordinated policy cannot be assumed to be identical with the rule of law. Quite often international organisations only decide on a framework and leave the actual resolution of conflicts to subsidiary levels, but even in organisations with 'supranational' features the implementation and enforcement of laws remains a continuous process and not a fixed state of affairs. Therefore regime theory has over-emphasised compliance with rules as a criterion for effectivity. As Snyder (1993, p. 26) points out, 'the implementation of law involves conflict, negotiation, compromise and mutual adjustment' and although it 'may be characterized by patterns and relative stability in the long term, it is not one-way but rather is recursive and circular'. In fact, the very same can be said with regard to compliance. Since it depends predominantly upon the behaviour of national administrations, country specific priorities, organisational features and standing operating procedures will have a strong, independent influence on the success of international policies (Young, 1989, p. 79). Therefore, it is insufficient to demonstrate a convergence of domestic interests among several countries, since it is also necessary to ask the complementary question of when and how interest-group influence can be decisive. Carruth (1989, pp. 17-38), for example, has shown that as well as traditional means such as sanctions, material incentives and symbolic action, the co-optation of societal groups at the domestic *and* at the international level can increase the legitimacy of policy-making, and in turn, the adherence to previously agreed rules.

In terms of evaluation, interest-group influence causes one further problem. Those who consider themselves to be the 'losers' or who perceive policy development as too slow, or even stagnating, will attempt to change the arena (Windhoff-Héritier, 1985, p. 22). They expect that by changing the structure of the game, there will be an improvement in their own position in domestic conflicts during the implementation phase of international policies. Yet the extent to which institutional alternatives are available determines the move to other domestic arenas, and erodes the structure of the horizontal arena as well. The correct identification of arenas, and of their scope and limits, becomes crucial in assessing correctly the credibility of threats by international institutions and the credibility of commitments by governments. *Prima vista* voluntary compliance with international rules appears to be feasible when there is a tight concentration of profits and the broadest possible dispersion of costs. The typology of domestic policies suggested by Wilson (1973, pp. 332-7), and presented in Figure 1.1, captures the nature of the resulting problem in an international context (Underdal, 1991, p. 110).

		Costs	
		Concentrated	*Diffuse*
Benefits	*Concentrated*	A	B
	Diffuse	C	D

Figure 1.1 Typology of domestic policies

The figure shows the incentive structure facing the actors at the national level when dealing with the implementation of international regulations. Broad goals and principles which are major part of the output of international institutions fit best into category D. Concrete attempts at problem-solving, such as a curb on subsidies to specific industries, would require implementation measures that would usually fall into cell C. We know from the pattern of interest group influence at the domestic level that the political decision-making process here introduces a bias in favour of policies located in cell B. The successful implementation of policy at the domestic or international level is facilitated in situations where the distribution of costs and benefits is concentrated (as in A). The bias towards diffuse costs arising from interest group pressure at the domestic level combined with the tendency of international institutions to be concerned with diffuse benefits leads to a situation which could be labelled the vertical *and* horizontal disintegration of 'effective' policies, i.e. a state of affairs where co-ordinated policies deviate significantly from what adequate solutions would require.

Any evaluation by international administrations themselves during the final phase of termination or policy reformulation undoubtedly misses this point if the main focus is put on the outputs or outcomes of their activities. While it is quite common to add to this a series of complaints about the insufficient supply of resources for fulfilling the organisational goals, it is much more difficult to establish a link between input and output. Criteria such as efficiency and effectiveness overemphasise what is really a purely formal relationship between the two. The previous paragraphs have instead tried to stress some of the more neglected aspects of a process which should be - but too rarely is - oriented towards problem-solving.

In conclusion, we can suggest that international institutions have the potential for distorting the preferences of governments in relation to policy co-ordination, even if that potential is not uniform but depends on the particular features of the institutions themselves. If, for example, the goal is to realise synergy gains, formal reorganisation according to the principle of subsidiarity will be necessary, though obviously not without questioning some of the theoretical concepts underlying the practical reform proposals. For this reason, I began my analysis with a rational choice approach but gradually extended and softened it by introducing ideational factors. In relation to empirical research, that implies drawing a dynamic picture, firstly by incorporating different levels of analysis and secondly, by taking seriously the interactions between those levels by means of a retrospective evaluation.

2 Co-operation, Co-ordination and Integration

This next chapter examines more closely the concept of co-ordination and argues that its interpretation should always be carefully related to the specific contexts in which it occurs. So far terms like co-operation and co-ordination have been used interchangeably and reference has sometimes been made to 'supranational' settings. There are many ways of dealing with this lack of conceptual clarity and expressing the different dimensions of related concepts. The Oxford English Dictionary, for example, defines co-operation as 'working together or acting in conjunction with another person or thing towards the same end, purpose or effect'; whereas co-ordination is contrasted with subordination and denotes 'the action of arranging or placing things in the same order, rank or degree in proper position relative to each other and to the system of which they form parts'. Finally, integration is defined as 'the making up or composition of a whole by adding together or combining separate parts or elements'. The same basic definitions can be maintained for the purposes of political science by virtue of the fact that they locate all three concepts on a continuum, with conflict and harmony as the two polar points between which states organise their interdependence.

Co-operation between states and the co-ordination of their policies are necessary prerequisites even in fully fledged federal systems. In the German system, for example, the principle of 'federal comity' demands to avoid interferences between different levels of government while simultaneously pursuing goals which are 'maximally community compatible' (Scharpf, 1992, pp. 11-4). However, activities under this label alone will not amount to integration (Scharpf, 1994b, pp. 226-7), which instead evolves as a process with several dimensions. When Galtung (1968, p. 377), for instance, speaks of a course of action, 'whereby two or more actors form a new actor and transfer loyalties to the new agent', he is mainly interested in the political decision-making aspect through common institutions. Deutsch (1957), on the other hand, insists that a move from regime creation to integration requires that member of two or more political units develop a sense of community, and thus highlights the socio-psychological aspects. Another alternative dimension would be to point to

47

societal interdependence creating an ever increasing number of economic transactions.

In Section 1 of this chapter, I will look at some of the recent discussions over institutional variation in reaction to economic interdependence, before proceeding to focus on one specific form of policy co-ordination that is particularly relevant to the activities of international and supranational organisations. This makes it possible in Section 2.2 to include the common value orientations factor and to draw some conclusions regarding the viability of a system which tries to reconcile different co-ordination mechanisms. Finally, Sections 2.3 and 2.4 place these findings within the context of the European Community (EC) and the Organisation for Economic Co-operation and Development (OECD). I then conclude by arguing that each institution follows a distinct organisational logic which prevents effective third order co-ordination.

2.1   Institutional Variation

Institutions can range from formal organisations shaped by diverse kinds of legal contract to very informal types of collective organisation characterised only by norms and conventions. For example, the task of securing free trade between countries can be carried out either by formal contract and enforcement through international treaties, or alternatively, through the emergence of norms and conventions which provide informal guidelines for state conduct; likewise it is possible to envisage intermediate categories which combine both contracts and conventions in hybrid forms. Although the specific policy-problem might remain the same, the strategic structure underlying the issues may well require different institutional responses. Authors such as Stein (1983), Snidal (1985) and Martin (1992) have all tried to explain this phenomenon by applying the tool of game theory. The Prisoner's Dilemma and a co-ordination game like the Battle of the Sexes can be taken as two 'polar' cases which catch the essence of what occurs, 'when the nature of interdependence between states, as reflected in the ways in which they affect and are affected by another, differs across issue areas' (Snidal, 1985, p. 924).

In Figure 2.1 both states choose policy option B rather than policy option A. Although both could potentially gain more from option A they decide to follow policy B in pursuit of their narrow self-interest, because it promises a higher payoff given the other state would be implementing policy A. Thus, by following its national interest, state I makes state II worse off regardless of what the latter does, and vice versa. But since both could benefit by a move away from their dominant strategy, there is room for co-operation instead of independent action and the simplest solution which suggests itself is a contract, thereby overcoming the previous stable, but inefficient, equilibrium. Through making binding agreements both states can achieve co-operation that is in their respective national interest in the form of policy A and gain a higher payoff than before. Therefore, in reality the political solution to this problem will leave an important role to contract like arrangements as provided by formal international organisations (Martin, 1992, p. 770).

		state II	
		A	B
state I	A	3,3	1,4
	B	4,1	2,2

Figure 2.1   Prisoner's dilemma

		state II	
		A	B
state I	A	4,3	1,1
	B	1,1	3,4

Figure 2.2   Battle of the sexes

In Figure 2.2 neither state is in a position to choose its most beneficial policy option without first knowing what the other intends to do. Though both states prefer one set of outcomes to another, i.e. they both favour the same policy option, they are not indifferent when it comes to effecting co-ordination on policy A or policy B. Due to the different payoff structure state I prefers option A, whereas state II is more likely to follow option B. However, once the two parties have settled on either one of the two efficient equilibria there is no need for a sanctioning mechanism. Since the single benefit accruing to each state is so much higher than in the case where both implement different policies, they have no incentive for departing from the agreed choice. The basic solution is therefore a convention including established traditions and shared principles, and which gives an orientation to mutually beneficial state policies in the same issue area.

This kind of theoretical reasoning about collective action problems and their respective institutional solutions on the basis of two by two matrices nevertheless has its limits. Potential solutions deriving from this type of analysis cannot simply be extrapolated to models which encompass a larger range of variables. Any more realistic scenario would of course have to include a full array of policy options where the relevant decision-makers are faces with choices other than purely dichotomous ones. In addition, most agreements concluded in an interstate context take place on a multilateral rather than a bilateral level, and there will nearly always be more than two actors participating in the different games. Finally, if we take proper account of the time factor, this might involve either specifying a time horizon, fixing discount rates for future benefits or measuring the speed of mutual policy adjustments, all of which modifications can be expected to have an independent impact on the particular institutional solution.

Consider, for example, the co-ordination game in Figure 2.2 and assume that it will be iterated. The participants now become more concerned with the exact distributional impact of their choice, because the short-term costs of forcing a move to a new equilibrium may be outweighed by the long-term benefits of another solution; those who are relatively disadvantaged by the existing convention will have the greatest incentive for changing it. Yet, as Figure 2.3 shows, if we make an additional modification in the number of participants, the players will be in an asymmetrical relation with one another from the very start (Snidal, 1985, p. 935).

state I	state III	state II
(4 / 3.5 / 3)	(3.5 / 4 / 3.5)	(3 / 3.5 / 4)

Figure 2.3   Three-state co-ordination

The state with a favoured payoff structure somewhere *between* that of the other states enjoys a comparatively better position than its partners with more specific preferences. Whatever the convention agreed upon, state III on the co-ordination axis will always secure a benefit with a ranking of at least 3.5, whereas at the very most only one of the other two countries will achieve the same result.

Therefore, a certain amount of caution is fully justified when transferring findings derived from basic game structures to concrete contexts. Rather than explaining actual outcomes as being a consequence of a particular institutional set-up, they provide a better understanding of how deficiencies in organisational performance can arise from variations in the degree of institutionalisation (Chisholm, 1989). Assuming that the strategic structure of a policy problem is adequately described by a co-ordination game, its formal organisation would then have to be restricted to the choice, interpretation and observance of a convention by means of information gathering and informal consultations. Conversely, if the situation resembles that of the Prisoner's Dilemma more formal arrangements will be needed in order to monitor and assess the degree of compliance with the rules and to overcome the continuing incentives for states to avoid following a co-operative policy (Martin, 1992). But this can only be the starting point for an exploration of the comparative utility of alternative organisational forms under different configurations of state interests: To refer back to the discussion in Section 4 of Chapter 1, the really important question to ask is whether, and to what extent, end-goals such as trade liberalisation can be reached under pre-existing institutions. Again, different institutional architectures and organising devices might lead to a choice of tools where a policy problem is set in the 'wrong' institutional context, i.e. a co-ordination problem is resolved through a contract and a Prisoner's Dilemma tackled with a convention. With regard to the former the creation of an unnecessary constraint leads to a waste of resources, whereas in the latter case the convention lacks sufficient restrictive power over the individual behaviour of states; in the first situation the outcome is inefficient, in the second ineffective.

There are, however, other attempts which try to include the observable institutional variety right from the start, such as the efforts to liberalise the international economic system. The subsequent paragraphs in this section therefore look at some of these inductive approaches in the light of their relevance to organisations like the EC and the OECD.

Those approaches based in the tradition of institutional economics have formulated a third model, located between the extremes of the market and hierarchical systems. Taking the form of a federation or teams, the respective participating units are assumed to remain statutorily independent but engage in pooling returns. By means of joint decision-making, profits will be shared, markets divided and orders allocated without the reliance on a central administration to monitor the members. In terms of more traditional inter-firm relations a cartel would approximate best to this intermediate form of *co-ordination mechanism;* only in cases where the degree of uncertainty, the size of transaction-specific investments and the frequency of recurrence of the transaction is very high, would a hierarchical order have to be established.

Arguing along similar lines, Yarbrough and Yarbrough (1992) have distinguished four institutional forms - uni-, bi-, mini- and multilateralism - in order to conceptualise institutional variation in trading arrangements. The novelty of their approach lies in the fact that they associate these four categories not with the number of parties to an agreement, but instead to particular enforcement mechanisms. Despite the fact that in diverse contexts the organisational dilemma may be essentially the same (Yarbrough and Yarbrough, 1992, p. 20),

> actors within a group have common interests in expanding the size of the relevant pie, but conflicting interests in dividing it. Cooperation increases the size of the pie, but unilateral defection enables a party to capture a larger share of the smaller pie. Cooperation requires keeping concerns over division of the pie from interfering with increasing the size of the pie.

The actual benefits deriving from trade agreements will ultimately depend on the pattern and extent of compliance; and the latter can be expected to vary according to different kinds of trade. Depending on the type of trade transaction involved, a specific enforcement mechanism is thus the deliberate *ex ante* choice of the participating countries for dealing effectively with the possibility of opportunist behaviour among their partners. If, for example, it is possible for a country to withdraw with low costs from transacting with a trading partner in response to a protectionist action, unilateral policies will still be viable and only a few institutional safeguards would be necessary to ensure compliance. If, on the other hand, considerable costs arise from withdrawal the enforcement of agreements will be under the control of a third party. This can either be done on a broad (multilateral) or, as is the case with the supranational dispute settlement procedures in the European Community, on a more limited (minilateral) scale. In cases where these mechanisms are not available for particular goods or products, 'bilateral' trade institutions - implying the setting of common standards or working with issue linkages - will be installed.

However, a major shortcoming of this positive approach to institutional variation stems from its central proposition, concerning the respective utility and success of organisational forms. Because it assumes that the parties anticipate non-compliance in advance of their agreements, the approach is unable to incorporate any *ex post* opportunism into the analysis. It is in fact a more general weakness of functional reasoning that there are in practice many stable paths to co-operation which cannot readily be differentiated in terms of their consequences for aggregate welfare. Indeed, why should those particular agreements and institutions that actually emerge represent uniquely efficient solutions to common problems? As Garrett (1992, pp. 559-60) points out,

> This approach ... downplays the fundamentally political nature of most bargaining over cooperative agreements. There are likely to be many political solutions to collective action problems that conform with Pareto criteria. ... However, in most instances, these different solutions are likely to have significant distributional consequences, and hence the preferences of participants with respect to choosing a solution may differ considerably. Thus, the focus on common problems should be supplemented by explicit attention to the dynamics of bargaining over the detailed form that cooperation will take.

Institutions need not be granted any 'supranational' powers for stable co-operation to be facilitated, as is true for example in the EC case. In certain circumstances, they only need to provide the information which is necessary for the effective punishment of members. Since it would be very costly (if not impossible) for actors to construct arrangements that offer an exhaustive set of rules which would be relevant to all their future interactions, the participants can only make 'incomplete contracts' outlining some 'general codes of conduct' rather than specifying how participants should behave under all possible conditions (Weingast and Garrett, 1993, p. 180; Majone, 1996, pp. 68-72). In contrast to the Yarbrough and Yarbrough approach, the much more pertinent question is how existing institutions actually deal with unanticipated contingencies when - in the absence of clear-cut rules - compliance again becomes a matter of dispute. Hence Weingast and Garrett's (1993, pp. 181-2) suggestion that current interpretations of institutional choice are inadequate in two related ways:

> First, they fail to explain how actors settle on particular rules of the game, including the relevant organizing principles and supporting institutions, from among the many sets that are available. Second, they do not consider the impact of ambiguity and unanticipated contingencies on the role of institutions in the implementation of these rules: how institutions arbitrate in disputes that are not directly covered by their mandates and why members might adhere to their decisions.

Weingast and Garrett's answer is based on the construction of focal points, which can resolve multiple equilibria problems in cases where the actors are indifferent as to the potential outcomes. They argue that ideational factors, in the form of shared beliefs about the spirit of agreements, can play a decisive role if *mechanisms* (such as mutual recognition in the EC example) can be devised that combine an informal notion like fairness with more formal elements of organisation (Weingast and Garrett, 1993, pp. 203-4). In other words, contract and convention can unite in one institutional solution, whilst not denying the simultaneous relevance of other variables to the understanding of institutional variation. Aside from ideas, economic interests and power resources can also be expected to have a significant influence on institutional choices within organisations, and it is precisely for this reason that the concrete context in which specific collective action problems are addressed matters so much. Regime theorists such as Haas and Keohane have accepted some of the arguments such as these, which are grouped together under the heading of institutional variation, and have responded by trying to establish some new categories that capture both differences in the internal coherence, authority, and legitimacy of regimes and also their organisational prerequisites (such as patterns of representation, secretariat autonomy, the status of experts, revenue base or the monitoring of compliance).

According to Haas, differences between regimes reflect different forms and intensities of state demand, e.g. when states ask for more effective national action, the pooling of information and aid to implement measures very often proves sufficient. *Co-ordination*, by contrast, is a more ambitious kind of 'regime responsibility', where 'states seek to negotiate agreements on how they should act individually in order to bring about some generally desired future state of affairs' (Haas, 1990, p. 198). Consequently, the implementation of the respective policy measures for achieving a particular outcome will remain completely in state hands and the resulting institutional structure will not imply either rule-making or conflict resolution. If, however, domestic policy measures have negative repercussions in other countries, a need for such commonly agreed mechanisms does indeed arise. And *regulation* in this typology thus becomes the 'most ambitious type of regime' (Haas, 1990, p. 198):

> Regulation implies that specific rules of conduct are agreed to and that institutions for resolving conflict over the rules be set up. As far as rule making and conflict resolution are concerned, regulation takes place in the organization; but the implementation of the rules usually remains the responsibility of the member states.

Keohane (1993, pp. 38-41), on the other hand, suggests applying a typology on the basis of different criteria for becoming a member of an international institution. If membership is in principle open to all states and, in turn, all members control organisational performance, then its function will be limited to 'consultation' through the exchange of opinions and the discussion of symbolic issues. Other institutions will accept members only if they are prepared to follow a set of prescribed commitments, and will foster 'collaboration', i.e. control for free riding, via the provision of reciprocal benefits for the participants. Finally, some institutions may restrict membership to a small number of states that have converging interests or that have similar domestic political arrangements; because these member states wish to realise potential gains *vis-à-vis* outsiders and/or try to build strong bonds of community, they will engage in 'cartelization'.

It is worth asking to what extent the activities of the OECD and the EC coincide with the above typologies. Is the former an example of co-ordination, along with regulation depending on the specific issue-area (Haas, 1990, p. 247)? Is the latter in practice *sui generis* and, therefore, not to be described under the international institution/regime label? Or do both, being cartels, fulfil the same role of exploitation of adversaries (Keohane, 1993, p. 40)? Although both authors attempt to pay more attention to contextual factors, their search for overarching principles ultimately fails to actually tie down institutional mechanisms to organisational settings. Despite the conceptual refinements, they still do not appreciate how policy co-ordination can be equally as well approached using a rule-based system (through the provision of resources to ease adjustment costs and rule clarification), as by a discretionary bargaining system (by means of brokerage, the provision of information and model building). The crucial questions, as to why certain types of regimes should be more conducive to desired outcomes and whether less institutionalised systems of national bargaining can under certain conditions produce similar results, are left unanswered.

From there, we can move to Kahler's (1989, p. 379; 1995, p. 4) definition of *co-ordination systems*. Kahler adds a decision-making level to the well-known rules-discretion dichotomy, i.e. whether the decision-making on the mutual adjustment of policies takes place primarily in the domestic or international setting. In figure 2.4 cell A represents a rule-governed model that relies on decentralised national decisions for co-ordination, whereas cell D stands for the broad use of discretion in international negotiations which are conducted without anything more than procedural guidelines; both could still produce the same outcome, depending on the specific context. If, for example, there is no underlying consensus with regard to the main variables along which national economic systems work, or no benign economic environment to facilitate adherence to commonly accepted rules, then neither of the two models will succeed. This in fact argues in favour of 'hybrid' solutions which try to bridge the gap between the two standard models of international policy co-ordination, and which also go beyond the extreme cases of either non-co-ordination with purely discretionary, national decisions (cell C) or unified

management of a multi-country economy similar to that of a national one
(cell B).

Levels of decision

Modality of co-ordination	*National*	*International*
Rules/Injunctions	A	B
Discretionary bargaining	C	D

Figure 2.4   Co-ordination systems

The discussion so far has shown that institutional variation presents us
with a conceptual dilemma that is rooted in the move from 'co-operation
under anarchy' to co-operation in an already institutionalised setting.
Though institutions and outcomes may well be connected in a systematic
way, the majority of existing approaches lack clarity and focus: what they
gain in terms of theory by constructing typologies is lost in their
applicability to concrete organisations and vice-versa. In the following
section I will try and suggest some improvements, firstly by concentrating
on the composite model of regulatory policy co-ordination, and secondly,
by comparing the respective mechanisms of the EC and the OECD.

2.2   Regulatory Policy Co-ordination

Selznick (1985, pp. 363-4) has defined regulation as the sustained and
focused control exercised by a public agency over activities that are valued
by a community. Hence, it is not limited to rule-making alone, but includes
other factors which play a role in the formation of laws, and it also finds
expression in less formalised ways such as standards and general norms.
Governmental agencies of different national affiliations do not simply
concentrate on the steering of societal activities by fiscal incentives, they
also resort to a wide range of legal-bureaucratic instruments; with
regulative intervention quite often becoming justified almost exclusively on
the basis of efficiency criteria. Yet as this section concludes, its relationship
to questions of legitimacy is frequently of greater significance. As Goodin
(1988, p. 248) remarks:

people have all sorts of wants, and decision-makers are obliged to respect them all if they respect any of them. People may, for example, desire equity, even at the cost of efficiency; or they may want to have certain procedures employed in making decisions, even if that is not the most efficient way of going about things.

The extent to which common value orientations influence and actually enter into the content of specific regulations is difficult to discern: according to the definition presented above, they would have to be *a priori* identical with the orientations and preferences of the regulators themselves. Given its emphasis on allocative efficiency, the general potential of regulative policy-making also faces other restrictions alongside those derived from normative reasoning, due to the existence of different rationality criteria in the actual practice of regulation. The neo-classical focus on market failure, for example, is based on microeconomic conceptions of rationality but the regulatory instruments to be employed are mainly legal ones, whose content is influenced by considerations of administrative applicability; yet, once the stage of implementation is reached, their success will depend on a mixture of all these dimensions.

It comes as no surprise that the solutions that appear more attractive are those which try to circumvent the procedural difficulties associated with the criteria just mentioned. One such example is the concept of self-regulation, implying a market with rules set up by the producers, firms and enterprises themselves, and where regulators become a subgroup of the suppliers. Though it is in the nature of most forms of regulation to involve an element of self-regulation (because it is concentrated on production activities), its general scope can be considered a function of the requisite technical knowledge. Those suppliers possessing an expertise in certain issue-areas will have an advantage in the political arena where regulatory decisions are taken, in the shape of a compromise between different interest groups. In short, the greater the need for specialised information the more likely becomes the recruitment of experts from a particular grouping. So should the resulting organisation of the market be evaluated in relation to welfare aspects? Producer interests answer this question positively, because incomplete markets and asymmetrical information would otherwise either make it impossible to assess the quality of goods correctly or only to do so at too late a stage. Consumer interests, on the other hand, would answer this question in the negative, because in their view self-regulation imposes market entry barriers in order to guarantee additional revenues for those suppliers already operating in the market. Nevertheless, the surplus income coming from the firms has to be distributed somehow. But as it is difficult to think in terms of self-regulation without the official support of state agencies, it is also impossible to answer the question of redistribution without active state participation.

As with what happens in domestic settings, the internationalisation of markets may ascribe a comparable task to international organisations: public agencies, which counterbalance the privileged position of transnational firms operating under conditions of geographically separated production and consumption. However, the analogy cannot be pushed too far. Apart from certain business sectors, there are problems in trying to identify something like a community at the international level, and even in the regional context of the EC, the continuing *Gemeinschaft versus Gesellschaft* debate has indicated how a missing sense of community can result in stagnation and indeed disintegration (Scharpf, 1988). For international institutions, facing budget constraints and delays in the contributions of their members, there is an incentive for increasing competencies by extending regulatory activities, which increase their influence without having large implementation costs attached.

At the international - just as at the national - level, issues of political economy attract supporters of pure market solutions as well as advocates of hierarchical allocation. In consequence international regimes vary both in form and in substance: they can either impose limits on the rights of states or restrict the activities of non-state actors; they can facilitate private exchange relationships or have a distorting influence on market arrangements; and in certain circumstances they may even provide for the political appropriation of resources. The acceptance of international regulation, and hence its impact, will in turn largely depend on the dominant 'mode of allocation' in the domestic policy arena that is the target of regulatory intervention. Similarly, at the unit level different modes - market, political regulation, direct state intervention - can be expected to have independent influences on the implementation of international rules (Kohler-Koch, 1989, p. 64). Since different distribution mechanisms will be used across countries, a degree of conflict with the instruments of international institutions is inevitable. This may lead to the purely technical problem of 'translating' rules into national political systems, but can also initiate co-ordination problems between government departments which try to protect their own turf by flexible interpretations of international regulations. In addition there will be further obstacles created, if established domestic distribution patterns are threatened. In particular, if national administrations have to relinquish some of their powers, they will tend to combine with status quo oriented groups to form political opposition to international arrangements. It is plausible to assume that, instead of abandoning already existing practices, new areas of regulation as well as multiple and overlapping rule-making will generally be favoured; only those instruments which are less rule-bound, or more flexible and loosely connected with interest group rents can be easily seceded to inter-governmental settings.

However, this cannot solve the problems of governments which experience the decreasing efficacy of their policy instruments under conditions of rising economic interdependence and globalised markets. Lindblom (1977, p. 174) has shown that in a bargaining situation between business and government the eventual outcome will usually favour the former. In return for maintaining essential investment functions, the government rewards the business with tax concessions, subsidies, loans and legal privileges. Since firms and enterprises can engage in an 'investment strike' with potentially negative effects on employment and the re-election prospects of governments, it is primarily their demand which will be reflected in official policies rather than those of others. But once the presence of more than one government is assumed, then business is no longer confined to this strategy and can now actively disinvest and move elsewhere. In relation to the original bargaining situation, for example, subsidies offered by country A can be used by firms to pry even greater subsidies from country B and vice-versa. Ultimately, this could lead to a situation where the potential gains from winning contracts and securing a corporate presence will be outweighed by the costs of permanent subsidies, but in the meantime capital can exploit its mobility by circumventing domestic regulation and undermining the efficacy of national measures.

The results of this process will differ from country to country depending on its industrial structure. National administrations will try to peal with the problem themselves, making discretionary use of a wide range of regulatory instruments - including sometimes resorting to cyclical regulation and deregulation contingent on the respective success of their industries. However, when all governments experience a decreasing efficacy in their policy instruments, co-operation in the form of regulatory exchange offers a more promising opportunity for the pursuit of individual goals than unilateral action, even though this response will again be insufficient because of the altered nature of the relationship between firms and governments and changes in international market structures. Following the logic of accumulation, more and more enterprises are forced to seek *additional* markets rather than simply moving to other ones, and state agencies and business enter into a symbiosis, where 'in return for state support, the firm more readily adapts its strategies to accommodate national political (including economic security) goals' (Stopford and Strange, 1991, p. 234). In practice, foreign policy interests may even merge with industrial policy to create a 'new diplomacy' aimed at obtaining the value-added within the respective home territory (Strange, 1992, p. 7).

Seen from this angle, the question is not so much one of whether it is possible for national governments to act as a cartel in regulatory matters in order to improve their bargaining position in relation to the private sector, or more particularly whether it is possible in this way to forestall business attempts to play states off against each other (Bowler, 1988, p. 525). Instead, it is much more that the transformed 'Lindblom problem' asks whether delegation to international fora makes any sense at all, given that states now seem to be more willing to compete with each other in collusion with the private sector. While the general proposition, according to which there are gains from co-ordinating regulatory policies when one state is affected by the respective decisions of another, may still hold, the circumstances under which it is in the national interest to do so (by giving up independence in regulatory matters) requires greater elaboration.

Concerning the study of firm-government relations and the case of export promotion, the main issue becomes whether enterprises within member states should be regulated at national, EC or OECD level. According to economic theory, regulations seek to compensate for market failure caused by the use of market power, the existence of externalities or information asymmetries between the participants. But although the recognition of market failures is a necessary condition for justifying regulatory intervention, it is in this case not a sufficient one (Fleisig and Hill, 1984, pp. 329-40). Therefore, aside from the possibility that institutional innovation may be more costly than the actual magnitude of market failures warrants, a particular kind of *regulatory failure* can often occur because there are also asymmetries of information between regulators and the economic agents whose activity they seek to control. Consequently, an argument in favour of regulatory intervention requires that in any one instance the costs associated with market failures are actually balanced and not increased by the activities of public agencies. In addition, delegation presupposes a situation where market failures can be ameliorated less effectively at the national than at the international level (Gatsios and Seabright, 1989, p. 38).

However, since many national regulations have become a strategic weapon in international competition, this latter distinction is not as straightforward as it at first seems. The example of particular relevance to this thesis is the use of state aids to industry, where national agencies not only ignore the behaviour of their counterparts but in fact deliberately adapt their own strategies to those of major competitors. While it is sometimes argued that subsidies reduce unemployment, provide a substitute for the reluctance of private capital markets to cover long-term risks and lead to product innovation, official involvement has instead often been used as an instrument for opening up new markets for domestic firms by gaining an advantage over potential rivals with a different domestic base.

It is not necessary to repeat here the discussion in Chapter 1 about the role of international institutions as a part of the co-ordination process, but it is worth stressing in addition that international solutions to regulatory failure will also entail significant costs and delays during negotiations and perhaps even more so once agreement has been reached. Section 1 of this chapter has also given some indications as to how institutional variation can matter in situations where not just one but several optimal solutions exist, differing only in their distribution of benefits. The bargaining situation in which participants have to agree on a particular corrective to market failure can be characterised exactly in this way, since each party will be better informed about the conditions in its own industries and will be concerned with distributional consequences.

A second and more important issue, in relation to the 'hybrid' case of regulatory policy co-ordination, is that of *credibility* towards other parties. The welfare potential of co-ordinated action can be exaggerated unless the reaction of the private sector is properly taken into account. For example, the behaviour of exporting firms cannot be considered to be a matter of indifference for any intergovernmental arrangement among major trading partners: an adverse reaction by private enterprises to co-operative agreements between national authorities can actually make things worse rather than better. The co-ordination of economic policy instruments sometimes means more, sometimes less regulation of the actors in the market. Depending on the national context the ability to enforce co-operative regulatory outcomes across countries will vary according to the degree of symmetry in the relations of each home government towards its nationally-based firms. While there is often uncertainty on the part of private enterprises about the likely severity of regulation, governments and international agencies, on the other hand, will not really know the actual costs it imposes on industrial sectors and the economy as a whole. Particularly, where international bodies set up terms of reference but national agencies decide on the rules in specific cases, it becomes quite difficult for firms (as well as for other participating states) to observe whether the aims and intentions of domestic regulatory decisions are consistent with what governments officially proclaim them to be. However, this kind of discretionary regulation is the very essence of a model that tries to mix certain features of rule-based and bargaining-based co-ordination systems, so international institutions with regulatory tasks will not therefore be immune to the credibility problem. Though doubts about the precise aims being pursued could be eased by greater publicity surrounding negotiations, the self-interest of governments normally dictates a desire for secrecy and confidentiality during most stages of the co-ordination process.

The credibility problem also crops up in relation to third countries which do not participate in the delegation of regulatory powers to a common agency. To take another example from trade policy, where firms from two countries, A and B, are competing for the market of C, an importing country, the question is how should they determine the optimum level of a common subsidy to their exporters in reaction to an import tax imposed by the third country. If the tariff set by C is comparatively lower in relation to A's subsidy level than that of B, then country B would be better off transferring power in order to achieve treatment equivalent to that given to country A. Likewise, if under the same conditions A and B delegate to a separate agency, which in turn determines a new subsidy level different to the original agreements, both countries would ultimately be worse off than had they taken a course of unilateral action. As Gatsios and Seabright (1989, p. 52) have argued:

> although a country may choose any level of export tax or subsidy it wishes, it is not within its power to have any reaction function it wishes. And the equilibrium of this game is determined by the reaction functions of the players, not simply by the strategies open to them. ... transferring powers to a separate agency could therefore be worse ... This warns us that even when there are gains from setting a common policy, a common agency may not be the best means to do so.

Although this remains conjectural and would require an empirical analysis of the participants' individual and joint reaction functions for it to be properly substantiated, the example illustrates the potentially counter-productive effects resulting from co-ordination by delegation.

More generally, there are three main reasons why regulatory policy co-ordination can have perverse effects. Firstly, and has been indicated above, transferring regulatory powers to more distant institutions might diminish the effectiveness of monitoring because of information deficits on the part of the regulators in relation to the activities of national industries. Secondly, and in line with the arguments presented in Chapter 1, the possibility of 'firm capture' and 'government capture' at the domestic level is matched by the possibility of 'bureaucratic capture' at the level of international organisations. Whereas the first type of regulatory capture describes the tendency of agencies to identify with the aims of the private enterprises themselves, the second refers to the involvement of their activities with *other* aims of government such as the securing of employment, attempts to gain competitive advantages or the furthering of foreign policy goals. In fact, the bureaucratic capture of international institutions, in which regulatory practice increasingly reflects the individual aims of the staff, may in certain organisational contexts also include political aims that go beyond the mere correction of regulatory failure at the unit level. Thirdly, it is one of the characteristics of international institutions that they only become selectively active, in terms of controlling limited policy areas rather than regulating an entire policy space, with the result that some of the relevant international repercussions of policy choices (i.e. externalities) are partially neglected (Gatsios and Seabright, 1989, p. 55). Particularly when agreements concerning regulatory policy co-ordination establish general frameworks for action, the decisions that are taken on a case by case basis will actually revive the process of bargaining, albeit whilst excluding cross-effects with related issues.

As will be shown in Chapter 6 the overall result proves negative if, for example, a regulatory arrangement also includes a spending budget that is to be distributed according to procedures which fail to compensate for the disproportionate influence of different parts of the membership.

The arguments put forward in this section reject the proposition that regulation has to be undertaken at the international level due to market globalisation. To begin with these arguments were more theoretical in nature, but are reflected in more practical problems as well. For example, the internationalisation of market segments for capital goods advances faster in some geographical areas than in others and consumption patterns vary enormously between industrialised and developing countries. Though a process of change in the traditional firm-government relationship can be identified in many countries, its actual impact needs to be differentiated on a regional, as well as country by country, basis. The introduction to this section also suggested some motives for regulation other than those of economic efficiency, such as on grounds of equity. But universal organisations with a large and heterogeneous membership will usually define equity in terms of equality of treatment, i.e. as regards their status and voting rights. Bargaining in a politicised atmosphere around already divisive themes is thus bound to produce compromise formulas instead of regulations which put the problem-solving onus on the participants, and hence no strong case can be made for a 'world regulatory agency'.

These limitations, together with a lack of political will to set up organisations with adequate power and authority, leads most authors to agree that regional organisations are the natural fall-back solution in regulatory matters (Tudyka, 1990, p. 147; Hurrell, 1995, p. 56). If the question is one of deciding whether or not to regulate at the national or the global level, the trade-offs between the negotiation costs of agreements and credibility towards third parties and between scale economies and diverse preferences, would suggest a solution in terms of overlapping jurisdictions, each dealing with specific policy issues in geographically demarcated areas. Nevertheless, as Section 2 of Chapter 1 indicated for international institutions in general and as Cooper (1976, p. 51) has remarked of this type of 'regionalism' in particular, a number of deficiencies continue to exist:

> A system of functional federalism would, in the absence of a higher authority willing and able to sacrifice its vested interests in particular jurisdictions, inhibit bargaining and political compromise across functional, jurisdictional boundaries. For much of the time it is useful to have each issue operate on its own track, with its own set of conventions and sanctions to influence behaviour. But from time to time the inability to bargain across issue areas would prevent communities from reaching an optimal configuration of public goods.

The same holds true for models of regulatory policy co-ordination where several states pool financial, technical and administrative resources in order to be in a better position to deal with regulatory problems. This kind of half-way house between unilateral action and centralised regulation, which brings together states with similar problems in consortia or compacts, will also require an institutional mechanism of third order co-ordination. Majone (1991, p. 32), for example, proposes for the EC context the incorporation of horizontal and vertical co-ordination in a system of different, but compatible, regulatory regimes by using a small agency that acts as a 'regulator of last resort' and 'regulatory clearing-house'. Yet the very existence of more than one such institution at *several* regional levels (even if it is internally consistent with an optimal assignment of policies and responsibilities) not only inserts another level of delegation, but creates in addition an external constraint on bargaining and compromise between socio-economic regions.

Rather than trying to suggest solutions for deficiencies in regulatory policy co-ordination, this section has attempted to show how the search for optimal organisational boundaries has reached a general impasse, to the extent that international regulatory activities actually appear to be part of the problem that they were originally designed to solve. Whilst there will always be significant externalities in national policy-making, a structure of regional variation is unable to compensate either for a missing sense of community or common value orientations: on the contrary, it implies the elimination of democratically legitimated all-purpose entities precisely because it renders superfluous the homogenising function that the nation-state used to fulfil for society as a whole. In consequence, international institutions work with a highly fragmentary range of co-ordination mechanisms that were previously applied to national systems. The next two sections go on to analyse how two different regional organisations with overlapping membership try and deal with this situation.

2.3 The EC Context

As has been suggested above, co-ordination requires mechanisms for defining a common interest and proposing problem-solving policies, thus allowing the participants to establish a mutually beneficial common programme aimed at influencing national policies in an agreed direction (even if individual governments will maintain well-defined spaces for discretionary decision-making). Since the partners in the co-ordination programme expect that its benefits will outweigh the costs of policy adjustment, power and coercion are generally considered to be inappropriate to national deviations in co-operation. State actors remain free to reject policy measures if they do not voluntarily agree on changes in their position by means of influence and persuasion. In the EC context, however, a *superordinate* goal - albeit vaguely defined - exists. Therefore we can expect that this goal will find its expression in an applied co-ordination concept.

This section analyses four elements essential for the examination of this hypothesis: (1) integration techniques standing on the output-side of internal decision-making; (2) issue-specific co-ordination on the basis of respective Treaty provisions; (3) co-ordination mechanisms in comparison to those under use in other international organisations; and (4) external (or third order) co-ordination to conceptualise interactions with third parties. This eclectic view will allow us to show how 'politicised issue areas' become a central feature of co-ordination in the EC context.

The voluntary character of the EC's policy programme is reflected in only one of the three stages in its co-ordination process. In the first phase, the relevant Commission Directorates draft proposals for specific policies on the basis of the general objectives outlined in the Treaty of Rome and its subsequent amendments. Formal procedures allow for the inclusion of advice, requests or initiatives from other parts of the Community's institutional ensemble. In addition, consultations will take place with representatives of organised interest groups, technical experts and delegations of the member states, but even at this early stage no important decision can be taken without the prior initiative of the Commission. By virtue of possessing this monopoly as well as the right of changing its proposals in the course of negotiations with both the Council and Parliament, the Commission makes a large impact on the framing and content of Community decisions. The *confrontation* of national policy positions with the views of the Commission opens up the second phase in the internal co-ordination process: once a proposal has been accepted by the different Directorates, it can be handed over to the Council of Ministers for approval. During these stages, the Committee of Permanent Representatives (COREPER) plays an essential role, both as an informal adviser to the Commission and also as an instrument of evaluation for the member states, playing a pivotal role in reconciling organisational goals with those of the membership (Taylor, 1990). Finally, the Council usually endorses regulations which are directly binding on the member states as well as on individuals, companies and other groups within them. The Commission oversees their implementation within national systems and can, if need be, activate the Court of Justice in order to initiate legal sanctions. Clearly, the discretionary aspect of policy co-ordination has by this point come to an end.

In general, legal instruments are of great importance in European policy-making. For example, the Commission's 1992 programme was essentially aimed at the elimination of market barriers caused by the existence of different regulatory regimes within the member states. The law thus became the object of moves towards integration because differences in treatment had to be gradually removed (even though the law has traditionally been seen more as a central agent in the integration process). By means of creating institutions equipped with law-making powers, the European Community had originally been in opposition to market forces; it was thought that unidirectional changes in legislation would transform the prevailing production conditions in national economies, and this is a legacy that still finds expression today. Since legal integration frequently 'takes the form of a replacement or an overlay of national norms by European ones', it 'remains largely a top-down process' (Dehousse and Weiler, 1990a, p. 243).

There are a broad range of integration techniques located on the output side of the decision-making process, some of which are of an essentially non-binding character. Recommendations and opinions, for example, are part of procedural requirements according to which the different partners in the institutional ensemble are obliged to co-ordinate their actions, disseminate information and participate in consultations. Most other techniques, however, rely on the force of law, as is true in three cases (Article 189 EC Treaty): (1) decisions which refer to the specific applicability of national laws to a person, company or state; (2) directives which require member states to regularly amend their national laws, and which are binding as regards the result to be achieved, but leave the form and methods through which individuals and companies are obliged to comply with these modified laws to the discretion of the national authorities; (3) lastly, regulations which are equivalent to national legislation because they are binding in their entirety and directly applicable to member states.

At the start of this chapter, it was pointed out that co-ordination is a necessary rather than a sufficient condition for integration, but it is nevertheless the conventional wisdom within the Community institutions to regard the multidimensional process as somehow oriented towards a remote end condition with a more centralised form of government. Although that assumption is increasingly questionable, it remains widely held among those involved in European policy-making. In practice, those drafting the Maastricht Treaty built upon experience and past practice in relying on an essentially *functionalist strategy* (Taylor, 1983, p. 13), which will then also be reflected in the activities of the Court of Justice. As Dehousse and Weiler (1990a, p. 246) have stressed, 'although they are generally regarded as mere interpreters of the law, courts sometimes take on a truly creative role'. Particularly, because of the fact that the 'provisions of European law merely concern fragments of national legal systems and do not totally transform national legal orders', there is a good deal of room for goal-oriented interpretation when dealing with the inconsistencies of 'selective expansion' (Joerges, 1994, p. 32). The case law resulting from decisions taken by the Court thus constitutes another kind of integration technique in addition to those already mentioned. In consequence, the Court's formal role of interpreting treaties affecting the Community, and of adjudicating in the event of disputes between the other Community institutions or between any of the latter and one or more member states, will not be a purely neutral one (Dehousse and Weiler, 1990a, p. 244; emphasis added):

> At the analytical level, the language of law can sometimes be of great importance. Since law is often a translation of policies into operational terms. The legal discourse sometimes demonstrates intentions which have not been explicitly formulated or confirms other signals. Far from being mere lip service to the idea of integration, the Court's language is symptomatic of the line of *teleological* interpretation it has adopted from the outset.

The Treaty of Rome already made wide use of co-ordination terminology in many substantive issues of economic and social policy as well as of agricultural, trade and transport policy (Everling, 1964). The Single European Act and the Maastricht Treaty further extended use of the concept into the areas of research and technology and industrial and development policy, but in doing so, it has been difficult to avoid a general confusion with other similar or closely related terms, especially since the various official languages of the Community have sometimes translated them interchangeably. When comparing the legal meaning of words such as 'alignment', 'convergence', 'adjustment', 'co-operation', 'co-ordination' and 'harmonisation' across alternative versions of treaties, for example, Lochner (1962) was unable to discern any fundamental differences: all made reference to processes or techniques of integration yet remained extremely *indeterminate* concerning concrete measures. The creation of these concepts was thus compromised by the uncertainty on the part of participating governments. Even though most member states shared a sense of dissatisfaction with the state of affairs in certain issue areas and agreed that measures had to be taken, they postponed a more precise decision as regards the content or scale of new policies (Mitrany, 1994, p. 91).

It is also difficult to construct some sort of grading in intensity. In general, activities by common institutions, member states or both together, would need to be initiated in order to reduce or remove the different effects of legislation on domestic systems. At the same time, is always room to manoeuvre for national governments, independently of whether the same effect can be achieved by other means or whether the means themselves have to be adjusted. The content and scope of this discretion can only - if at all - be deduced from the basic goals set by the European Community, which are then served by individual Treaty provisions and their amendments. However, if the general aims are as far reaching as those outlined in Article B of the Treaty on European Union (TEU) the concept of co-ordination (and its derivatives) is potentially compatible with complete unification. Alternatively, 'unified' and 'common' policies could be restrictively employed to produce an end state that makes use of other forms of co-operation. Any other efforts at juxtaposing, say, co-ordination with harmonisation and reserving the latter term for a common policy which 'emerges from different policies of equal validity, amongst which a common denominator may nevertheless be identified', are more or less bound to fail (Taylor, 1990, p. 41). As is the case with similar and related terms, harmonisation leaves room for the adaptation of national policies in a number of ways, ranging from minor to total congruence.

The lack of clarity in the formation of concepts provokes consequences in several areas, to the extent that some commentators have suggested defining co-ordination purely by reference to the specific circumstances of the respective policy issues. Equally, however, the infamous example of industrial policy co-ordination has - in the eyes of many observers - revealed a generally negative potential for interventionism on a European scale (Streit, 1993). Article 130 (2) of the EC Treaty states:

The Member States shall consult each other in liaison with the Commission and, where necessary, shall coordinate their action. The Commission may take any useful initiative to promote such coordination.

Since the official view of the Commission is that it is economic systems rather than private companies which compete on global markets, their organisation by national governments is considered to be decisive for the international distribution of wealth and political power, and because these competing systems do not follow equally the rules of a free market economy, industrial policy objectives have come back on to the European agenda. In fact, the provisions of the Treaty do not simply limit the role of the Commission to that of a mere consultant; it may eventually come to manage considerable areas within the national economies. But, as Joerges (1994, p. 55) has indicated, once the commitment to a competition-based economic system is eroded, 'the Community cannot credibly impose principles, based on its competitive Economic Constitution, upon national policy makers'. This brief digression into a specific issue area thus confirms a more general point, namely that an applied co-ordination concept still opens up various lines of (political) interpretation, which lead to one-sided definitions of the 'common good'.

The legal foundation to the EC's operational structure provides a number of instruments that can be usefully described as co-ordination mechanisms. Some of these represent functional equivalents to similar techniques used in international organisations (Ansari, 1986; Majone, 1994, pp. 162-70; Bryant, 1995, pp. 11-6), whilst others cannot properly be reconciled with one of the cardinal principles in the overall legal structure, i.e. the idea of exclusive competencies. In certain policy areas the member states are not only precluded from enacting measures contrary to EC law, but they are also forbidden from taking any action at all. Moreover, the potential for co-ordination is unevenly distributed between a number of different mechanisms.

Mutual recognition, fits best with the concept of co-ordination that has been developed so far: it is primarily a negative obligation imposed on the member states to prevent them from applying their individual regulations to imports. In other words, any goods and services legally available in one country should have unrestricted access to other markets as well. On the one hand it has the advantage to be compatible with the 'free movement' objective of the Treaty of Rome, on the other hand this mechanism still allows for decisions by the member states as to what is considered to be a sufficient adjustment. While in this respect it served the purposes of the member states, the aims of the Commission were also clear: reliance on a much less integrated technique was the only feasible means of relaunching the common market project and restoring the momentum for more far-reaching steps towards integration in the future. Initially, the single market programme was even presented as part of a neo-liberal agenda intending to move towards deregulation and enhanced competition. The translation of the purpose behind the Single European Act into the day-to-day operation of the internal market was basically aimed at domestic legal systems, and not at enterprises active on a European scale. Regulatory competition between systems, rather than the creation of uniform frameworks, was thought likely to speed up the process of market integration.

Harmonisation, by way of contrast, makes the goal of integration much more visible by fostering the adoption of norms on a Community-wide basis. At the same time, it is far more difficult in practical terms to get the member states to collectively define the standards a given product must meet in order for it to circulate freely within the community. although harmonisation may at first sight appear to be equally likely to attain a given target, it possesses the drawback of imposing a positive obligation on the member states. Despite problems with harmonisation due to delays in implementation and innovative responses by private enterprises, the Commission continually persisted with this approach when formulating its policies - but with little success, because it proved to be extremely cumbersome to harmonise thousands of laws and regulations in countries where levels of economic development still diverge and different legal, administrative, and also cultural traditions continue to exist. Hence (Dehousse and Majone, 1993, pp. 6-7),

> the impasse reached at the end of the 1970s was due not only to external causes like economic crises and the consequent revival of protectionism, but also, and more seriously, to basic flaws in the prevailing mode of Community policymaking and in the very philosophy of integration

With the completion of the internal market, however, there has been no fundamental break with the functionalist logic. Instead, the principal Community actors seriously believed that it was possible to achieve the same result by encouraging both the harmonisation of national regulations and the mutual recognition of their basic equivalence. In practice, the new approach still involves a large degree of regulation in terms of the harmonisation of basic standards and supervisory rules. The approach could therefore be more correctly characterised as being a combination of the two original co-ordination mechanisms, amounting to less than detailed harmonisation but more than regulatory competition (Dehousse and Majone, 1993, p. 22; Joerges, 1994, p. 51). In short, it is a hybrid solution falling between national deregulation and re-regulation at the European level, in order to facilitate faster progress towards the overall project of a political union.

The creation of semi-autonomous *European agencies* would appear to be a logical institutional consequence of this type of policy-making, thus enabling the pooling together of the expertise available at the national level, which is absolutely essential to the process of internal review and commentary. Joerges (1994, p. 46), for example, envisages them being confined to advisory functions, in order to 'mediate between the interests of economic actors and various technological, industrial and trade policy ambitions and calculations'. At the same time, it should not be forgotten that the creation of new institutions with their potential for action (both legal and financial) is by far the most visible aspect of the whole integration process. As Dehousse and Weiler (1990a, p. 252) rightly argue, there is of course no absolute correlation between institutional and substantive integration, i.e. 'a more supranational structure will not necessarily end up producing more integrated norms'; yet if some of these agencies were to control their own spending budgets at some point in the foreseeable future, then doubts would inevitably arise as to their ability to act in a co-ordinating capacity. It is not easy to deny that the potential for intervention and the development of centralist institutions clearly exists.

Despite the primary importance of formal legislation, it would be a gross oversimplification to view European policy-making as being confined to the use of hard law. At the current stage of integration, implementation is mainly left in the hands of national administrations. Whilst the Commission has had to accept this fact, it has also created new means of coping with the situation. By operating with *soft law,* rather than refining the rules themselves. Being the European institution which has the task of defining the 'common interest', the Commission realised that general rules of conduct without any legally binding force can nevertheless produce certain desirable effects. Precisely because soft law consists of broad principles changing in application from case to case, it came to be seen as an attractive, additional co-ordination tool possessing considerable value. For better or worse, and in common with the other co-ordination mechanisms applied in the EC context, it is characterised by being highly indeterminate in substance.

To take the example of the quasi-legal official Commission *communication,* it can be seen how, by drawing on Treaty provisions, the Commission was able to extend its power to include explanations of Court of Justice judgements, thus turning its interpretation of their implications for national governments into a formal device. In the context of the creation of the Single Market, which put more emphasis on mutual recognition, the Commission started to perceive an additional need to make the

'Community' view concerning certain competencies better known to the public. As an instrument of soft law, the communication is tailor-made for the purposes of its user: in contrast to the usual co-ordination process, it enables the Commission to by-pass the Council, to present its interpretation of an issue without procedural delays and 'to stake out its position concerning entire economic sectors' (Snyder, 1993, p. 33), while moving beyond activities categorised under such terms as information, declaration or interpretation. In practice, co-ordination mechanisms of this type help induce a drift towards integration by identifying what has already been agreed upon and what is still in dispute. In other words, by determining the agenda in a particular way, certain substantive solutions can be anticipated and others excluded.

Finally, soft law can become hard law, a tendency reflected in the Community's external relations, ranging from Political Co-operation (EPC) outside the original legal framework to the codification of its procedures in the Single European Act, and ultimately, the Common Foreign and Security Policy (CFSP) of the Maastricht Treaty. The latter is again an instance of how the co-ordination terminology proliferates in the Union's relations with third countries and international organisations. As has been noted above, such key phrases as mutual consultation, common positions and joint actions indicate that the notion of a common policy remains indeterminate, leaving wide room for discretion in the internal and external policy processes. The precise competencies involved in policy formulation, the actual content of a common policy and its particular aims can only be determined subsequently by political considerations (Boulouis, 1988). Incremental institutional changes, like those brought about by Treaty amendments, cannot fail to re-politicise foreign policy and security issues, but each time new 'legal signposts in a landscape of ever moving boundaries' are set up, a particular path to integration is reinforced (Dehousse and Weiler, 1990b, p. 23).

In the case of the traditional relationship between the European Community and the OECD, where co-ordination between the two has - in comparison to other international organisations - taken a much more formalised form, the Commission usually aims for the creation of a specific EC-clause, which in practice is implemented through working arrangements that regulate the exchange of information, consultation, or the form of participation at meetings (Ferretti, 1984; Schricke, 1989). Moreover, since the Treaty of Rome sought common action by international organisations whenever questions relating to the creation of a common market are touched upon, the Council was obliged to submit general guidelines, but left their specification to others. In distinguishing between the status of the Community as a whole and the form of its external representation (through a permanent delegation from the Commission) the example of the OECD thus demonstrates how a degree of autonomy was granted to one particular institution, a general point that was also later on confirmed in the EPC context, where the Commission's formal recognition paved the way for its becoming a policy initiator (almost in the same way as the usual co-ordination process in other policy areas). In fact, the CFSP provisions of the Maastricht Treaty further strengthened the position of the Commission, by explicitly acknowledging its right of proposal and participation in all stages of policy formation.

Officially, it is usually argued that the vertical structure separating EC institutions and international organisations facilitates an interactive mode of policy-making (Commission of the European Communities, 1989). Section 5 of Chapter 6 will refer to the Commission's role in helping co-ordinate aid from the G-24 countries (the former OECD membership) towards Eastern Europe, and other issues such as monetary policy can likewise involve responses at the European level to decisions made in an international institutional setting (though the latter without being under the remit of the legal framework of the Community). For now, it will suffice to note the central feature of the co-ordination concept in the EC context: if integration is to be achieved 'through law', then only some facets of the overall co-ordination process can maintain their voluntary character in the long run, and it has been argued that even co-ordination mechanisms of the soft law type share this common attribute. The indeterminacy in concept formation should thus be interpreted not as being paradoxical, but as a deliberate choice to encourage the politicisation of concepts by the salient actors in the Community's institutional ensemble.

2.4   The OECD Context

The OECD essentially constitutes a forum for discussion aimed at achieving a balance between the economic interests of its member states and basic principles of good conduct and behaviour, and evolved from being a regional organisation into a world-wide institution made up of similarly structured national economies. Its organisational logic follows rules according to which it should progressively develop from being a mediator between its own members, between groups among them, and with third countries (where its relationship to developing countries is of particular importance). However, mediation in the OECD is not goal specific: as it was conceived, it has neither the aim nor the instruments for creating a new political or economic order, but instead provides a communication link for the discussion and co-ordination of national policies, albeit with the latter term having to be clearly distinguished from the way it is used in the EC context. The OECD also relies on the advice of experts, but does not require their recommendations to maintain an exclusive focus on national policies, a point reflected in the freedom of the Directorates within the Secretariat to conduct their own studies and disseminate new ideas, e.g. by making use of consultants and expert committees from national administrations.

The basic organisational features are those of a think-tank and watchdog institution that draws heavily on co-ordination procedures as part of a never-ending cycle with no final consensus (Haas, Williams and Babai, 1977). The majority of the internal work consists of policy comparison, assessment and mutual criticism, through which governments can be induced to adapt their policies in situations where they would never accept a formal obligation to do so. The organisation therefore keeps deliberately a low profile and tries to keep internal disputes away from public view, which also forms a prerequisite for the necessary flexibility in negotiations and the success of mutual persuasion. As long as it is possible to keep political demands separate from pragmatical recommendations, the chances for successful implementation at the national level seem to increase (Bayne, 1987). The OECD can be viewed as an instrument of co-ordination relating to specific tasks, and even though there is no formal transfer of authority, the pressures of international opinion and the effectiveness of moral suasion in consultative meetings tend to grow over time.

Article I of the OECD Convention which came into force on 30th September 1961 specifies that its three goals are: (1) 'to achieve the highest sustainable economic growth and employment and a rising standard of living in Member countries, while maintaining financial stability, and thus to contribute to the development of the world economy'; (2) 'to contribute to sound economic expansion in Member as well as non-member countries in the process of economic development'; and (3) 'to contribute to the expansion of world trade on a multilateral, non-discriminatory basis in accordance with international obligations'. While this wording leaves much to the bargaining process between participants as to which policy goal should have priority under changing economic circumstances, there is an obvious, built-in organisational bias towards the long-term promotion and facilitation of market-oriented economic policies (Henderson, 1988, p. 214). The OEEC (Organisation for European Economic Co-operation) Code of Liberalisation, for example, had already laid down obligations for non-discrimination towards other European countries, yet on their part, the Europeans (and the French in particular) wanted to do without them, because the need to harmonise policies to make better use of American aid and national resources initially called for a comprehensive overview of the entire economy in the member countries (Aubrey, 1967, p. 23). Nevertheless, Article I of the OECD Convention repeated the demand for an expansion of world trade on a non-discriminatory basis, aside from promoting stability and growth in member countries and economic development among non-members.

There are other differences between the OEEC and its successor organisation: the objectives of the OECD are broader than those of the OEEC, while the obligations are fewer and considerably less demanding; its charter essentially provides for consultation and *voluntary* co-operation. The OEEC, by way of contrast, entailed rules and obligations to which each of its members were bound (Aubrey, 1967, pp. 29-30). Under the OECD Convention, member states 'agreed to pursue, both individually and jointly, policies' whose impact will necessarily be indirect. Since a member government cannot be expected to consult the others about each individual step, a prerequisite of co-ordination is that each government must explain its position and put forward its views about the direction of future policies. Ideally, every country's general approach would become known to the others before difficulties arise, and in cases where common or parallel actions are desirable, prior discussion would make it easier to formulate them. In short, the essence of working jointly on a problem is to provide a supply of background information in order to influence national policy-making at the formative stage.

There are typically two formal instruments which go to make up on the output side of the OECD's decision-making process. Firstly, there are the *decisions* which carry an obligation for all member states and which establish legal duties in terms of national behaviour. They are based on international law and have to work without any sanctioning device. The precepts and restrictions that form the substance of decisions are directed solely towards states, their content is not therefore suitable for immediate implementation in domestic systems. All decisions still require detailed specification through national legislation and administrative acts. Secondly, *recommendations* do not imply any obligation on the part of the member states for domestic implementation, but should instead be understood as an incentive for giving additional consideration to whether a proposed measure would achieve the desired result; they thus contain requests for information from the member states.

The organisation's economic law reveals a particular tendency towards a permanent reduction and erosion of legal instruments. However, that decline is accompanied by an advance in the use of diplomatic instruments. There has been a change of emphasis: the organisational structure increasingly works towards the setting up and maintenance of an institutional framework for a permanent conference between states. In this context, laws might continue to have an ordering effect, but any claim to exclusivity is deliberately precluded (Hahn and Weber, 1976, p. 308). As in other institutional contexts, it is not possible to directly correlate legal instruments for the implementation of norms with their actual effectiveness. A rule possessing little or no safeguards in the form of sanctions can nevertheless be executed or carried out by the respective addressees, due to the interplay of interest constellation and political-economic influence of other actors. Soft law and diplomacy acting in concert would seem to provide an effective guarantee for the organisation of economic relations among the participating states.

The OECD has no court with general competencies: International surveillance and monitoring through its own organs constitute the only available instruments for the implementation of its rules and codes. But who actually ensures that states follow the stipulations of international law and correct any relevant divergences in national practice? In this instance, the OECD relies on the formation of an independent judgement by its Council, on the basis of regular investigations conducted by the Secretariat (including the preparation of statistical data and the collection of information). Three organisational features demonstrate a special capacity to co-ordinate policies: (1) high-level national officials, who hold a significant responsibility for the formation of policy in their own countries, participate in negotiations; (2) the internal structure is equipped to deal with all the interlocking aspects of a problem, by the employment of subsidiary bodies that are set up specifically for that purpose; (3) the role of the Secretariat is confined to that of servant to the member states, i.e. to the permanent delegations representing them.

The process of policy co-ordination at the OECD level deals with a wide range of interests and concerns (Henderson, 1993). Numerous issues and related policy problems that would otherwise be functionally divided in different international organisations are addressed jointly. In this respect, an additional advantage stems from its forum-like character as a 'club' of industrialised countries. As in other international institutions, direct pressure exerted by developing countries is formally excluded, while the low profile of the organisation ensures that it is not reintroduced through public discussions within the individual member states. Among the organisation's most important policy areas are trade, international payments, transport, economic policy, energy, environmental protection and development aid, with most of these activities having as their main aim the facilitation of economic relations between *private actors,* thus pushing back state intervention in the respective sectors of the economy.

On the other hand, this situation only allows for a normative treatment of policy issues in terms of their reciprocal relation to their overall political significance: states are obliged to rely on instruments of political influence. Particularly in the broad field of economic policy, the committee structure of the OECD creates a conducive environment and good preconditions for the unfolding of political involvement since corrective surveillance and declaratory resolutions are coupled with the participating governments' duty to submit reports and to concede to the OECD certain rights of surveillance. In the field of international trade, the OECD was able to establish itself as a forum for mutual information exchange and discussion (Cooper, 1983, p. 49), by means of receiving regular reports on its members' external trade figures, by the use of *enquête* commissions to analyse long-term economic processes, and of course, through the examination of complaints from individual members when confronted with objections from other member states.

As early as the mid-1950s, the OEEC Council was alerted to the impact of state intervention because of its detrimental consequences for trade flows. Without any further specification, a general *standstill clause* for export promotion measures was brought into effect, with possibility for complaints in cases of non-observance initiating some procedural safeguards (of which some member states then made use). After the transformation of the OEEC into the OECD these activities continued, including an especially strong interest in export credits and export credit insurance. However, the complexity of these issues necessitated an extremely careful investigation of their potential consequences. A general stock-taking of their harmful effects was followed by a gradation of criteria that would comprise the basis for an official OECD interpretation, in cases of conflicts among member states. In practice, this meant the introduction of the new procedural mechanism of *prior consultation*, which was introduced in what was a very sensitive policy area, because interference with traditional trade flows through the interventionist device of export promotion not only had external economic effects but also produced repercussions at the level of domestic politics. Governments making use of these instruments thus shared concerns relating to external geographical restrictions, and also internal problems with respect to the selection of particular industrial sectors and branches.

As happens in the Council and other OECD committees, the technique of surveillance is applied in trade matters as well, with gathering of information and the comparative examination of specific trade problems forming the basis of what should in principle be sanction-free *value judgements*. When combined with the presentation of facts, expert evaluations and advice, these judgements should then help avoid conflicts between major economic areas. It is primarily diplomatic methods that are employed for balancing diverging interests among its own members, as well as for co-ordinating policies towards third countries. Frequently, however, attempts to co-operate in economic policy-making rely on the existence of complementary interests, when it often suffices for there to be a mutual exchange of information about the evaluation of the effects of the policy instruments controlled by each member state. After consultation has taken place, the individual state proceeds autonomously, but its specific policy will be supported by other governments without it having any immediate effect on their own domestic economies.

There are several possible reasons as to why an international organisation such as the OECD enjoys a comparative advantage in the provision of information, for example, because of the gathering and compilation of comparable data from a large number of countries, or due to the quality of its economic forecasts. But in the latter case, a degree of caution is necessary: if member countries are in a position to influence the forecasts of an institution, then its clients can justifiably question the value of the services which they are purchasing. They could even end up with inferior policies as a result of politically or bureaucratically adjusted predictions, which have been significantly altered in order to introduce bias. In reviewing some of the literature on OECD performance, Fratianni and Pattison (1982) found that its forecasts were inferior to 'naive' forecasts, i.e. an informed guess concerning, say, fixed balance of payments would actually have been more accurate than what the official figures indicated. Furthermore, since the forecasts have not improved over time, Fratianni and Pattison (1982, p. 259) assume that:

> each country has a say in what the forecast is concerning the country's performance. These forecasts need not be good in a statistical sense, but may be useful politically. A policymaker may desire the public release of false or misleading information in order to pursue certain stabilization policies despite the fact that private economic agents may efficiently assess all of the information available in the market.

In matters of trade policy, there are some important roles reserved for the OECD. Although primarily an institutionalised platform for concerting the views of the industrial nations on trade policies *vis-à-vis* other groups (such as the least developed and post-communist countries), in certain limited areas of major importance to its membership the organisation has the additional aim of promoting rule-making before these issues end up in negotiating fora that contain a more diverse membership. Finally, there is a far-reaching third role, dealing with the industrial and structural aspects of trade, where many closely related issues join together in the co-ordination process. Tariffs and subsidies, non-tariff trade barriers and environmental controls have in common that governmental policies directly affect patterns of production. Attempts are therefore made to arrive at special arrangements for particular sectors, which aim at regulation in the fields of company law, foreign investment, and science and technology policy, in order to influence private sector decisions on who is producing what, where, how and when.

The OEEC had already been an innovator in institutional procedures: with the help of small working groups of experts, it was able to create sufficient authority and negotiating skill to work out compromise solutions even during periods of crisis. Just as important was the development of *co-ordination mechanisms* that were later taken over, adapted, and expanded by the OECD, but the success of those mechanisms was not only due to its being an institutional device - also crucial was its location in an atmosphere where the participating parties shared 'a sense of corporate responsibility' for joint undertakings (Aubrey, 1967, p. 27). The method that proved most useful in attaining a consensus, or at least a workable compromise capable of having an impact on policy-making in its formative stage, was the procedure of *confrontation*. In the annual country review, for example, each member is obliged to submit a statement on the status of its economy and on its policies to the other members. Criticism exchanged among experts can be influential in the early stages of policy formation, and as long as it is voiced in closed session, the maintenance of confidentiality ensures that concerns among governments about their reputation do not constantly inhibit discussion (after all it might be not that easy 'to hold out against a thoroughly documented and well-reasoned case developed by one of the expert bodies'). Despite its informal character, confrontation is considered to be an effective instrument of persuasion. An equally important factor is the expectation that over time the member states will become even more aware of the economic problems of their partners, thereby acquiring a common sense of policy interdependence. The number of unilateral actions against the interests of other governments can then be reduced, since the use of self-restraint would bring with it the implication that each member would be entitled to reciprocal behaviour were similar difficulties involving its own vital interests to arise at some future point.

However, to employ the term *harmonisation* to describe the whole set of organisational concepts and methods used by the OECD membership would be a misnomer, so long as no congruent national policies had emerged, nor a common understanding of their principles been reached (Harrrison and Mungall, 1990). The formulation of voluntary guidelines, the drawing up of standardised rules for the purposes of regulation, and the holding of consultations before the enaction of measures potentially harmful to other members, do not really reveal a general tendency towards international agreements or binding decisions and neither do they postulate a common policy for the participating governments. Instead, the OECD's goal is to achieve parallel action, through the achievement of policy co-ordination in a consultative form. To that end, general resolutions and informal recommendations suggest desirable policies, define common objectives and point out directions for domestic policies: in short, they provide common standards by which national governments can assess their own actions. The subsequent translation of such standards into broadly generalised rules of international conduct, and sometimes into fully-fledged *codes of conduct*, are deemed to ensure that individual policies develop in step with each other.

Common problems do not automatically require a common policy, but will encourage a joint search for acceptable solutions. Being an economic organisation of sovereign states, the OECD cannot create the necessary political will alone, though it can certainly act as a catalyst in its formation. During the *periodical review* of national policies, the process of notification and consultation necessitates (despite its voluntary nature) a certain amount of corresponding information, generally accepted interpretation, and agreement on relevant values in pursuing separate policies. Crucially, the effectiveness of *multilateral surveillance* depends on the results obtained from the organisation's general research efforts and their subsequent evaluation by the secretariat and the member governments. Here again, it is necessary to be quite clear about the underlying logic of the co-ordination mechanisms: the main organisational task is to provide a framework where co-ordination still predominantly takes place through the market; surveillance essentially defines the market as a universal co-ordination mechanism. The development of additional instruments through political co-ordination efforts therefore has to be limited to a corrective and supplementary function (Kloten, 1985, p. 395). In consequence, the process of *mutual cross-examination* between the senior national officials responsible for particular policy-areas cannot be directed towards the actual amendment of domestic approaches or structures in the interest of a common programme. Secrecy and confidentiality should instead allow governments to avoid anticipating too many of their own obligations and, preferably, to delay any policy modifications until the careful deliberations within the OECD are over. Or as Camps (1975, p. 21) once put it:

> willingness to *discuss* anything but no prior commitment to *do* anything are both important, for no one really knows where the stopping points, or breaks, lie on the continuum of policy measures.

Finally, the OECD's *forum* activities can themselves be considered as an independent co-ordination mechanism. Via the interaction of the executive organ - the Council - with various specialist committees, working parties and problem-oriented *ad hoc* groups, there emerge very general declarations of principle on current policy issues. Because it is an institutional setting without any supranational meta-principle (Klenk, 1994, p. 356), the OECD can circumvent more fundamental controversies about its internal operations, legitimacy and organisational aspirations, whilst in the eyes of the political elites, the aforementioned mechanisms help reinforce the national policy process. Since no structural transformation is envisaged at present, the OECD maintains its appeal to the self-interest of governmental actors through its approach to the resolution of interdependence problems.

In its vertical relationships with other international institutions, the OECD's co-ordination process reveals yet another advantage. In comparison with the GATT organisation, which had more than ninety members, and the IMF with over one hundred and fifty, the number of participants is no more than twenty-nine countries (Bayne, 1997, p. 365). The modalities of interactions with the former provide for permanent information and consultation between the respective secretariats, through an on-going exchange of observers and official documents; representatives from other organisations have the right to attend and speak at internal meetings, but are not entitled to participate in voting procedures. The comments and statements given by member states to the recommendations of the OECD imply a commitment to uphold the same (or at least an uncontradictory) position in any other international organisation.

When considering the role of advanced country co-ordination in the general area of monetary and economic policy, there still remains a major tension between action taken at the OECD level and similar action within the European Community, because both are to some extent alternative 'solutions' located in an intermediate position between the nation and the global system. Extensive co-ordination of policy at the OECD level could weaken the impetus towards the co-ordination of policy at the EC level and vice-versa, the more so since the EC is set on a course of economic and political union and will therefore continue to follow a distinct organisational logic in its co-ordination mechanisms. The OECD formally accepted the right of the EC to be represented within its organisation as early as 1960, mainly because of a certain similarity as regards the aims of the two organisations (Commission of the European Communities, 1991, p. 261). Delegates from the Commission are allowed to participate on all OECD bodies independently of the representatives from individual member states with the exception of the Budget Committee, but since the

Commission does not possess full member status, it has no hope of opposing resolutions passed unanimously (even if its formal rights do include the possibility of putting forward proposals). Any suggestions made by the EC tend to go beyond mere rhetorical exercises, as their substance would usually have been discussed beforehand with the respective European member governments and ultimately takes on the appearance of a single negotiating position once each national representative has submitted a congruent statement.

However, these formal rights of representation cannot hide some fundamental differences, from which new points of conflict can sometimes arise. The role of the OECD is a much more flexible one, experimenting as it does with new kinds of international action. If there are indications that 'rule making' becomes feasible and can be expected to be effective, further functional implementation will normally be transferred to a broader (global) forum, while the OECD in turn makes the necessary adjustments in its own program. Internally, its central task will be to spot new problems and to stimulate reactions to them before they reach a 'critical mass', whereas externally, it serves the industrialised countries in formulating a strategy in response to demands from developing countries. When taken together, the two activities amount to *system tending* rather than transformation.

PART II
EMPIRICAL
INTEREST STRUCTURES

3 Britain: Export Promotion and 'Levelling the Playing Field'

> Exports are the life blood of the British economy and the competition for orders is increasingly fierce. I am determined that our exporters should continue to meet the challenge of this competition, and win.
>
> *Michael Heseltine*
> *President of the Board of Trade*

This opening chapter of the second part of the book examines the export promotion policy of Britain. In moving from a broad three-level conception of co-ordination to the concrete policy-making context, emphasis is put on the different institutional factors that determine the formulation of interests in national promotion systems. Based on this methodological step, this part of the book attempts to link main features of the domestic co-ordination process in Britain, France and Germany with several output indicators for the period between the early 1980s and 1990s. In the overall structure of the argument it also provides the empirical background for the evaluation of institutional choices at the European and international level that constitutes Part III of the book.

Similarly to other European trading states the British system has characteristics including export credit insurance, export finance and aid finance as constitutive elements of the policy space in export promotion. Section 3.2 shows how sectional interests within the governmental hierarchy dominate the interministerial decision-making process, especially in the area of aid finance, and how the required expertise is provided by particular groupings. By looking into data on the use of official resources Section 3.3 considers the privileged position of specific industries as recipients of subsidies, before Section 3.4 widens the picture to include the political motives standing behind the distribution of export support measures. Finally, Section 3.5 describes changes in the institutional set-up of the national promotion systems. In reaction to domestic pressures and international regulations policy measures in Britain have been concentrated on export credit insurance in order to maintain control over an important policy instrument.

3.1   System Characteristics

When analysing responses to the recession after the first oil price shock in the early 1970s, Katzenstein (1978, pp. 302-7) defined export promotion as being the main objective in Britain's foreign economic policy, and claimed that consensus ideology, institutional innovation and macroeconomic policy were the principal instruments working towards that end. Hall (1986) expanded this argument further by focusing on the organisation of the state and the organisation of capital. Hall found, for example, that - in contrast to the situation in France and Germany - the Treasury's main responsibility in the post-war period has been the control of public expenditure, rather than industrial performance. For the majority of the period, there was no cabinet-level Ministry of Industry and hence no institutionalised means of assessing the impact of policy measures on industry. As economic policy-making always took place under the bureaucratic control of the Treasury, it was only possible to make marginal innovations (Hall, 1986, p. 248), such as occurred in the early 1960s with the creation of the Department of Economic Affairs (DEA), which eventually assumed certain responsibilities for regional development. The original goal - to create a rival institution to the Treasury - had failed because the DEA could not engage other government departments in an effort to promote industry (Zysman, 1983, pp. 215).

The prominent position of financial capital is one of the most salient features of the British economic system. The international orientation of the financial sector is accompanied by a relatively strict division between the managers of financial and industrial capital, and government policies on exchange rates are a good illustration in point: thanks to a persistent overvaluation of the pound sterling, the perceived interests of finance capital have been better served than those of industry (Strange, 1971). In general, the City's definition of economic interests are insulated from the concerns of British industry. In keeping with the considerable political importance attached to issues of international confidence and economic status, conventional diplomacy has had to take these definitions into account (Hall, 1986, p. 58).

In consequence, industrial policy-making was mainly confined to the maintenance of employment in economically depressed areas rather than being concerned with a real structural reorganisation. Official subsidies were unable to substitute for a more extensive influence on a particular industry's sources of external finance. When the British government created mechanisms for state industrial intervention, these have not, as for example in France, been directly linked to the allocation of credit by the banking system (Zysman, 1983, p. 227). Furthermore, even when the political will to introduce changes in industrial sectors did exist, the internal division of responsibility between ministries made their implementation impossible. Export credit policy, which could in theory have been part of a comprehensive industrial strategy, likewise 'has tended to be short-term, *ad-hoc* and to some extent determined by what competitors do' (Pearce, 1980, p. 11). Instead of being an independent determining factor in overall economic policy, export credit policy was formulated within the parameters set by this general strategy and in this way it also became possible to establish it as a subsidiary area of policy largely protected from public scrutiny.

In contrast to France and Germany, the official activities dealing with export financing and insurance are combined in one institutional setting. The Export Credits Guarantee Department (ECGD) holds the most important position, as a government department which is directly responsible to the Minister of Trade and Industry. Its incorporation into the ministerial hierarchy underlines the fact that export promotion measures are viewed as a central element in foreign economic policy (Dieckmann, 1986). Although in principle the defraying of credits is left to registered banks, the department performs a steering function by distributing subsidies in support of guarantees and interest rates. Despite the basically liberal-conservative outlook of recent economic policy-making, the various demands to leave export promotion as far as possible to the market have not fundamentally altered these organisational features. Within the Department of Trade and Industry, there is still a basic agreement as to there being a direct and close correlation between credit competitiveness and export performance, particularly in the case of long-term credit for capital projects.

Under the terms of the Export Guarantees and Overseas Investment Act, the ECGD takes up activity in the field of *export credit insurance*, and the agency can conduct business relating to commercial risks as well as to operations undertaken in the 'national interest' (OECD, 1990, pp. 135-42). However, according to the provisions set down by law, it has to satisfy two interrelated objectives: to encourage British exports and to do so without any costs to public funds, which means that the premium charges on its policies have to form the major source of income. All the funds provided to the ECGD for the purposes of trading activities are supplied annually by Parliament, which also sets certain statutory liability ceilings on its commitments.

Before a part of the agency's services were privatised (cf. Section 3.5, below), the department usually employed a fairly flexible approach, using specific, tailor-made policies to suit the needs of individual customers. One exception to this rule prior to 1992 were the comprehensive short-term policies designed for all types of export business, which offered credit terms of up to half a year's duration. In addition, and in a way similar to other European agencies, the insurance programme provides bond risk cover, investment insurance and cover for foreign exchange risks. In the area of bank guarantees, a broader range of services is available. The British agency is able to offer supplier credits with 100 per cent guarantees to facilitate those transactions that are already insured with the ECGD; likewise, in the case of buyer credits, guarantees are given to the lending bank for the repayment of a loan made to an overseas borrower for the purchase of British capital goods. At the same time, cover is available for lines of credits extended by lending banks to special overseas borrowers, which may include guarantees for a number of supply contracts made under a single financing agreement, in order to support the placing of orders for the domestic capital goods industry. Finally, as in the French system, there is the possibility of insuring against exchange rate risks, even if this service has rarely been used by customers, due to the existence of an effectively functioning foreign currency market.

In Britain there is no official institution for *export credit financing* or refinancing: the ECGD instead directly provides interest rate support from public funds (Taylor, 1984, p. 30), and while these subsidies are not limited to an annual ceiling, they are still subject to overall public expenditure control. Both domestic producers and foreign borrowers have access to bank finance at fixed rates of interest for exports, with credit terms of two years or more. The commercial banks receive a guarantee from the agency that their lending will be repaid at a commercial rate of return on both sterling and foreign currency lending, with all banks registered under the 1987 Banking Act being eligible in principle, either as sole lenders or as members of syndicates. To a certain extent, official control is maintained in so far as the Department has discretionary power to determine the role played by any individual bank, and to refuse or modify its support depending on the specific matter in question.

In the British case, the state's involvement in influencing the cost of finance is evidently linked to the sophistication of the domestic financial market (Gill, 1986, p. 267). The few limitations placed on the movement of capital have positively influenced the availability of finance. But at the same time, the particular link between insurance and finance was intended to work in the opposite direction, with constraints being imposed on the use of official resources in cases where credits could only be supported in connection with public export credit insurance (Deutsches Institut für Wirtschaftsforschung, 1991, p. 127). In practice, however, a shift of power between the major actors in the export promotion system has brought about a reversal of this effect. To quote Pearce (1980, p. 8):

In the past three decades, ECGD has evolved from an organization concerned exclusively with insuring export credit, to the agency responsible for administering a comprehensive programme of official support for export finance. The crucial characteristic of this programme is that it is operated by the banks: within it, the function of the ECGD is to facilitate the provision of export credit at the fixed rates by the banks. This entails satisfying the banks' concern for their security, liquidity and rate of return.

On the whole, both, the advanced financial markets and the linkage of insurance with finance have worked to the advantage of domestic producers, albeit with varying costs to the public budget. The large-scale subsidisation of the finance sector began in 1972, when the aim of the fixed-rate scheme to 'offer exporters a rate broadly equivalent to domestic market rates but which was not subject to the continual fluctuations of the market' was changed to that of 'providing export credit at levels of interest based not upon domestic rates but upon those charged by trading competitors' (Pearce, 1980, p. 10). Just five years later, the credit agency was soon pressurised for budgetary reasons into breaking new ground by subsidising the interest on export contracts that had been fixed in Euro-dollars and, to a lesser extent, German marks. The result of the new move was that the cost of subsidising interest rates at internationally competitive levels was sharply reduced, as long as market rates on Sterling remained above those on Euro-dollars of comparable maturity (Cizauskas, 1983, p. 2).

In the field of *aid finance*, Britain demonstrates some important differences when compared to its European partners. There is, for example, only a non-cabinet Minister for Overseas Development, who directs an aid programme that is administered by a part of the Foreign and Commonwealth Office, namely the Overseas Development Administration (ODA). It is important to note that since 1977 aid finance has included an Aid and Trade Provision (ATP), which from 1985 onwards has also contained a single integrated loan facility. The ATP resources constitute a separate allocation within the bilateral aid programme, and are usually deployed in the form of an aid grant in conjunction with an export credit under two separate financial contracts. These mixed credits are under the joint control of the ODA and the Department of Trade and Industry; the former examines projects in relation to developmental criteria, whilst the latter evaluates their industrial and commercial relevance to the national economy. In recent years, the use of a soft loan facility, which allows for the extension of long-term loans at concessional rates of interest under one contract, has become popular and this method of financing has commonly opted for lines of credit to specific countries rather than engaging in individual contracts. Exceptions to this policy are usually only made either to meet the preference of the buyers or to match more effectively the practice of other OECD countries.

3.2   Domestic Co-ordination

Domestic co-ordination links together different decision-making centres in order to formulate a policy which is consistent with the requirement to establish a national preference structure that creates order among various policy goals in their internal and external dimension. In the context of export promotion policy, this primarily refers to the ECGD's formal obligation to consult the Treasury and the Export Guarantee Advisory Council (EGAC), whose members are appointed by the President of the Board of Trade and, as Table 3.1 shows, are mainly drawn from senior levels of the banking, commercial and industrial sectors. The original task of the Council was to give expert advice in relation to commercial matters, rather than to interfere with the conduct of business when national interests were considered to be at stake. However, as a result of legislative reforms, the new Export and Investment Guarantees Act of 1991 has significantly widened the influence of this statutory body. It now states that,

> the function of the Council shall be to give advice to the Secretary of State, at his request, in respect of any matter relating to the exercise of his functions under this Act.

Through regular monthly meetings, the EGAC recommends to the ECGD how to handle sovereign risk underwriting and, in particular, suggests the market ceilings and controls that the official agency should impose on its exposure. In addition, it has been assigned the task of providing guidance in reinsurance, portfolio and debt management, as well as in provisioning for sovereign debt and overseas investment insurance, and the President of the Board of Trade is also required to consult the Council about the provision of short-term national interest reinsurance. The new Act has imposed an obligation on the Secretary of State, in consultation with the Council, to determine whether or not there exists a national interest case which allows him to use his general enabling powers to provide reinsurance for private insurance companies. This obligation is permanent and wide-ranging, and covers all the reinsurance facilities which the government proposes to put in place after the privatisation of part of its insurance services.

Table 3.1   Advisory council members 1990-1993

Member	Company
Peter Leslie	Commonwealth Development Corporation
Allan Gormly	Trafalgar House
Robin Fox	Kleinwort Benson Group
David Douglas Home	Morgan Grenfell & Co
Derek Thomas	NM Rothschild & Son
Dudley Eustace	British Aerospace
Robert Davidson	Balfour Beatty
Christopher Smallwood	TSB Group
John Melbourn	National Westminster Bank
Viscount Weir	The Weir Group
Geoffrey Lynch	Roberts & Hiscox Underwriting Agencies
Bernard Dewe Mathews	J Henry Schroder Wagg & Co
Timothy Evans	Foster Wheeler
David Newlands	GEC
Frank Lampl	The Bovis Construction Group

Source: ECGD (1994).

The participation and influence of sectional interests within the governmental hierarchy is ensured through the Export Credit Guarantee Committee, with virtually any Whitehall department, or the Bank of England, able to be represented at its meetings depending on what is on the agenda. Under the Treasury's guidance, the committee tries to balance short-term considerations of credit risk with more political interests, reflected in long-term trading relations, domestic unemployment rates and foreign policy objectives. For example when commenting on to what extent commercial criteria should be relaxed, the Foreign and Commonwealth Office often presses the case for some countries more than others. If a particular contract appears problematical from a commercial perspective, but would still be of major developmental value to the partner country and also establish a useful foothold for British exporters in the future, then the representative from the ODA might be able to tip the balance in favour of its approval (though this influence will not bear on any questions regarding the precise terms of particular export credits).

Another keen participant on the committee and possessing a strong interest in policy formulation, is a division from the Ministry of Defence, the Defence Export Service Organisation (DESO), which takes part in the negotiations that determine individual country credit limits because of its remit to promote and secure British arms exports. Since the ECGD provides cover for both military and civilian sales, the composition and variation of the respective country lists is the main target of the organisation's activities (Phythian and Little, 1993, p. 274).

Most official long-term insurance and credit contracts are given almost exclusively to developing countries, and it is in relation to this area that the co-ordination of decision-making has faced much general criticism. The complaints essentially refer to an inability to establish any meaningful capacity or administrative arrangement for persistent interministerial linkages in the area of foreign economic policy. Responsibility is instead divided between departments which, as in the case of the Treasury, have competence in short-term economic management or, as with the Department of Trade and Industry, in the management of commercial policy in conjunction with manufacturing industry. The existing institutional arrangements have not yet been able to facilitate a mode of policy-making that is insulated from the pressures of short-term events and domestic interest groups. In short, foreign economic policies have become merely *ad hoc* responses to particular problems (Morrissey, Smith and Horesh, 1992, p. 75).

Two attempts have already been made in the past to improve on the domestic co-ordination process and to compensate for the absence of a department concerned with long- or medium-term economic planning. An initial measure tried to assist departmental planning by setting up medium-term (five year) 'real' spending targets, but this has invariably been disrupted by changes in government or short-term crises requiring emergency cuts. The second effort tried to off-set the fragmented nature of departmental responsibilities by emphasising the dominant role of the Foreign Office in economic policy co-ordination. Although both attempts implicitly adopt a similar piecemeal approach towards improving the domestic co-ordination process, the latter is usually considered to be more successful. At times the Foreign Office has itself attempted to ensure consistency, by accommodating several different policy strands rather than pushing for its sectional interests alone (Cable, 1982, p. 190).

From an institutional perspective and in terms of policy formulation towards the developing countries, this strategy should have been much easier to follow than in countries like France or Germany. Britain's ODA, for example, has since 1979 been a department within the Foreign and Commonwealth Office, and the demotion of the Ministry of Overseas Development to the status of a separate administration within the Foreign Office signalled the incoming government's commitment to give greater weight to the political and commercial aspects of aid. Statements made by the ODA underline the compatibility between aid and foreign policy objectives, a point which should come as no surprise since the Overseas

Development Minister is responsible to the Foreign Secretary, who represents both the diplomatic wing of the Foreign Office and the ODA in cabinet. Britain's aid and development policy can, therefore, be seen as both informing and reflecting the government's overall foreign policy objectives.

On the other hand, a closer look at the institutional structure in a particular policy area suggests that the overall co-ordination capacity has not actually increased. Other government departments such as the DTI, the Treasury and the ECGD continue to make an input into aid management and hold responsibilities for other policies with a potentially major impact on the conduct of foreign economic policy. Hence, it can be argued that the influence of diverse interests is now much more significant, because of the proliferation of subministerial committees. There currently exists an Aid Policy Board and an Aid Policy Management Group, which comprises senior civil servants from the ODA and the Foreign Office's diplomatic wing. However, it is the Joint Aid Policy Committee (JAPC) that has become the main forum for consultation on aid policy, enabling interested government departments to put forward their own perspectives on key issues. The staff brings together various representatives from the ODA, DTI, ECGD, Treasury, Bank of England and the diplomatic wing of the Foreign Office. In addition, a JAPC sub-committee on Aid and Trade (SCAT) which relies on the participation of exactly the same departments, is responsible for the day-to-day running of aid and trade affairs (Randel and German, 1993, p. 56). Given this dispersal of co-ordination efforts, it is not unexpected that the former Labour opposition in Parliament favoured a return to an independent department headed by a minister of cabinet rank, in order to underline the importance of development co-operation in its own right.

Similarly revealing is a brief examination of the actual co-ordination mechanisms in the field of aid finance, where the support of exports credits using resources from the aid budget has been a major concern of all the industrialised nations. In Britain, the basic conflict derives from the requirement that ATP projects have to be soundly based from a developmental viewpoint, but at the same time, comply with one of the commercial objectives stipulated by the scheme. Five specific aims were enumerated by Parliament for justifying official intervention on economic grounds: (1) the facilitation of entry into a new market or sector; (2) the establishment or maintenance of technological links; (3) the retention of a traditional market that is temporarily under threat; (4) to counteract the use of aid by trading competitors; (5) to help British industries secure orders of commercial and industrial importance. There was, apparently, no order established as to which of the different objectives should prevail over the others in cases of conflict, nor was the aggressive use of aid by trading competitors made a necessary condition for the approval of particular projects, with the result that 'the question of which commercial purposes were to be given priority at any moment was left entirely to the discretion of the DTI' (Toye and Clark, 1986, p. 294).

As it stands the particular co-ordination mechanism undoubtedly creates a privileged position for industry. In a first stage applications from firms are filtered by the DTI and cases are subsequently passed to other interested Whitehall departments. Only at this point are the pros and cons of combining credits discussed interdepartmentally, e.g. among the ODA, Treasury, ECGD and the Bank of England. In the next step, applications are then handed over to the ODA to gain final approval for the granting of money from the aid budget. The different character to the institutional procedures that are involved in distributing the non-ATP bilateral aid, within the ongoing framework of country aid, thereby produces effective outcomes; the ATP scheme diverts aid to countries that would otherwise not qualify for support and, in addition, with conditions much more favourable than those of normal aid (Toye and Clark, 1986, p. 298).

3.3   The Interests of Firms

Due to changes in its institutional set-up in 1972, the British system of export promotion had already moved towards a closer relationship with the private sector. The National Export Council, which had operated under the regulations of private law, was succeeded by the British Overseas Trade Board (BOTB), an organisation fully in public hands (Shutt, 1985, pp. 94-6). A further manifestation of the same trend was the creation of a central institution for export promotion through the merger of the Departments of Trade and Industry in 1983. Many members of the European business community envy the influence that their competitors possess in the governmental hierarchy. For European business, Britain appears to be an efficient organisational model because private enterprises are included within the conceptional framework of export support measures, and as long as the BOTB membership remains representative of the national business community as a whole, it guarantees what seems an effective implementation of trade policies from a comparative perspective.

It is the high degree of concentration in British industry that has encouraged direct contacts between private firms and government. Major exporting firms could gain direct access to decision-making within the Department of Trade and Industry by becoming a member of the BOTB, which has seventeen Area Advisory Groups, each dealing with a major trading region and consisting of business representatives who have 'an intimate knowledge of trade' with that particular part of the world. Among the twenty-one members of the Board are delegates from major companies, the Confederation of British Industry (CBI), the Foreign and Commonwealth Office and the ECGD, with the presidency being held by the Secretary of State for Trade and Industry (Morrissey, Smith and Horesh, 1992, p. 61).

As can be expected, the CBI wholeheartedly supports the promotion system, because of its conceptual clarity, strong centralisation and efficient use of human resources (CBI, 1982, p. 14). But as a consequence of this direct involvement, it has to be recognised that the Confederation's own organisational characteristics come to bear on the decisions taken within the governmental hierarchy, so that - as in the German case - the composition of membership favours the views held by the larger firms and only gives an unequal amount of influence to small and medium-sized companies. Moreover, since the general interest group's policy is usually formulated by specialist committees that tend to be dominated by big firms, this policy input bias is further reinforced.

Table 3.2   British official export credit insurance[a]

	Premium income	Claims paid	Recoveries	Total
1982	161.2	207.7	48.8	2.3
1983	248.3	421.5	75.0	- 98.2
1984	138.2	571.3	112.7	- 320.4
1985	120.9	645.6	248.6	- 276.1
1986	141.8	644.5	224.8	- 277.9
1987	121.3	591.3	299.4	- 170.6
1988	106.9	734.0	239.4	- 387.7
1989	156.3	663.0	266.8	- 239.9
1990	138.3	671.7	278.8	- 254.6
1991	122.3	803.0	365.5	- 315.2
1992	144.6	867.6	430.1	- 292.9
1993[b]	117.6	620.5	132.0	- 370.9

[a]SDR millions;
[b]capital goods and project business only.

Source: ECGD (1992-1994) and own calculations.

The ECGD's business performance relates to the output side of the domestic co-ordination process, and gives some indication of how the government-firm relationship has developed over time. Throughout the

1980's, the pressure to make official concessions to the demands of the business community increased considerably, to the extent that, in the period between 1982 and 1993, the requirement to run the export insurance system on a self-financing basis was not met. However, with an overall deficit of approximately 3 billion SDR (special drawing rights), the total amount of money was comparatively low. As Table 3.2 shows, the British export promotion system did not resort to an 'excessive' use of official insurance in order to cope with the changing economic environment of the mid to late-1980s.

This picture changes somewhat if we look at another closely related policy area. Owing to the fact that the system characteristics are such as to leave the majority of export financing to private banks, the official interest rate support scheme becomes an important instrument for the distribution of subsidies (cf. Table 5.4 in Chapter 5, below). Indeed, while Britain between 1984 and 1992 had one of the lowest official export credit volumes in the OECD (cf. Figure 4.3 in Chapter 4, below), the amount of subsidies - as measured by the annual costs of fixed rate export finance - came to more than 2 billion SDR over the same period. Moreover, as Table 3.3 indicates, these costs were at their highest in the early 1980s, when the granting of insurance cover through the ECGD was more or less congruent with the relevant commercial criteria.

Table 3.3   Fixed rate export finance in sterling and foreign currency[a]

	Total outstanding	Annual costs
1982	5238	342
1983	6658	394
1984	9225	281
1985	8216	327
1986	8714	319
1987	7099	172
1988	6192	120
1989	6334	112
1990	5558	257
1991	5592	316
1992	6653	216
1993	5872	103

[a] SDR millions.

Source: ECGD (1992-1994) and own calculations.

A report made to the British Parliament undertaking an analysis of the wider economic effects of subsidising exports (either in the form of interest rate support or by means of resources from the aid budget) criticised this practice and in particular challenged the typical accompanying argument that promotion efforts are required in order to catch up with the rival programmes of major competitors (Byatt, 1984). By contrast, the document raised some far-reaching public policy doubts as to the overall effect of subsidies, maintaining that, as a rule, favourable support granted to one sector simply imposed extra costs on another. In trying to look beyond the benefits accruing to only one sector, the report argued that the automatic matching of other countries' contract conditions could not be justified on economic grounds. Finally, the study concluded that there was no systematic evidence for believing that substantial follow-up orders resulted from contracts won through the provision of export-credit subsidies (Byatt, 1984, p. 165).

In reaction to this, a number of firms engaged in exporting capital goods suggested that the authors of the *Byatt report* were 'out of touch with commercial reality'. Their response was supported by findings from the National Economic Development Office, which looked into the cost and benefit structure of a single project, and concluded that matching is not only justified but actually essential, because 'it is quite easy to lose manufacturing capability quickly, but it is a long and costly process to reenter a market once abandoned, if it is possible at all' (Morris, 1984, p. 343). Despite some broad agreement as to potentially negative long-run effects in terms of the distortion of trade and competition, the question nevertheless remained concerning what to do in the short term, given that other countries were supporting their business projects.

Although all this implies the need for a further increase in ATP resources, the experts reporting to the Parliament felt unable to give their support to such demands. Despite the fact that a good case for government involvement could be made on industrial policy grounds, it was argued that money coming from the aid budget would be far too crude an instrument for supporting those objectives. The authors of the report went on to say that the sectors which had benefited so far were not in fact the target of any particular state strategy, thus making it very difficult to use export support measures as a basis for selecting suitable cases to be included within a broader industrial policy (Byatt, 1984, p. 173).

What this dispute underlines is the relevance of the tying of aid as a third option for serving the special interests of private firms. Indeed, it is in this category that Britain regularly allocates more resources in relative terms than France and Germany (Brown and O'Connor, 1996, p. 95). Moreover, as shown in Table 3.4 (based on the report to the Development

Table 3.4   Official tying of aid based on reporting to DAC[a]

	Britain	France	Germany	DAC average
1977-1979:				
Untied	18	41	76	40
Partially untied	18	8	0	12
Tied	64	51	24	48
1982-1983:				
Untied	24	37	70	46
Partially untied	1	9	0	10
Tied	75	54	30	44
1985:				
Untied	28	43	64	46
Partially untied	2	0	0	7
Tied	70	57	36	47
1987:				
Untied	24	54	58	-
Partially untied	0	4	0	-
Tied	76	42	42	-

[a]per cent.
Source: Jepma (1991, p. 66).

Figure 3.1   Tied aid in Britain, France and Germany
Source: Jepma (1991, p. 66).

Assistance Committee of the OECD), the level of tied aid in Britain was always well above that of untied aid spending in the period between 1977 and 1987. At the end of this period, as Figure 3.1 indicates, France and Germany had converged to the same level of aid tying, whereas Britain continued to stay well above the DAC average of previous years. This is the more striking considering that the aid budget was cut in absolute terms over the same period (Morrissey, Smith and Horesh, 1992, p. 90); clearly, it was not business that was forced to bear the burden of public expenditure restraint. Using tied aid the government compensated British firms for the limited availablity of export credit insurance and finance from the public sector.

Much can also be learned from seeing how the ATP promotion scheme came into being as a 'contingency provision' for financing developmentally sound projects. During the early and mid-1970s, large manufacturing firms successfully lobbied the government through their trade associations, the media and Parliament by arguing two main points: foreign competitors would use development aid to back their own national producers, giving them an unfair advantage in the competition for market shares, and secondly, that the Department of Trade and Industry should have at its disposal a defensive instrument for safeguarding manufacturing jobs in domestic industries. All that seemed to be necessary, therefore, was for a certain per cent of the bilateral aid programme to be allocated to commercial purposes.

But while most arguments of this kind tended to point to the potentially positive effects on employment, little was said in public about the motivation of the individual firms lending their support to such a scheme. Given that the primary aim of all exporting firms is to increase turnover and generate higher profits, their basic interests are unlikely to coincide with the retention of competing international subsidies, nor will they be much concerned with improvements in the performance of the macroeconomic variables that are uppermost in the minds of policy-makers. Instead, assuming that ATP support is available, firms will be most interested in the possibility of additional foreign sales. In practice, the handling of decision-making rules and procedures probably favours private over public interests. Toye and Clark (1986, p. 295), for example, point out that the approval of official support has to be made 'in an extremely short time span (one week or less) under the constant pressure of firms claiming that, in the absence of a favourable response, a valuable export order will be lost'. Likewise, changes in the rules regarding the apportioning of resources have further underlined the privileged position of business. Since 1980, when the doctrine of 'generalised matching' was introduced, it has been enough to demonstrate that the country offering a contract that is eligible for ATP money appears on a list of countries where 'spoiled markets' are deemed to prevail.

The effects are much as to be expected. The distribution of public money has been highly uneven between both sectors and firms, with mechanical and electrical engineering, shipping and other transport systems being the main beneficiaries among the industrial sectors. In the meantime, the Overseas Development Administration itself began to doubt the worth of the employment argument, which had been at the root of the discussions about the tying of aid and the mixing of credits. According to estimates produced in 1991, 55 per cent of the available funds spent during the first seven years of the programme were absorbed by just five firms (Biwater, Balfour Beatty, GEC, NEI and Davy McKee).

Almost precisely analogous to the linkage between official interest rate support and private banking interests, is the closely existing connection between the ATP scheme and industrial interests. In both these areas of the British export promotion scheme a well organised lobby has developed, possessing a strong influence on the form official subsidies take, whilst at the same time, the system characteristics are such as to allow for more restraint in the area of official credit insurance. It will be the task of the next two sections to look at how government has reconciled these particular interests with its own political ends.

3.4   The Political Dimension

In general, the political dimension to export promotion policies has been badly neglected in the studies of economists (Neary, 1991). In the standard account by Pearce (1980, p. 13), for example, it is claimed that changes of governments or ministers might bring about some shifts in emphasis but will certainly not involve sharp breaks in policy-making. It is often argued that the constraints that are put on individual actors in terms of budget limits and technicalities of contracting do not allow for politically motivated responses, but as will be shown in this section, that interpretation leaves several distinctive features of British export promotion policy unexplained.

To begin with, and as has already been indicated the employment argument simply does not square with economic reality (Letovsky, 1990, p. 33). Even though the *Byatt report* produced some econometric estimates suggesting the phasing out of official support measures in the form of interest subsidies, they continue to be justified in this way. So why exactly do British policy-makers still stick to an extremely expensive way of reducing unemployment (Cassen et al., 1994, p. 208)? The costs of handing out subsidies in the form of an interest support scheme are especially high, because there is an ongoing obligation to make payments for the whole credit period. Moreover, neither the fluctuation of commercial interest rates in general, nor that of the American markets in particular, are under the control of any British government, though in 1993, the US dollar nevertheless accounted for almost half of Britain's outstanding credits held in foreign currencies (ECGD, 1994, p. 20).

By the same token, the employment argument has been used to bolster support for the mixing of aid and trade policies, but here too, empirical findings can refute the proposition that the tying of aid is an efficient way of achieving macroeconomic gains (Morrissey, Smith and Horesh, 1992, p. 159). In fact, even if economic gains are the primary motivation behind this particular type of export promotion, these benefits will be much higher in the case of multilateral rather than bilateral aid. In any case, this kind of policy choice cannot be explained solely by the privileged position of business; as Morrissey, Smith and Horesh (1992, p. 160) have suggested, political considerations must enter into the analysis as well:

> In effect, ATP sheltered a number of large firms from the commercial costs of the reduced budget; insider status was not the only factor explaining why they were sheltered: the international markets where matching mixed credits are required tend to be for capital-intensive projects which require large contractors; only large firms can maintain the local contacts to operate in LDCs; large projects are easier to administer and are of high visibility for political purposes.

Both examples point to the conclusion that government is willing to accept domestic costs in exchange for having an instrument at its disposal for the furthering of foreign policy goals, and this is an aspect that finds its most obvious expression in the existing regional ties with major trading partners. In 1989/90, for instance, the Middle East accounted for almost a third of all project business, a share lower than 40 per cent of the previous year (cf. Table 3.5, below), but making it still by far ECGD's largest foreign market despite the upturn in project activity in Asia. A significant proportion of projects, approximately 660 million SDR, were Iraqi insurance risks, a situation which changed dramatically after the Gulf War, when Iraq was taken off cover completely. In a similar way, cover policy towards Iran also came under review and the country will not be eligible for insurance guarantees until 'outstanding political issues' are resolved (Marks, 1991, p. 14).

These issues were addressed by an official inquiry in 1996 focusing on the period between December 1984 and the invasion of Kuwait in August 1990. After the Iran-Iraq cease-fire in August 1988, the government's official policy in relation to the export of equipment with military potential was subject to alteration. This could lead to frictions between the government's commercial interests and the guidelines it had introduced in 1984 to implement restrictive policies with regard to export licensing (Doig, 1997, p. 144). Therefore the Foreign Office, the Ministry of Defence and the DTI faced the task of co-ordinating their positions and acting in accordance with the government's policy priorities (Tomkins, 1997, p.110). In practice, however, each ministry defended its autonomy to the effect that the DTI could extend ECGD cover that served the main purpose of attracting additional finance for the sale of defence-related products to Iraq (Doig, 1997, p. 148). At the same time, Parliament had been divested of its scrutinising role, since Ministers did not provide information about the support of these sales through the official ECGD scheme.

Following the end of the Gulf War, Kuwait rapidly became one of the most promising markets. At first the Secretary of State for Trade and Industry refused to confirm in Parliament whether or not that ECGD cover would be made available for reconstruction. A prompt reaction to this hesitation came from exporters, to whom it signalled an alarming Treasury determination to cut back on ECGD support, even in the most pressing and potentially lucrative markets of the Middle East. Ultimately, however, the ECGD felt compelled to restore medium and long-term cover, and the reconstruction of Kuwait has subsequently seen the British government and industry acting together in a manner previously eschewed by reticent diplomats (Marks, 1994). The Prime Minister, the Secretary of State for Foreign and Commonwealth Affairs, and the Ministers of Defence, Energy, Environment and Trade and Industry have all visited Kuwait since its liberation, lobbying hard for British business and offering the backing of state guarantees, which gives again a good illustration of how official insurance becomes the medium through which a positive political standing is exploited in order to achieve sustained commercial success.

As Table 3.5 shows, the British support system has a strong orientation towards essentially three markets in terms of project business: Africa, Asia/Pacific and the Middle East go to make up more than two thirds of all contract values. Though the exposure within the regions remained relatively stable between 1989 and 1991 several shifts occurred in the distribution of project business insured by the ECGD. The emerging markets in the Asia/Pacific region with a more than 37 per cent share, take up by far the largest proportion of projects. With the exception of Africa, which still experienced a rise in business volume despite the highest regional exposure (27.3 and 31.5 per cent respectively), all other markets including those of the Middle East reveal a reduction in projects with official insurance.

Table 3.5   Project business by region[a]

	Insured		Exposure[b]	
	1989/90	1990/91	1989/90	1990/91
Africa	22.6	30.6	27.3	31.5
Asia/Pacific	15.8	37.2	26.6	25.9
Eastern Europe	9.8	3.8	13.5	13.6
Middle East	33.1	19.2	14.8	12.4
North/Central America	6.1	2.2	8.6	7.3
South America	4.2	1.0	7.4	7.9
Western Europe	8.4	2.2	1.9	1.4

[a]per cent;
[b]unrecovered claims and interest plus amounts at risk.

Source: ECGD (1992).

Table 3.6   ECGD exposure 'Top Ten Markets'[a]

Market	1992	Market	1993
Nigeria	2054	Nigeria	2130
Poland	1414	Hong Kong	2003
Hong Kong	1403	China	1380
South Africa	1322	South Africa	1272
China	1200	Indonesia	1092
Brazil	1020	Malaysia	1027
Malaysia	995	Brazil	982
United States	787	Egypt	740
Indonesia	747	CIS	675
Mexico	747	Mexico	639
Subtotal	11689	Subtotal	11940
Total (all markets)	23825	Total (all markets)	22872

[a]SDR millions, unrecovered claims and interest plus amounts at risk.

Source: ECGD (1992-1994) and own calculations.

Project business in Asian countries promises high profits despite a mixed repayment record, especially for the British merchant banks (cf. Table 3.6). However, even in the case of trade relations with regions where private markets seem to function reasonably well, a political dimension is again clearly evident. Malaysia, which enjoys an annual growth rate of eight per cent, belongs to the ranks of the most prosperous countries in Asia. That notwithstanding, the British government approved £ 234 million of official financial support for the Pergau Hydro-Electric Project, which had been rejected by the World Bank because of doubts regarding its economic efficiency. The provision of these resources from the aid budget were at first directly, and later indirectly tied to arm sales from Britain, and additional information that has been made public confirmed several other examples whereby, under the Thatcher government, payments from the ATP programme went to countries like Nigeria, Indonesia and Thailand in return for contracts with British arms manufacturers (Foreign Affairs Committee, 1994; Schulz, 1994, p. 17; Economist, 1997, p. 22).

Table 3.7   British capital goods and project business by sector[a]

	Aerospace	Defence	Other civil	Total[b]
1989	5.0	29.2	65.8	1692
1990	9.6	19.3	71.1	1441
1991	14.8	27.8	57.4	1758
1992	18.0	13.2	68.8	1905
1993	8.7	41.8	49.5	3525

[a]per cent;
[b]SDRmillions.

Source: ECGD (1994).

What is more, as Table 3.7 indicates, the defence sector has also become central to the ECGD's business performance: in 1993 the aerospace and defence sectors, for the first time amounted to together more than 50 per cent of Britain's capital and project business. This becomes even more remarkable when it is considered that in the same year the total value of contracts supported by the ECGD more than doubled in comparison to the years between 1989 and 1991. The specific importance of cover for arms sales had already manifested itself in 1988, at which point it became increasingly difficult to meet the demands of British arms manufacturers involved in large-scale contracts because there still had to be enough resources left over to include civil exports within existing country limits. In consequence,

Ministers announced the authorisation of new arrangements for large contracts for defence goods whereby, subject to ministerial approval, such contracts could be underwritten up to a ceiling of one billion Sterling (ECGD, 1994, p. 10).

The political nature of export credit policy is immediately obvious from the way in which the ordinary country lists are set up. The future availability of long-term credit is determined in line with the categorisation accorded to each country, in the case of Britain, these lists are organised into four categories. Category A, for example, includes those countries presenting little or no risk of default, i.e. mainly NATO countries and EC members; those on lists B and C consist of a number of developing countries, while category D largely comprises African states with a bad repayment record. In the course of time, individual states might be removed from the list entirely or, as in the case of Iran, later be readmitted as a potential destination for exports (Phythian and Little, 1993, p. 266).

3.5   Reform

Several reform efforts in the field of export promotion began in the early 1980s, when the Thatcher government set up a committee of inquiry with the task of finding out whether a government department such as the ECGD was the best institutional solution for serving the interests of British business. Three leading representatives from the private sector participated in the consultations: the chairman of Britain's biggest engineering exporter, Vickers; a senior general manager from Barclays Bank International, and the director of Royal Insurance, an important company active on the private export insurance market. According to this committee's analysis, the problems encountered during the government's promotion efforts mainly stemmed from an expensive premium system, inadequate insurance policies and cumbersome procedures for the settlement of claims. As a potential solution, the Conservative government considered the possibility of privatising the official services, but concrete reform steps and the direction they should take soon became a matter of controversy.

One proposal suggested leaving the public funds in the hands of the Treasury before channelling them directly to private companies, without having the Department of Trade and Industry (DTI) act as an intermediary. As a second alternative, the 'three wise (business) men' discussed a step in the opposite direction, and closer to the promotion systems on the continent under which the powers of the ECGD would be extended to let it borrow and lend on its own account and thus enter into competition with commercial banks. Ultimately, a third option was recommended by the committee: all business hitherto conducted on the commercial account of the department would be handed over to the private market, while contracts with long-term risks would remain under official control.

From a purely economic point of view, this proposal came as a complete surprise to the outside observer. Indeed, its implications were akin 'to selling off British Leyland's profitable Jaguar division while leaving the rest to drain the public purse' (Economist, 1983, p. 80). For government officials on the other hand, it held out the promise of fulfilling two of their major ambitions: firstly, to have a political instrument at their disposal for dealing with large-scale, long-term contracts, and secondly, to signal to the financial sector their aversion to meddling in any form of state banking (Gill, 1986, p. 267).

Despite the recommendations being made, no definite moves were made towards their implementation. The institutional set-up of the ECGD remained intact, though its business performance now came under much closer scrutiny from the government with the result that several official reports were presented in the mid-1980s, suggesting that the agency should either be transformed into a public corporation or else steps should be taken to ensure a greater operating efficiency. Some attempt has been made to achieve the latter through the recruitment of managers from the private sector, rather than by altering the structure of the department itself.

Finally, in the late 1980s, the government again tried to restructure the British export promotion system by means of a new 'export initiative'. In contrast to earlier attempts, the focus of support measures was now switched to 'export-newcomers' rather than already well-established firms. On this occasion, there was a much stronger commitment on the part of the policy-makers to end their involvement by handing parts of the official promotion schemes back into private hands (absolutely convinced as they were that the free market principle also had to find its expression in one of the core areas of state intervention). In practical terms, this meant yet another assessment of ECGD performance and further recommendations for its improvement. The respective findings were published in 1989 with the conclusion that the two main insurance operations should be run as separate businesses, but with an official reinsurance link being retained (Project and Trade Finance, 1993b, p. 110).

In 1990, the government started putting this reform proposal into practice by privatising the ECGD's short-term section - the so-called insurance service group. As Table 3.8 shows for three programme features, this is an area where Britain's support system is unable to match that of France and with the exception of the 'Foreign Content' category, that of Germany. The British official short-term support scheme always ranks behind those of major competitors. Hence, it is not surprising that, in the context of the European Community's 1992 programme, the ECGD guarantee section has strongly pushed for the idea of a *level playing field* throughout Europe. Where other governments have responded to these demands with a series of alliances between national and private insurance agencies, Britain chose a much more radical path.

Table 3.8   Competitiveness of short-term programme features

	Fees/Premium	Risk cover	Foreign content
1	*France*	*France*	*France*/Japan
2	Japan	Italy	Canada
3	Italy	Japan	Italy
4	Canada/US	Canada	*Germany/Britain*
5	*Germany*	*Germany*	US
6	*Britain*	*Britain*	
7		US	

Source: Export-Import Bank of the United Sates (1993, p. 29).

This situation created a dilemma in that, although the public programme has not been particularly successful, neither has the private sector really been able to develop an efficient structure to cope with its new role. The route towards privatisation therefore produced many more difficulties than had been anticipated in the official plans, and of the originally interested companies, eventually only two stuck by their offers (which, incidentally, were based on prices far below the government's expectations). In the end, the former ECGD branch was sold to a Dutch insurance conglomerate, NCM Credit Insurance Services, after a private insurance company from Britain had withdrawn its offer, out of dissatisfaction with the government's refusal to change some of the conditions of the take-over or to maintain a reinsurance facility to cover the political risks connected with credits extended to developing countries.

Since 1992, the remnants of the export credit department has been active in three areas only: arranging lines of credits for small-scale capital goods, providing project finance (especially in complex financing structures), and offering investment insurance. All these activities are supported by a new method of risk assessment, the Portfolio Management System (PMS), which attempts to closely match fee levels to the risk involved in each transaction by using a case-specific evaluation of the probabilities of default and expected loss. To this end, the PMS draws on a sophisticated econometric model for assessing the risks associated with export contracts, and it is hoped that the real choice facing the exporter is between having no cover at all or having some cover, but at a higher premium rate than in the past. By taking a purely technical approach towards risk appraisal, the government department expected to get rid of its deficits by directing exporters towards more active markets with good repayment flows and active buyers. So far, however, the actual business results tell a different story: a considerable amount of project business had in fact already been redirected towards the Asian markets in 1991 (cf. Table 3.5, above), and ironically, official export credit insurance in 1992/1993 amounting to 370.9 million SDR ran up one of the highest deficits in the last ten years (cf. Table 3.2, above).

The new system has been widely criticised by representatives of the national export industries, who feel that they are at a competitive disadvantage in international markets in relation to rival firms. In response, the government announced a considerable lowering of fees over the course of the next two years, but this has scarcely obviated the demands for re-nationalisation of the short-term branch. The ECGD has thus made available a package of reinsurance arrangements in order to smooth the path of the privatised business into the commercial sector, and the government will still provide a reinsurance facility for three years to supplement the services on offer by the private market. In addition, the official agency will even reinsure the whole contract value, in cases of high risk countries not deemed appropriate for inclusion in the main insurance programme. This national interest facility has no time restrictions and, subject to satisfactory performance, will continue for as long as the Department of Trade and Industry considers it to be necessary (Project and Trade Finance, 1993b, p. 115).

These partial policy reversals were accompanied by a reluctance to take any reform steps in the closely related sector of aid finance, where an arguably more urgent need for reform existed because of the 'osmosis effect' of ATP resources on normal aid. This latter term describes the tendency for each allocation of aid to be conditional on the acceptance of other forms of (tied) aid. Large-scale capital projects in particular often involve such 'package deals' with all kinds of subsidies cropping up, ranging from grants out of the regular bilateral aid budget, to local cost aid, ATP grants, ECGD loans and so on. Thus, the regular bilateral aid programme is in effect used as an extra incentive for recipient countries to accept offers that include trade-related forms of aid. If the government's real intention were to control spending, it would be more meaningful to remove ATP from ODA participation and simply allow the DTI to generate its own scheme of assistance to British firms.

Be that as it may, the specific linkage between export credit insurance and aid finance already became evident to most exporting firms in 1991, when they were obliged to recognise that, because of the whole privatisation issue, that year's entire tied aid and trade provision budget had been exhausted within one month. But this was only one of several reasons why reform discussions at the ministerial level did not touch upon the aforementioned issues. Extending the notion of a *level playing field* to other sectors would have implied taking away major policy instruments for circumventing the anti-protectionist rules of international institutions. Paradoxically, therefore, Britain's obligations arising from membership of the European Community and the OECD have prevented more fundamental reforms from taking place and created further incentives for including resources from the aid budget in the national promotion scheme.

Given that it went against the perceived interests of exporting firms, it can then be asked why the policy shift towards privatisation took place at all. This can be explained by acknowledging the pre-eminent position of the British insurance market, especially with regard to the insurance of political risks. London is the centre of a market that operates with considerable restrictions in other European countries. It is a place where companies like Trade Indemnity Corporation, American International Underwriters, Pan Financial, Commercial Union, and Investment Insurance International can work in co-operation with Lloyds, the market leader, to provide cover for commercial *and* political risks (Maule, 1992; Haufler, 1997, pp. 85-9). These companies are in a position to provide cover without any of the classic country ceilings, off-cover regulations, 'national interest' requirements and payment modalities, which is a great advantage when selling cover for sensitive product areas such as arms and weapon systems. On the other hand, the most important drawback to the services they provide consists of the relatively short time spans under cover and an expensive premium system, but it was noticeably in the area of short-term business that the ECGD handed the market over to private competitors. Ironically, the Single Market project thus allowed the Anglo-American insurance model to take precedence over the traditional continental model; whereas in the latter instance insurance used to be charged with the protection of common interests, in the former case it is the profitable management of markets that has become paramount (Albert, 1994, pp. 90-1).

This chapter began by locating British export credit policy within the broader framework of organisational features of capital, and went on to show that, as well as the banking sector, insurance companies should be considered as part of finance capital as well. Insurance companies account for half the net overseas earnings of the City, a large part of which is occupied in Lloyds members' underwriting activities - mainly reinsurance. In fact, the growth of reinsurance activity has largely compensated British concerns for the loss of direct insurance business in less developed countries (due to the spread of controls and take-overs by foreign companies). Newly established national companies have invariably required reinsurance because of the narrow spread of risks in limited domestic markets, and have nearly always turned to London. The shape and pace of the reform process has therefore not only been determined by traditionally strong banking interests, but equally by an increasingly important international export insurance market.

4 France: Export Promotion and 'Libéralisme Organisé'

Dans ce contexte incertain, la Coface est forte de son expérience des marchés difficiles, d'une compétence reconnue, d'une situation financiére solide. Si elle sait rester à l'écoute de son marché, elle pourrait profiter des opportunités que la crise, comme toute crise, ne manquera pas de susciter.

Pierre-Yves Cossé
Président-Directeur Général de la Coface

During the 1980s the French state directed more public funds to the promotion of exports than either Britain or Germany. The research objective of evaluating the role of international institutions can be achieved by going beyond this quantitative result and by disaggregating the policy sector into three interrelated instruments which are used to intervene in the economy. As in the preceding chapter the analysis is divided into five parts. Section 4.1 presents the main domestic institutions that link export insurance, finance and development aid with the requirements of the French economy. Section 4.2 then emphasises the centralised nature of the co-ordination process under control of the Ministry of Economics and Finance. In the period under consideration, as Sections 4.3 and 4.4 show, the outcome of this process has changed because of realignments between business and foreign policy interests. However, as Section 4.5 concludes, the reform of the French export credit agency has not eroded the capacity of the state to provide selective subsidies to national industries.

4.1 System Characteristics

Although the domestic institutional settings tend to lead to choices displaying a recognisable pattern, these frameworks will also reflect changing state objectives over time. The guiding principle of the French system of export promotion has often been described as *libéralisme organisé*, reflecting the conviction among decision-makers that there is a definite need to closely organise the expansion of trade and, more generally, that interventionist economic policies are legitimate (Machin and Wright, 1985, p. 32). In near accordance with the organisation of the

111

internal political system, the orientation and main features of the export support system in France are comparatively highly centralised.

In recent years, there has been a tendency in France to incorporate the institutions of export financing and insurance into a tight network comprising all organisations concerned with the promotion of trade (Schultz, Volz and Weise, 1991, pp. 14-5). The central nodal point is formed by the *Centre Français du Commerce Extérieur* (CFCE), which maintains close contacts with the official export credit insurance agency, the *Compagnie Française d'Assurance du Commerce Extérieur* (Coface), and the export bank *Banque Française du Commerce Extérieur* (BFCE). The first of these institutions deals with insurance and guarantee business, while the second one represents the most important institution in the field of financing. Both are typically heavily concerned with the organisation of large-scale projects (*grand contrats*), involving the supply of airplanes, industrial equipment and military goods.

The BFCE can provide financing with or without state guarantees for almost any form of international trade, either by using its own funds or through refinancing on the private capital market (Loriaux, 1991, p. 112). Together with Coface and a few other state-owned credit institutions, it is also the largest shareholder in financing institutions, which concentrate on supporting small and medium-sized firms.

To draw again on the description given by Hall (1986, p. 243), the relations between industrial and financial capital are such as to give French banking institutions a detailed knowledge of the affairs of many firms in the industrial sector and hence considerable influence over their strategies, due to the heavy dependence of industrial firms on long-term debt financing. French banks are in a position to exercise great influence over the affairs of industry; they can do so by taking an active interest in the production and marketing strategies of the firms supported by them.

In the French case, the organisation of capital is distinguished by a strong state influence in the banking sector. After the Second World War, a series of state controlled institutions such as the *Banque Nationale de Paris* (BNP), the *Société Genérale* and the *Crédit Lyonnais* were established for the collection of savings. Other institutions took on more specialised tasks, like the *Crédit National* providing funds for industry, or the BFCE helping facilitate and encourage non-colonial exports. The BFCE, which has a yearly capital sum of about ten billion francs at its disposal, is a particularly good example of how public funds can be used to enter into joint ventures with private banks, with the result that the state is then in a position to exercise substantial leverage over the activities of the private banking sector (Cohen, Galbraith and Zysman, 1982, p. 61). In France, therefore, there exists a relationship based on mutual dependence whereby finance capital is closely involved in the affairs of industry and, in turn, the state exercises substantial control over finance capital.

As has been mentioned above, the *insurance and guarantee* business rests largely with Coface, a formally semi-public, joint stock company that counts the major nationalised banks and insurance companies among its capital holders (the most important being the *Caisse des Dépôts et Consignations*, the *Crédit National*, the BFCE and the *Société Française d'Assurance Crédit*, SFAC). The Coface insurance company is liable on its own private account for business relating to commercial risks with a credit period of up to three years, although in this area it can also take on business of 'national interest' on behalf of the state account (*compte de l'Etat*). However, even the short-term commercial risks which form part of the agency's private business are still reinsured by the French Ministry of Economics and Finance: so long as Coface pays an annual fee out of the premium it receives and accepts certain credit ceilings, the state will provide excess-of-loss cover in this area. In the cases of commercial risks with a contract length of more than three years, political risks, or the insurance of military equipment, Coface acts as the official insurer in accordance with the country ceilings that are set each year by the government. Here, the French system usually differentiates according to country risk and duration terms, whilst disregarding the difference between private and public buyers in the importing countries (OECD, 1990, pp. 43-8).

The official side of Coface's insurance service includes cover for exporters, guarantees for banks and programmes in the fields of foreign exchange risk and cost escalation. The terms of cover, and hence the costs for exporters, differ according to the categories of goods. In the case of capital goods and large-scale projects, insurance is shaped in terms of individual policies covering both commercial and political risks. For example, a supplier credit could be insured in a deal under which Coface accepted 85 per cent of the commercial risk and 90 per cent of the political risk associated with the contract. A buyer credit, by contrast, might be covered by the company at 95 per cent of the contract value for all risk categories. A second category of products, mass-produced light manufactured goods, can be insured in one of two ways: either by means of a comprehensive policy which covers commercial and political risks, but leaves it up to the exporter to decide the country of destination, or through an open policy mainly covering political risks and only including commercial risks if specifically required. In the class of consumer goods, raw materials and equipment, cover is available on the company's own account, which includes the insurance against political risks.

In a way similar to the role played by the Coface in the field of insurance, the BFCE conducts business in the area of *export finance* both on its own account, in line with general banking rules, and also on behalf of the government. When fulfilling the function of a government agency, it supplies direct credits with maturities exceeding seven years to countries placed in the second and third categories on the list of the OECD Arrangement. The overall financing process always involves very close co-operation between the commercial banks and the public institution, perhaps most evident in the fact that the BFCE manages a special mechanism for stabilising the costs of credits granted in both French francs and foreign exchange. It further compensates other banks for the difference between an internal reference rate, plus a current bank margin, and the cost of financing in accordance with the OECD Arrangement rules. The application of this mechanism is limited to medium-term export credits (two to seven years) and the medium-term portion of long-term credits (Thomas, 1982). In order to provide the resources for these transactions, the export bank itself operates on the national and international financial markets, but with governmental support in the shape of subsidies and sureties.

From an institutional standpoint, the most important feature of *aid finance* in the French system is the strong position of the Republic's President (due partly to the Constitution but more importantly to Gaullist legacy), even if in formal terms the Minister for Co-operation and Development controls the aid budget, and the Ministry of Foreign Affairs, the Ministry of Economics and Finance and the Ministry of Home Affairs are also involved in decisions on the distribution of resources (Hessel, 1987, p. 326). Together with an agency that is responsible for the implementation of aid transactions (the *Caisse Française du Développement*), each of the above government departments disposes of its own representatives in this area.

As far as the technicalities are concerned, funds from the Ministry of Economics and Finance are generally linked to officially guaranteed private export credits. Since the early 1960s, when this scheme for mixed credits was first established, export credits have usually been extended under special agreements, or *protocoles*, negotiated with the recipient governments. These agreements fix the amount and conditions attached to the aid that is made available, detail its objectives with regard to specific projects, and determine the respective proportions of aid funds and export credits. The development aid component is funded by the Ministry of Economics and Finance at concessional rates, whereas the private credit is extended under the terms of the OECD Arrangement. While the ratio between the two parts can range from 30 up to 65 per cent, the total grant component of these tied aid credits must still comply with international regulations. Direct control remains with the BFCE, because it is responsible for administering the private credit part for the commercial banks and for specifying the general terms of the credits. When making concrete project appraisals, the Ministry of Economics and Finance consults other parts of the administration in order to strike a balance between the application of developmental criteria and the tying of funds to procurement in France. To take the year 1990 as an example, in practice this meant that the share of resources from the Ministry of Economics and Finance was distributed at extremely low interest rates ranging from 1.5 per cent to less than 3 per cent, in combination with long overall credit periods of up to 33 years and repayment-free periods of up to 13 years. Official sources nevertheless stress that in principle credit conditions are not used for matching objectives, since they are agreed on under the *protocoles* before the offers from competing foreign exporters are known.

In addition to this mixed credit scheme, a less traditional programme for integrated credits has also been introduced; even though the latter scarcely differs from the former as regards decision-making, project appraisal and the tying of aid, it is still officially presented as a novel response to demands made by the recipient countries. The Ministry of Economics and Finance, with the joint support of the *Crédit National* and the BFCE, extends single credits in the form of 'monobloc' loans, which combine budget funds and market resources in a single package. At the same time, a third pillar of French official export finance, namely the *Caisse Centrale de Coopération Economique* (CCCE), also provides concessional loans, commercial loans or combinations of both the two, to 40 independent developing countries in Sub-Saharan Africa, the Indian Ocean and the Caribbean.

4.2 Domestic Co-ordination

One of the main functions usually ascribed to French planning is that of improving the degree to which policies are co-ordinated with one another, which in practice means synchronic co-ordination, so that policies complement rather than contradict each other, and diachronic co-ordination, so that short-term targets are assimilated into medium- and long-range goals. As in Britain and Germany, French planners have tried to improve co-ordination between certain policy agencies by encouraging their participation on a variety of interministerial committees (Hayward, 1986, p. 22), but two factors have hindered their efforts. On the one hand, the Ministry of Economics and Finance has ended up playing the central role in the shaping of overall macroeconomic policy while simultaneously, inter-departmental rivalry has led to a selection of specific industries related to particular crises at the microeconomic level (Machin and Wright, 1985, pp. 11-2; Hall, 1986, p. 161). Taken together, these two characteristics mean that France is another example of negative co-ordination, where only the demands of a particular department are considered in the policy process.

The French state has itself often been interpreted as being a kind of co-ordinated and directed institution in its own right, because of its partial insulation from outside interference by pressure groups or Parliament. As Zysman (1978, p. 266) has put it:

> once a choice is made, strategic coordination led by the chief executive may be simplified in a centralized state because the number of individuals who are involved in the choice and whose active cooperation is required is substantially reduced.

Likewise, the formal procedure to be followed at the micro-level for the receipt of official finance is completed by approval from the *Commission des Garanties et du Crédit au Commerce Extérieur* (CGCE), a committee chaired by the *Direction des Relations Economiques Extérieures* (DREE) of the Ministry of Economics and Finance.

A brief look at the CGCE membership indicates that the French system is able to do without direct business involvement in the shape of expert advisory councils. Its fifteen members include representatives from the Ministry of Foreign Affairs, the technically relevant ministries of Industry, Public Resources, Agriculture and Defence, the Bank of France, Coface and BFCE. In its weekly meetings, the committee examines demands for guarantees from enterprises on the basis of reports presented by the director for medium-term business at the Coface. In practice, the technical ministries play a comparatively minor role in the decision-making process, with the leadership function being assigned to the DREE, whose director holds the chair of the commission and thus plays the dominant role in dealing with disputes or deviations from standard routine business.

In France, the export credit mechanism works in such a way that all the commercial banks (most of which are still nationalised) as well as the highly specialised BFCE can grant export credits on favourable terms. However, in order to enjoy state guarantees for the preferential rates of interest, the banks are obliged to present their case files to the interministerial committee, and it is the commission which then decides on the conditions and terms of export credits, rather than the commercial banks. By virtue of its being the central forum for discussion, it enables the participants to resolve their potential policy differences and to exercise discretion whenever possible. Due to the confidential nature of the meetings, it is virtually impossible to trace individual decisions back to the varying influence of particular state agencies, and the situation is further complicated by the fact that the policy instruments are set up in such a way as to operate selectively and to open up different degrees of bureaucratic involvement.

The number of actors involved at the decision-making centre is quite high compared to France's other European partners, but it nevertheless constitutes a successful means of linking the nodal points in the financing network with industrial interests through its promotion of exports and its efforts to increase the competitiveness of French products. At least part of this success can be explained by a more general capacity to co-ordinate high-level decision-making, thanks to an education system which channels a small number of students from the *École Nationale d'Administration* (ENA) and the *École Polytechnique* into top bureaucratic positions from which they may enter positions in public and private enterprises (Zysman, 1983, p. 131).

A second, closely related factor, which helps to explain the French form of interministerial co-ordination without direct business involvement, is to be found in the domestic system of corporate governance. About 60 per cent of the leading positions within the major enterprises and financial institutions - be they private or public - are occupied by former ENA graduates. At the same time, the managers of nationalised firms, or even of companies likely to be privatised in the industrial, banking and insurance sectors, are regularly appointed by government. It is usually argued that this helps prevent foreign take-overs and preserves the essential nature of French business culture, but the negative consequences of the existence of such a small, elitist circle are often overlooked: for example, because most managers preside as *Président-Directeur Général* over their own supervisory boards and very often can choose its membership as well, there is little or no possibility for effective control over them.

An additional reason for the French style of domestic co-ordination is the prevalence of a more aggressive commercial attitude which is backed by determined state assistance at all stages of an export deal. State officials frequently co-ordinate proposals from French private banks, engineering companies or other suppliers, and then adapt accordingly any state contribution, such as mixed credit packages. It also seems to be quite common for senior civil servants to head the commercial selling and negotiate many parts of a deal even when it comprises both private and public elements (Franko and Stephenson, 1980; Pearce, 1980, p. 32).

Obviously, domestic co-ordination in the distribution of state aids to promote exports has to take into account the international environment, but this is probably more true of France than for any other of the three countries under comparison. Due to the particular organisation of the bureaucracy and its close relation to business via state ownership, policy-makers are in some sense insulated from certain pressures and are able to impose some kind of direction on the economy, thereby forming a basis from which to disrupt and complicate the actions of those possessing a stronger influence on the workings of the international system. Or as one observer noted of the 1970s oil crisis: 'Not a maker of the system, though an occasional breaker, the French situated themselves to take and maintain the benefits of an order others had established' (Zysman, 1978, p. 270).

A good example to illustrate this specifically French type of export promotion is provided by the organisational dispersion of aid finance. Despite a fairly broad division of responsibilities, a more assertive conduct of aid policy by means of export credits becomes possible because the allocation of resources is accompanied by informal channels of communication between officials of the *grand corps de l'état*. While the Ministry of Economics and Finance still remains at the centre of the domestic co-ordination process, several other state agencies have their own delegations within embassies abroad independent of ambassadorial control. The Ministry for Co-operation and Development, for instance, is represented through the *conseillers financiers*, who hold responsibilities for whole groups of countries; the Foreign Ministry likewise has its *conseillers culturels*, who remain answerable to the respective ambassador but are centrally co-ordinated by the ministry from home. Finally, a special implementing agency for development policy, has branches of its own in certain selected countries and these enjoy a large degree of autonomy.

In recent years, the problematic nature of centralised co-ordination has been brought to the fore in the context of *Cohabitation*: when a Conservative government held power under a Socialist President. As the Constitution confers general and specific powers in the area of foreign policy on the President which the Gaullist legacy emphasises as the *domaine réservé*, the Head of State enjoys a certain influence on aid and foreign financial matters even when a hostile government is in power. At least unofficially, it is well-known that in the field of aid finance in particular, the various actors (presidential staff versus government ministries) pursue conflicting strategies which are hidden from view throughout the decision-making process. The fact that fairly substantial sums are usually involved is disguised by complex distribution procedures and fragmented budgets which are beyond proper parliamentary control. It is only possible to speculate on the handling of the comparatively flexible and subtle export credit instruments in the context of activities which often do not easily pass the test of having national welfare or economic development as their primary purpose.

4.3 The Interests of Firms

An all-encompassing identity of interests between firm and state was to a great extent predetermined even prior to the creation of the Fifth Republic. Under the guidance of the Ministry of Economics and Finance, post-war reconstruction concentrated on a few selected sectors, in which state funds were used to put pressure on individual firms to comply with an official strategy that resulted in the building of 'national champions' in response to the perceived threat from transnational companies. Because they were something of a latecomer in the development of a strongly export-oriented industry, the state actors decided to transfer resources into high-tech products, of which aircraft and atomic power became the most prominent examples. In organisational terms, this meant an involvement in business decision-making of a directness and intensity that could hardly be matched by other Western governments. While other countries essentially try to control and regulate business activities, the French case is invariably characterised by direct promotion and assistance to industry, which finds expression in such groups as business people and government officials working together co-operatively to draw up guideline economic plans that specify their intentions and common aims.

Despite the considerable public expenditure costs and the constraints that impose on the use of monetary policy, the government has remained firmly committed to expanding the country's industrial power. A vital part of this strategy has been the support for capital goods exports via the use of subsidised credits. Although this was justified domestically as a way of opening up export markets, the extensive use of promotion instruments has not actually brought about major shifts in relative country shares: the French performance has not been markedly better than that of Germany or Britain, who have much less interventionist systems. A more convincing explanation for adopting this strategy should begin with the close working relationship between business and government, in the form of partial or complete state ownership of export firms. Over time, this structural feature has more or less reduced the firm-government relationship to a two way channel where ten industrial groups (comprising about two dozen companies) are in an effective position to make their voice heard when official support is needed (Messerlin, 1986, pp. 394-97).

One good example of the nexus of interests between the insurance companies and export industries is Alcatel Alsthom, one of the major companies to benefit from official export subsidies. Among the members of the company's board are the presidents of banks such as the *Société Générale* and the *Crédit Lyonnais* and the insurance company UAP, which in turn jointly hold 16 per cent of the capital in Coface; moreover, the *Société Générale* is also the largest creditor and shareholder of Alcatel Alsthom.

Some observers argue that the ties binding French business to government have been loosened in recent years (Schmidt, 1995, p. 14), and fundamental changes have indeed occurred in firm-government relations between the mid-1980s and the mid-1990s, but this still begs the question of whether deregulatory policies in France have really divested the state of its *dirigiste* instruments. A closer look at export promotion actually suggest the opposite conclusion: whilst business is increasingly subject to the imperatives of world competition, the constraints imposed by the market and the demands made by technological progress, its links with government have in fact been tightened further. After 1982, export subsidies were still allowed to grow despite the restrictive path that the government pursued in its monetary and fiscal policy (Loriaux, 1991, p. 219). Similarly, modified instruments in the export finance and insurance sector such as 'foreign content support' and 'multi-sourcing contracts', enabled state agencies to maintain their links with large industrial groups despite foreign take-overs and strategic alliances (Hollenbach, 1992). The latter concurs with the hypothesis that it is the structure of the financial system, rather than the issue of ownership, which defines the options open to the French government in the formulation of its industrial policy (Zysman, 1983, p. 112).

The data on French export finance reported to the Trade Committee of the OECD show a decrease in the official export credit volume when compared to the early 1980s. Figure 4.1 indicates that a convergence with German and British targets towards lower spending took place in the first half of the 1980s. After that period, however, all three countries continued to diverge in their allocation of export credits. By 1991 France was overtaken as Europe's most active supplier of special financing arrangements by Germany, who experienced the largest growth in long-term financing activities as a result of increased business with countries of the former Soviet Union.

The French proportion of official versus private export finance (48.8 per cent) was still above that of Germany (25.5 per cent) and Britain (2.2 per cent) for the period between 1985 and 1990 (cf. Table 5.4 in Chapter 5, below). Despite the growth in alternative sources of financing, French

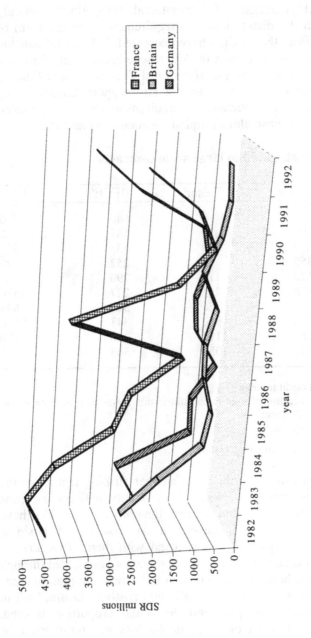

Figure 4.1   Official export credits with over five year repayment period
Source: Export-Import Bank of the United States (1993, p. 8).

business was forced to turn to government for more rather than less support, as Table 4.1 illustrates in the case of large-scale contracts, where the above-mentioned conditions of international competition certainly applied. Even though the direct financing requirements - in the form of interest rate support from the BFCE - have decreased, indirect refinancing requirements have increased because of debt rescheduling, with the result that the additional costs borne by the Ministry of Economics and Finance regularly outweigh the reductions in interest rate support. Lastly, taking into account the financing requirements for credit insurance, it can be noted that the total budget costs have almost tripled between 1983 and 1992.

Table 4.1   Budget costs of aid to large-scale contracts[a]

	Coface[b]	Trésor[c]	BFCE[d]	Total
1983	137	- 7	640	770
1984	- 106	- 19	587	462
1985	0	- 20	538	518
1986	355	72	252	679
1987	1122	172	290	1584
1988	1226	417	227	1870
1989	1578	736	520	2834
1990	1233	980	343	2556
1991	787	1117	216	2120
1992	832	1057	343	2232

[a] SDR millions;
[b] financing requirements of credit insurance;
[c] refinancing requirements because of debt-rescheduling; the Trésor is a division of the Ministry of Economics and Finance;
[d] export credit interest rate support.

Source: Schwartz (1993, p. 7) and own calculations.

The latter situation can be attributed to another striking feature of the French system that runs contrary to economic rationality: both trading firms and their partners in the provision of finance, the commercial banks, have surprisingly chosen public sector buyers in the conduct of business transactions, despite the higher risks associated with them. This adverse selection can only be explained by the respective incentives offered through the national insurance scheme. In retrospect, it has turned out that, in cases of default, such contracts were systematically less costly to insure, both in terms of the premiums to be paid and the actual proportion insured. Moreover, it also became clear that a particular loss was reimbursed far more quickly by Coface than claims deriving from a contract with a private sector buyer.

Table 4.2   French official export credit insurance[a]

	Premium income	Claims paid	Recoveries	Total
1980	242.9	652.4	250.7	- 158.8
1981	270.6	584.8	321.0	6.8
1982	280.0	864.6	275.3	- 309.3
1983	335.5	1090.3	383.0	- 371.8
1984	375.7	955.1	774.5	195.1
1985	-	-	-	-
1986	468.2	1711.9	701.0	- 542.7
1987	322.3	2409.0	1314.0	- 772.7
1988	227.6	2196.0	548.0	-1420.4
1989	275.9	2738.4	1138.0	- 1324.5
1990	243.5	2685.0	891.0	- 1550.5
1991	266.0	2476.0	1053.0	- 1157.0
1992	195.9	2067.0	1033.0	-838.1

[a]SDR millions.

Source: Coface (1980-1992) and own calculations.

As Table 4.2 indicates, Coface has extended its technical role of risk evaluation and risk cover into becoming an agency for distributing subsidies. In the period between 1980 and 1992, there were only three years that returned a positive balance; for most of the period, operating costs far exceeded the income from premiums and recoveries and in 1992, the cumulative deficit amounted to more than 8 billion SDR. Especially from the mid-1980s onwards the annual deficits rose considerably and remained well above the level of the early 1980s. In comparison to Britain, the French state insurance system incurred much higher costs in absolute terms for the state budget, while in the second half of the 1980s the German insurance system (as will be seen in Chapter 5) reached deficit levels placing it in a midway position between the other two countries.

Figures 4.2 and 4.3 present data submitted by the official export credit insurance agencies to the Berne Union, an international non-governmental organisation whose membership includes the French public and private agencies. These figures indicate that none of the three export credit insurance agencies operate their systems on anything like a self-financing basis according to purely commercial criteria, a point that can be illustrated

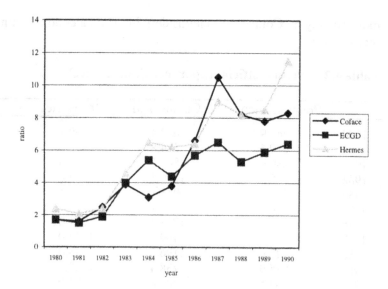

Figure 4.2　　**Ratio of claims paid to value of insurance operations**
Source:　　　　Ruberti (1992).

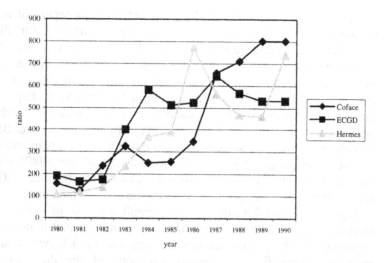

Figure 4.3　　**Ratio of claims paid to premium income**
Source:　　　　Ruberti (1992).

by looking at the flow of resources over the last decade. Whichever method of accounting is used, either taking the ratio of claims paid to the value of insurance operations or using the ratio of claims paid to premium income, the data reveals an almost constant increase in the expenditure component. When expressed in this comparative manner, the position held by each of the three countries is not as clear-cut as in the case of the overall deficits.

The index given in Figure 4.2 shows that for the period in question, the British insurance agency always performs better than its German counterpart: it always maintains a lower ratio between claims paid and value of insurance operations than the German agency, Hermes, and for the second half of the 1980s, the same holds true in relation to the French operator, Coface. However, the relative positions of France and Germany change over time: whereas in 1982, 1986 and 1988, both end up with the same or very similar ratios, Hermes more often had higher claims to pay in relation to its insurance operations. The picture alters again if we look at the second index given in Figure 4.3. From 1987 onwards, the French insurance system displays the highest ratio between claims paid and premium income. What is particularly remarkable is the comparatively high value of the index for Britain's ECGD, which from 1983 until 1986 was higher than that of the French Coface; in addition, with the exception of 1986 and 1990, it is always higher than the corresponding figure for the German Hermes. Seen from this comparative perspective, therefore, the French example of providing subsidies through official insurance is not nearly as exceptional as some observers have suggested. Although in the late 1980s Coface does demonstrate the largest deviation from a self-financing system, that position had been more frequently occupied by the ECGD in the years previously.

The boundaries marking off Coface operations to correct market failures from those to support the particular interests of exporting groups are imprecisely delineated and fluid. As in the case of the other two countries, three product areas, namely nuclear power plants, commercial jet aircraft and steel mills, have benefited enormously from export subsidies. Aside from official insurance, preferential financing conditions are another decisive factor for the award of contracts, and here, the findings of empirical studies tend to agree with the view among French officials and businessmen that the export-credit system is monopolised by just a few persistent applicants, who manage to be influential because they are owned by the state. All in all, no more than five industries (machine tools, electrical equipment, metalworking, aircraft/shipping and construction) have secured the majority of benefits. Thus, in subsidised interest on credits, a particular bias is observable towards sectional interests, in the guise of national interest, and while the gains from this practice are heavily concentrated in a few industries, its costs are borne by the rest of the economy thanks to the tax revenues in the state budget (Melitz and Messerlin, 1987, pp. 161-3).

Export insurance on the part of the state is distributed among these sectors in similar fashion. Table 4.3 registers a decline in contract values for the period between 1982 and 1992, a pattern that is precisely the reverse of developments in the German system, where the comparable contract values more than doubled during the same period (see Table 5.3 in Chapter 5, below). Despite the falling value of the transactions being covered, the industrial plants and machinery/transport sector made up for more than half of the official insurance business for most of that time. In the early 1990s, the sectors of aerospace/shipping and construction work stabilised at approximately the same relative proportions of contract values, which meant a considerable increase in exports for the aerospace/shipping sector and a further drop in those related to construction work in comparison to the early 1980s.

Table 4.3   **French large-scale contracts by sector**[a]

	Plants	Machinery/ Transport	Aerospace/ Shipping	Construction work	Total[b]
1982	33.0	23.0	6.0	38.0	19,816
1983	19.0	31.0	6.0	44.0	11,328
1984	35.0	32.0	7.0	26.0	9,891
1985	32.0	32.8	14.7	20.5	10,837
1986	40.6	22.8	13.5	18.1	9,625
1987	22.6	24.8	39.5	13.1	7,524
1988	22.6	33.4	18.9	25.1	8,217
1989	26.6	28.6	31.5	13.3	8,282
1990	34.6	25.9	20.2	19.3	9,086
1991	26.9	20.5	25.1	27.5	9,433
1992	30.0	30.0	21.0	19.0	8,056

[a] per cent of contract value;
[b] SDR millions.

Source: Coface (1982-1992) and own calculations.

It would be quite wrong to conclude that all firms within the sector benefit equally from the various support measures: in practice, the system favours large firms over small and medium-sized ones. In the latter case, the likelihood of making non-routinised applications leads to much higher administrative costs, while large firms generally export a much higher proportion of their output and hence can disperse their costs more easily. Be that as it may, although there is good reason for believing that implicit subsidies are substantial, export credits have not greatly improved the competitiveness of the benefiting branches: In fact, a study by Messerlin (1986, pp. 396) did not observe any substantial improvement in the net exports of industries receiving export subsidies between 1974 and 1982. On the contrary, many well known firms in this group, such as Airbus Industries, Renault and Technip continued to make losses, but the assistance received was enough to ensure the survival of vulnerable firms and industries in the face of strong international competition.

The arguments raised in all three countries to support state intervention in the export sector do not touch on distributional issues. Instead, it is stressed that domestic producers offer goods of high quality and fulfil international standards, but suffer from a general backwardness in terms of marketing and finance. Similar to the other country examples, some caveats apply in the French example. First, convincing criteria for deciding which industries should be supported and why some should enjoy more support than others are hard to come by. Second, even if subsidies are justified in order to achieve economies of scale, this line of reasoning will not hold true for all industries. In the classical sectors of aircraft production and arms manufacture, for example, the first production runs are usually destined for French users at fairly expensive prices. Therefore, what remains as the residual justification for the various promotion measures is their decisive role in winning contested contracts for domestic firms, either in specific product markets or in certain geographical areas.

4.4   The Political Dimension

The use of export promotion instruments reveals its foreign policy dimension most clearly in relations with developing countries, in respect of which France has always explicitly stressed the political and security aspects of its foreign economic policy (Bressand, 1982). The institutional potential for political considerations to enter into the operational side of official export insurance are evident in the 'double sided nature' of the Coface agency, both with respect to its legal status and the recruitment of its personnel. For example, if the management intends to make any changes in capital composition or company regulations, this will require the consent of the Ministry of Economics and Finance; likewise, both the *Président-directeur général* and *Directeur général* are nominated by the public authorities, and two government officials are obliged to be represented on its administrative board (Dutet, 1982, p. 80).

Further indication of political factors lying behind export promotion is to be found in the field of aid financing, this time on the side of policy-outputs. Economists have tried to explain French practice in the mixed credit field in the same way as they have in the case of official insurance. According to standard 'matching theory', subsidies for export credits are necessary in order to be able to face up to unfair competition from foreign suppliers and, as has been pointed out above, to respond to the practice of other countries. Yet, as Messerlin (1986, p. 405) suggests, 'this argument fits relatively badly with French practice with regard to subsidised export credits, namely to grant the lowest possible rates of interest'. A strategy of immediately offering one's lowest price and then systematically ignoring the reactions of competitors does not really allow the BFCE to be characterised as a bank exploiting its resources solely to level out disparities in contract offers; on the contrary, such myopic, rigid behaviour can only be properly understood in terms of the primarily political motivations for supporting specific export contracts.

Table 4.4   Competitiveness of medium-/long-term programme features

	Fees	Risk cover	Project support	Local cost support	Foreign content	Tied aid
1	Italy	*France*	*France*	*France*/Japan	Japan	*France*
2	Japan	Japan	Canada	Italy	*France*	Japan
3	*France*	Italy	Japan	Canada	Italy	Italy
4	US	Canada	Italy	*Germany*	Canada	*Germany*
5	Canada	US	*Germany*	*Britain*	*Germany*	*Britain*
6	*Germany*	Britain/ Germany	*Britain*	US	*Britain*	US
7	*Britain*	-	US	-	US	-

Source: Export-Import Bank of the United States (1993, p. 30).

The other European agencies did succeed in catching up by providing similar or related support measures. By the early 1990s, for example, programmes that lent official support to the foreign component in export goods or to the local costs of projects came to be frequently used by Britain and Germany as well (see Table 5.5 in Chapter 5, below). However, as Table 4.4 clearly indicates, with the possible exception of Italy, the French schemes were always way ahead of those of its major European partners in terms of competitiveness: securing the top ranking in four out of six categories and coming second and third only with respect to fees and foreign content support.

In retrospect, France represents the best example of how official credit and insurance became an issue of high politics. During the 1970s, policy-makers had already made use of this instrument in order to reorient and reinforce export sales of capital goods away from traditional European markets and towards buyers in developing countries, a goal attained remarkably successfully in less then seven years. Once a decision on the selection of strategic sectors had been made, it was easy to implement this policy because export industries had only to be exempted from the quantitative credit restrictions (*encadrement du crédit*) on individual banks (Cohen, Galbraith and Zysman, 1982, p. 58-9; Hall, 1986, p. 153; Loriaux, 1991, p. 43). Moreover, export performance improved even in the American market: given the unfavourable domestic environment, i.e. a much higher rate of inflation than that of the United States, as well as a 12 per cent appreciation of the franc against the dollar on the foreign exchange markets - increased export sales in new markets could according to standard trade theory hardly be expected (Franco and Stephenson, 1980; Wahl, 1982, p. 48). Nevertheless, the obstacles were overcome thanks to the concerted efforts of a number of different government policies focused on the common goal of export promotion. During exactly the same period, different kinds of support measures in Britain and Germany only gained a degree of political significance with regard to certain specific contracts, but in France these instruments had themselves become a primary object of politics. From 1974 onwards, selling goods to foreign markets emerged as one of the highest priorities in economic policy and was explicitly included as a major aim of the seventh and eighth French economic plan (Wahl, 1982, p. 70).

This then raises the issue of whether the distinction between 'high' and 'low' politics is less valid in the French case and the evidence presented here suggests that the time factor is of crucial importance (Kahler, 1982, p. 87). Depending on the motivations behind the economic exchange relationships with particular countries or groups of countries, the relative significance of policy instruments will change accordingly. France for a long time tried to pursue its geopolitical ends by the means of promotion policy, i.e. securing a sphere of influence over an entire geographical area, as is suggested in the following statement by a senior bureaucrat within the DREE, the foreign economic relations division of the Ministry of Economics and Finance (Robson, 1986, p. 136):

> We have been giving aid regularly for years, it is very stable in the way it is spent. We give to Morocco, for instance, almost always the same amount each year. Our aid is given for political reasons.

But more generally speaking, trade relations cannot be separated from politics in the entire area of 'commercial diplomacy', which covers a range of activities associated with the opening up of foreign markets. France's prime concern was not to seal international agreements in order to make domestic subsidies obsolete, it was much more a case of there being a growing awareness on the part of policy-makers that credit and insurance could create an ideal link between the need to boost exports and confirm foreign policy commitments.

The most visible manifestation of such a connection is of course given by the succession of presidential and prime ministerial visits to oil producing states and to the more rapidly growing developing countries, that were oriented at least as much to political ends as they were to the selling of aircraft, subways and power plants. Over time this type of marketing has also become a part of the day-to-day business of ordinary diplomats, with many French embassies now having special *attachés* for transport systems, who are directly responsible for co-ordination between the French government, industry and the administration of the buyer country (Frankfurter Allgemeine Zeitung, 1993b, p. 11). In the case of the recent, contested contract for the export of high-speed trains to South Korea advantages accruing from these organisational features came strongly to the fore: because of more generous financing conditions and better official marketing (as well as the fact that the South Korean negotiating team was led by a former student of ENA), the contract was eventually given to a French consortium led by GEC Alsthom, rather than to the German group headed by Siemens and AEG (Schumann, 1994, p. 157).

The nexus between commerce and politics, which was such a major characteristic of the 1970s, has continued to flourish throughout the 1980s (Hoffmann, 1987, p. 297). France persisted in its efforts to increase arms sales to Arab countries, especially to members of the Organisation of Petroleum Exporting Countries (OPEC), but later focused increasingly on Iraq, Iran and Saudi-Arabia (Loriaux, 1991, p. 275). The principal motivation for this behaviour was the desire to obtain secure and constant flows of crude oil at preferential prices, but unlike the previous decade the strategy initially met with a degree of failure. In the case of Iraq, for instance, it has been estimated that about 20 per cent of its total arms supply was provided by France over a ten-year period. Then in 1982, as a result of the war with Iran, Iraq was simply unable to meet import payments, due to a combination of a global boycott of many of its exports and a collapse in petrol sales to France from 29 million tonnes in 1980 to 1.5 million tonnes in 1982. Nevertheless, French exports to the country have since increased by around 20 per cent and France became its second most important trading partner. Through successive rescheduling agreements in 1983, 1984, 1986 and finally 1990, the outstanding debts towards France have accumulated to a sum of approximately 4 billion SDR, about half of which are covered by garanties from Coface (Agir Ici, 1991a, pp. 7-8). Furthermore, it is reckoned that almost 60 per cent of these debts are owed on French arms sales.

Table 4.5   Regional distribution of medium-/long-term contracts[a]

	North America	Latin America	West Europe	East/Central Europe	Middle East	Africa	Asia/ Pacific
1982	2.6	10.1	5.4	7.2	30.6	33.7	10.5
1983	4.9	9.9	5.4	6.3	12.5	52.8	8.0
1984	6.0	6.0	5.0	8.0	12.0	48.0	15.0
1985	1.2	11.0	4.9	9.5	8.9	49.5	15.0
1986	2.1	16.4	4.8	4.3	8.6	34.0	29.8
1987	2.4	12.7	7.1	4.4	7.2	31.0	35.2
1988	7.6	9.9	1.8	12.6	10.0	27.5	30.6
1989	8.8	5.4	10.6	8.1	5.1	34.1	27.9
1990[b]	-	-	-	16.0	-	-	-
1991[c]	-	-	-	16.0	-	-	-
1992[d]	-	-	8.0	16.0	17.0	21.0	29.0

[a] per cent;
[b] change in categories: OPEC 33 per cent, industrial countries 6 per cent, developing countries of the Franc zone 6 per cent, other developing countries 39 per cent;
[c] change in categories: OPEC 33 per cent, industrial countries 16 per cent, developing countries of the Franc zone 5 per cent, other developing countries 30 per cent;
[d] change in category: Americas 9 per cent.

Source: Coface (1982-1992).

The business reports published by the Coface unfortunately do not allow comprehensive comparisons with the performance of the German Hermes and the British ECGD. There is, for example, no detailed information available as to the spread of official French market exposure, i.e. the country distribution of unrecovered claims and amounts at risk. The official sources neither give a detailed country-by-country breakdown nor provide a separation of large-scale contracts according to their civil or military use. Nevertheless, the figures given in Table 4.5 display certain broad trends in the development of the official insurance business, though it should of course be appreciated that the regional composition of medium and long-term contracts refers to vast geographical areas containing heterogeneous sub-regions and countries in different stages of economic development.

Whereas in the North American, Latin American and West European markets, changes in the granting of cover for medium and long-term contracts were fairly moderate, the other four regional markets show much greater variation. The insurance for exports to Middle Eastern states lost a good deal of their importance: the number of contracts receiving official support almost halved in the decade after the early 1980s. The trend was even more pronounced with regard to Africa, with over 50 per cent of the medium and long-term business being conducted with this region in 1983, but down to only 21 per cent by 1992. Almost the exact opposite occurred in the markets of East/Central Europe and Asia/Pacific. In the former case, the early 1990s show a steady increase, bringing a doubling of contracts that amounted to 16 per cent of overall insurance business, while in the latter case, the trend is stronger still. Since the second half of the 1980s, the Asian/Pacific region has become the single most important destination for French medium and long-term contracts, to the extent that these relative changes in distribution between the four main markets suggest a deliberate re-orientation of traditional trade relationships (Kahler, 1982, p. 84).

In the field of export finance, it is common knowledge that the main recipients of mixed credits are former French colonies, and it is not therefore unreasonable to assume that their area of distribution is not significantly different from the flow of aid sources as a whole (Cassen et al., 1994, p. 207). In general, aid has tended to be directed towards the francophone countries of *le champ*: in 1990-91, for example, Sub-Saharan Africa received 57 per cent of French aid, while 21 per cent went to Asia and Oceania, 15 per cent to the Middle East and North Africa and only 5 per cent was given to Latin America and the Caribbean; in 1993, out of an approximate total of 5 billion SDR of development aid, two-thirds was channelled towards African states.

It is well-known that much of this aid is often spent in very unproductive ways. According to the Development Assistance Committee (DAC) of the OECD, in the years between 1977 and 1987 an average 51 per cent of French aid was tied to exports (see Table 3.4 in Chapter 3, above), and in absolute terms it is estimated that at least one billion SDR is used for expensive projects from which only the French supplier firms and established elites in the importing countries regularly benefit (Brown and O'Connor, 1996, p. 93). However, this aspect of aid policy is not due to a failure in implementation; because these payments are intended to contribute to the political stability of friendly African states, their use instead reflects much more the interests and objectives of the French government (Hook, 1995, pp. 47-68). Moreover, since politicians in the recipient countries know exactly where to address their demands within the aid administration and the leadership of the three major French political parties, the current system is based on long-term personal exchange relationships rather than on criteria of economic efficiency. It is only very recently that the changes initiated in the export insurance sector have begun to filter through to the area of aid finance.

In the light of these developments in the French practice of export promotion, other policy changes at the macroeconomic level appear to be comparatively less spectacular. At the beginning of 1994, the franc-tied currencies in Africa were devalued by 50 per cent, thus giving another signal to those countries that France is in the process of redefining its interests in the region. Similarly, a series of statements by the then Prime Minister Balladur suggested that with the end of a bi-polar world system, the African continent would cease to be a worthwhile investment in economic as well as in political terms; Balladur maintained that the French government had to pay greater attention to its economic requirements and would therefore be less willing to make concessions out of political considerations. The French Junior Minister of Development Co-operation has argued along very similar lines, suggesting that given the economic crisis in France, it is virtually impossible to fund substantial development in that part of the world, and claiming that the present problems of debt payments to multilateral finance institutions and the burdens of the provision of development programmes would exceed the financial capacities of France. The official explanation for continuing economic decline in Africa lays the blame with the recipient states themselves, for not following stringently enough the conditionality requirements set out by the World Bank and the International Monetary Fund (IMF).

Under such circumstances, the French business community would also welcome a more widespread exploitation of aid financing facilities and a move away from the focus on Africa, where the market potential has considerably shrunk in comparison to the 1970s and 1980s (Adams, 1995, p. 97). This attitude on the part of companies is mainly explained by the relationship between aid spending and the procurement of domestic products. Rough calculations suggest that only about 60 to 70 per cent of regionally focused bilateral aid returns to France in the form of purchases, while in the case of multilateral aid the equivalent figure amounts to 140 per cent. From this point of view, the official confirmation of approval by the French trade board towards the UN target that development aid be earmarked for multilateral institutions, comes as no great surprise. In addition, the same body, together with its foreign-based economic advisors, agreed to start a new campaign for improved sensitivity to the needs of French exporters and companies when planning aid policies.

Government and business interests would thus appear to be in broad agreement again, meaning that France provides perhaps the best example of how microeconomic instruments of export promotion can be used to combine perceived political and economic interests. In the long run, this strategy has encouraged a high concentration of trade with particular regions rather than a wide dispersion of subsidies irrespective of the importing countries involved. Yet, as this section has shown, when changes in the definition of economic and political interests occur, the promotion instruments are flexible enough to transfer these new demands to the level of contract relations between firms.

4.5   Reform

During the 1980s, the failure of domestic reform efforts made evident the negative side of French export promotion policy. The Bank of France was forced to cope with the financial burden created by having to refinance medium-term export credits. As long as exporters had almost unlimited access to finance at fixed concessionary interest rates through the banking system, enormous costs were created for the national budget and the sums that piled up placed an enormous strain on the conduct of French monetary policy. In particular, because the administration of the interest rate equalisation scheme created long-term refinancing requirements, the whole monetary set-up came under serious threat, because of its basic dependence on the management of interest rates. When confronted with the possibility of a 'non-functioning of the system' the governors of the bank launched several attempts at reform. However, due to the fact that the central bank was at that time still embedded within the governmental hierarchy, the radical changes that were envisaged never took place, owing to the unbroken resistance of successive Ministers of Finance (Pearce, 1980, p. 31). The main characteristics of the financial support scheme thus remained much as they were, albeit with the gradual introduction of some slight modifications on the operational side, such as the temporary suspension of interest rate support (in foreign currencies and francs) for the duration of export credits that were ranked according to specific country categories (Project and Trade Finance, 1993a, p. 35).

In the light of this experience, there is little use in trying to re-design the *Commission des Garanties* as one of the main institutions involved in deciding on the distribution of resources. Even if it were feasible to transfer the direction of this interministerial body away from spending institutions like the DREE and BFCE to those actually paying, namely the Ministry of Economics and Finance and the Coface, neither of the latter have previously favoured systemic self-restraint. In the early eighties, for example, the Ministry of Economics and Finance strongly resisted the creation of an independent agency for development co-operation, which would have ensured a greater consistency in the financial management of the French aid programme (Hessel, 1987, p. 334). A number of arguments have also been raised in support of a general reduction of the Coface monopoly in operational terms (Messerlin, 1986, pp. 406-7). Given the fact that the information on the various features of a contract is disseminated asymmetrically, the potential for exploiting the system lies with the benefiting industries. One way of opposing this tendency consists in a more effective monitoring mechanism, perhaps by means of a degree of specialisation among insurers, which could then be followed up by a kind of risk pooling among these more specialised insurers. In doing so, an additional advantage would result from the fact that the technically-speaking unconnected parts of the system, such as mixed credits or economic risks, would be made more prominent, thus introducing more transparency and creating an incentive for reducing state involvement in those cases where intervention unambiguously serves the purposes of the state.

Leaving these more theoretical arguments aside, the most constant pressure for reform during the 1980s and early 1990s came from the increasing deficits associated with the cover of contracts for large capital goods, until the rapid growth of defaults in the aftermath of the Gulf War finally created pressure for reform. At that moment, the political will to alter the structure of export guarantees given on behalf of the French state manifested itself amongst all the parties in the National Assembly. In a first draft bill, the Government mentioned changes in world economic and political conditions as the justification for concrete measures in the export credit insurance sector, i.e. the exclusion of the underwriting of risks on arms sales and the application of a general limit to the volume of garanties in the case of high risk countries (Handelsblatt, 1991, p. 8).

While it has become generally accepted that some limitations on the old form of state aids are desirable, there is less agreement as to how the National Assembly could effectively control the official expenditures. As a result of the common dissatisfaction with the present form of the Coface business reports, various proposals were made by members of the National Assembly (Agir Ici, 1991b), which contained pleas for more transparency and suggested the annual publication of two separate reports in order to effectively distinguish between civil and military contracts. With regard to the use of statistical material, it was felt to be essential to follow the lead already taken by their British, and to a lesser extent German, counterparts and differentiate the geographical spread of contracts, official guarantees and other financial contributions by public or semi-public institutions on a country by country basis. To complete these efforts at easing pressure on the budget, it was proposed that information be made available which would also include at least a medium-term assessment of each country's debt structure in terms of rescheduling, refinancing or even the writing-off of bad debts. Other members of the Assembly demanded the employment of a similar *single country - two reports* approach for the presentation of reports on the obligations faced by the Ministry of Economics and Finance that derive from defaults, indemnities or delays in payments.

In practice, however, the implementation of something akin to 'freedom of information' still seems to be a long way off (Agir-Ici, 1991a, pp. 17-9). Some modest reform proposals that tried to uphold a certain level of secrecy were unable to produce a consensus in Parliament, and the question of whether or not there should be some kind of control technique presided over by a parliamentary delegation, an *enquête* commission on arms exports or a control commission on public credit agencies, remains open to dispute (or as in the case of the second idea, has already been rejected by the *Commission des Finances*).

In the meantime, the Coface began to follow a new, self-proclaimed strategy of international growth in a competitive environment. From 1985 onwards, gradual modifications were woven into the conduct of everyday business and the company statute was eventually changed in 1991 through a regulation that permits the company to make interventions on a European-wide scale. The company's directors tried to strengthen their position on three levels, prior to the intended reforms by the EC Commission reaching their implementation stage: first, through the development of partnerships with other agencies in the field of credit insurance (for example, the Coface developed a new policy in conjunction with SFAC as one of the leading private export credit insurers, and also pushed for new partnerships with credit insurers from Italy, Ireland and Poland); second, the decision to participate jointly with the *Société Commerciale de Réassurance* (SCOR) in a specialised pool for political risk cover (the so-called Unistrat - Paris Pool). Last, the insurance agency endeavoured to secure a stronger presence in the related complementary service sectors of business information, debt recovery and exchange rate cover.

It is in the last of these sectors where the French export promotion system lived up to its reputation as one of the most innovative instruments in the field. At a time when their use of mixed credits was already becoming notorious, other forms of domestic support measures were discovered. In the mid-1980s, when the agency first started offering foreign exchange hedges, the requisite risk management techniques that had been developed in the private sector were then skilfully assimilated by the agency, and it became a specialist intermediary between exporters and the forward currency and currency options markets by providing a unique possibility of covering contingent risks (i.e. tenders), as well as actual exchange risks. In this particular area what is by now a fully developed scheme, handled by an associated company, 'Forex finance' has become one of the latest weapons in the armoury of the more sophisticated export credit agencies. Within the scope of this programme, the Coface offers a total of eight different types of exchange rate cover, one of which gives a good example of its potential as a domestic support measure: the 'framework' guarantee, for instance, constitutes a single measure for ensuring a specific exchange rate, up to a limit of five years, on all orders received by an exporter under one overall contract.

The major internal reforms came to an end in 1992, when a restructuring of the Coface capital took place under the direction of the Ministry of Economics and Finance (Schwartz, 1993, p. 8). The principal motivation behind this step was to involve the most important French reinsurance agencies which were known to be in favour of more market-oriented operations and activities in foreign markets. At the same time, however, these activities were intended to remain a purely national enterprise, with the traditional relationship between the national credit institutions being further consolidated in so far as resources from the *Caisse des Dépots et Consignations*, the *Crédit National*, the three big banks (the BNP, *Crédit Lyonnais*, and the *Sociéte Générale*) and the export bank BFCE together account for slightly more than fifty per cent of the agency's total capital. This observation clearly fits into the broader picture of French policy-making under internationalised market conditions (Hall, 1994, p. 187; Coleman, 1997, p. 274): the domestic institutional setting is modified to render the instruments of state interventionism more effective.

5 Germany: Export Promotion and 'Ordnungspolitik'

Die staatliche Exportkreditversicherung leistet einen entscheidenden Beitrag zur Aufrechterhaltung des Ressourcenflusses in die Entwicklungsländer und hilft den Entwicklungsländern so im Überwinden der Schuldenkrise und ihrer Integration in ein offenes Welthandelssystem.

Bundesministerium für Wirtschaft

At the beginning of the 1990s Germany's large deficits in the export credit insurance sector received growing attention by officials in national as well as international administrations. These observers did usually not include in their assessment other instruments of export promotion policy or make comparisons with other European trading states. The first section of this chapter shows that this comparison is both possible and necessary, because the policy space of export promotion can be described in the same terms as in Britain and France. Moreover, as Section 5.2 argues, the German pattern of negative co-ordination is similar to the process of interministerial co-ordination in the other two countries. As in the French case, the output indicators presented in Section 5.3, identify the trend towards a use of official insurance services for promotion purposes in the mid-eighties. Moreover, by broadening the analysis in Sections 5.4 and 5.5, it can be shown how interest groups influence the direction and content of institutional reform in the German system.

5.1 System Characteristics

In Germany, the nature of the domestic structure has led to a recognisable pattern in political choices. Hall's (1986) account describes the most striking feature of economic policy-making in the Federal Republic as being the close relationship between financial and industrial capital, where the latter can basically be considered to be under the control of the former due to the potential for large shareholdings on the part of banks. Arguing along similar lines, Zysman (1983) has defined the financial system as credit based and dominated by the banks; as regards the instruments of foreign economic policy-making, Katzenstein (1978, pp. 302-7) has

138

stressed the respective significance of an exporting ideology, the dominance of a deflationary macroeconomic policy and a tendency in order to defend what was then an undervalued currency to pursue export-led growth. In comparison, more specific instruments like credit guarantees, tax remissions and interest rate subsidies were considered less important, or as Kreile, writing in 1978, thought, that though such instruments of foreign economic policy were available, their actual use could not match the degree of mercantilism practised by other major industrialised nations (Kreile, 1978, pp. 191-224). However, the evidence collected here suggests that the export dependency of the economy has been translated into a political influence on the part of particular sectors, which often finds expression in a close co-operative relationship between the ministerial bureaucracy and interest groups in industry, trade and banking.

During the post-war period, instruments of export promotion played an important role in West Germany's economic relations with Eastern Germany. Historically, it was the revaluation of the German mark in 1958 and 1971 as well as the first post-war recession which placed issues of economic security at the top of the agenda for policy-makers, with goals such as those expressed in the Stability and Growth Act of 1967 often being ignored: the following of a strategy that repeatedly assigned priority to the most endangered goal within the 'magic quadrangle' meant that balanced trade relations were sometimes given short shrift. From the late 1960's onwards, the Ministry of Economics also embarked on an active policy of concentrating its attention on sectors heavily subsidised by the government or dependent on state agencies as their major customers. As in other European countries, the main rationale was to build up 'national champions' that were able to compete effectively in international markets, where sooner or later instruments of export promotion would eventually be forced to adopt a more prominent position.

Under the terms of the official German *export credit insurance* scheme, the Federal government assumes responsibility for both political and commercial risks: the *Hermes Kreditversicherungs-Aktiengesellschaft* constitutes a private company which was appointed by the government in 1949 to issue all export credit insurance entirely on behalf of the state, and any insurance transactions conducted by Hermes in this capacity immediately place a burden on the Federal Budget (Bellers, 1990, p. 139). The job of distributing export guarantees in practice rests with an interministerial committee (*Interministerieller Ausschuß*, IMA) under the control of the Ministry of Economics, where representatives from the Ministry of Finance, the Foreign Office, the Ministry for Economic Co-operation and the two official financing institutions (the *Kreditanstalt für Wiederaufbau* and the *Ausfuhrkredit-Gesellschaft*) meet together in corporatist fashion with delegates from industry, the banks and the export trade.

All official cover is accompanied by an exposure limit on total commitments, a credit frame that is fixed annually by Parliament once already existing commitments, premium payments and recoveries from earlier claims have been taken into account. In this respect, the relevant provision in the Budget Law makes an explicit distinction between cover intended for the promotion of exports and cover for exports of 'national interest', but without this leading to preferential conditions for either of the two types of cover or for exports to particular groups of countries. In other words, although some transactions which are of particular interest to the government may carry a higher risk, they are not subject to special credit ceilings. The way in which cover is granted establishes a close relationship with those banks that provide direct finance, because government insurance becomes an essential prerequisite for their lending activities.

Like its British and French counterparts, Hermes does not just simply provide guarantees for banks - the insurance programme includes many risks associated with export contracts such as insolvencies and changes in exchange rates. One exceptional feature of the German system resides in the various types of cover which are available to exporters (Glotzbach, 1973; Kageneck, 1990). Depending on the nature of the contracting partner, 'guarantee' business is the term applied in the case of private enterprises, while 'surety' business refers to transactions with foreign governments or bodies constituted under public law. Single transaction cover deals distinctly with short, medium or long-term transactions by an exporter or with medium or long-term loans given by German banks to a domestic exporter, whereas revolving (multiple transaction) cover makes provision for the full amount of the seller's annual short-term turnover with a particular foreign buyer. A third option, the so-called *Ausfuhr-Pauschal-Gewährleistung*, allows for up to two years comprehensive cover of short-term turnover with several foreign buyers at a flat rate (OECD, 1990, p. 60).

In addition, seven of the Federal states in the area of former West Germany offer more detailed facilities, which are basically intended to compensate for the existing gaps within the central promotion system. To date, only a handful of *Länder* governments have interpreted their own programmes as being competitive instruments to be employed in preference to their national counterparts. Instead, these schemes usually take on additional guarantees in order to cover pre-payment and supplier risks, as a support to small and medium-sized firms, and the resources of the *Länder* are generally used only as supplements to Federal programmes, in line with the principle of subsidiarity.

West Germany has usually preferred to rely more on market forces, and only decided to subsidise export credit in specific instances, as was the case with shipbuilding (because it was suffering a prolonged depression) and the Airbus project (because it was a new product that needed help to try and penetrate foreign markets). In addition, the fact that commercial interest rates have generally tended to be quite low has usually meant reduced possibilities for subsidising credit, but it was only really in the early 1970's, when the government was attempting to combat inflation by means of a tight monetary policy, that it occasionally became difficult to obtain export finance and pressure increased to create new official support facilities. On balance, however, German exporters were relatively satisfied with the competitiveness of their export finance facilities, which reflected the country's advantage in having a highly liquid and efficient banking system rather than access to particular instruments of subsidisation. Hence it seems reasonable to agree with Pearce's overall evaluation that, despite the role of the size and strength of the export sector as a key factor in producing economic prosperity in the 1970s and early 1980s, West German governments have held the view that they should interfere with market forces as little as possible (Pearce, 1980, p. 34).

Among the export financing institutions, the *Ausfuhrkredit-Gesellschaft* (AKA) is of comparatively minor importance since only a small portion of its activity draws on preferential refinancing sources from the *Bundesbank* (Ausfuhrkredit-Gesellschaft, 1991, p. 25). In terms of the distribution of official sources, the *Kreditanstalt für Wiederaufbau* (KfW), is far more significant. When this state-owned bank was established in 1948, its initial task was to finance the reconstruction of the economy by means of low-interest, domestic investment loans, but since 1955 this role has been extended to include the provision of finance for German exports and from 1961 onwards, the institution has also extended loans and grants on behalf of the Federal government within the framework of financial co-operation with developing countries (Sickenberger, 1992, p. 114).

There are two main sources by which the bank supports its external activities, firstly, through two export promotion funds under the management of the KfW but ultimately dependent on the approval of the Ministry of Economics for each loan that it proposes to make. Approximately one fourth of the credits stemming from the promotion funds are financed by special government money originally deriving from the European Recovery Programme (ERP), and the *Kreditanstalt für Wiederaufbau* combines these ERP funds with sources raised on the capital market in order to arrive at a blended interest rate. Secondly, additional support comes through entirely market-generated funds that are raised either on the German or the international capital markets, in exactly the same way as is customary for commercial banks.

Government influence is brought into play when the bank grants official support in the form of credits refinanced either wholly or partly from public funds, or in the form of interest subsidies also taken out of the same funds. This applies to credits from the export promotion funds, to mixed credits and to loans in connection with ship and aircraft financing, although in the case of the former, its use is limited to contracts made by domestic exporters for the delivery of capital goods to developing countries. Due to certain restrictions on the maximum amounts that can be financed out of these funds, additional market sources are necessary in order to provide the capital required for large export transactions, with a series of regulations stipulating that the amount of market funds used has to be limited to the same thresholds, and granted under the same financing schemes, as the officially supported ones.

Certain organisational features help explain the existence of this kind of low profile policy. In the first place, although government intervention is limited in terms of regulating the economy, there is nevertheless substantial intervention in the form of ownership of industry on the part of the Federal and state governments. At the same time, the banking sector is comparatively much more closely bound to industry, and consequently more willing to share risks, than in most other countries and the extent of integration between government banking and industry may in some measure offset the potential drawback of providing only a relatively small amount of subsidy for export credit. Most exporters are basically in favour of keeping German subsidies to a minimum as long as they are not at too great a disadvantage *vis-à-vis* foreign competitors who benefit from subsidies. The overriding idea for much of the post-war period has been to promote exports on the basis of quality, service and reputation rather than relying on preferential financing terms.

In contrast to France and Britain, the Ministry for Economic Co-operation clearly enjoys control over the aid budget and, together with the Ministry of Economics and the Foreign Office, constitutes the most important actor in the *aid finance* field. The bilateral programme is implemented by agencies specialising in technical and financial co-operation. Within the system of 'mixed financing', single concessional loans are offered as packages for combining resources from the budget of the Ministry for Economic Co-operation and KfW funds, and this forms a major part of German development policy, because the *Kreditanstalt* implements the aid programme dealing with bilateral financial co-operation. The selection criteria and appraisal procedures for operations involving these joint credits are the same as for projects entirely funded from the ministerial budget.

Of the overall aid total, 80.6 per cent was provided in the form of grants and only 9.3 per cent was given in loans; the remaining 10 per cent was either made available as capital, or as subscriptions to international financial institutions. In practice, however, more than half of German bilateral aid is tied to the purchase of goods and services in Germany and aid policy with regard to local procurement is very weak. As in other European countries, the government argues that it would only be willing to consider discontinuing its policy of tying aid on the condition that all the other important industrial countries did so as well. In the meantime, the alternative strategy implies the use of 'mixed credits' estimated at 0.7 billion SDR in 1991, which accounted for 14.3 per cent of official development assistance (ODA) that year and therefore represented a slight increase on the 1990 figure of 13.2 per cent, or 0.63 billion SDR in absolute figures.

In the area of mixed financing, resources stemming from financial co-operation are supplemented by commercial funds from the KfW, which happens in such a way that the total amount given in a uniform credit contract contains a grant element of at least 25 per cent so that it can be registered as official development aid (ODA). Two details are of particular importance here: firstly, the repayment of financial co-operation resources only begins after the repayment of the KfW financial credit, which rapidly produces quite a negative influence on net-transfers from the recipient country; secondly, the entire sum of credit *de facto* becomes a supply-tied capital aid, because the KfW portion has to be covered by Hermes, which - as it is an official agency - only provides this service to German exporters. On the supply side, mixed financing by and large attracts the same industries as financial co-operation as a whole. Given the fact that mixed financing is influenced by commercial considerations (i.e. it is directed towards specific projects in the fields of infrastructure or investment goods in the slightly more developed countries), its quantity influences both the sector and the country structure of development aid. If mixed financing increases beyond a certain level, it eventually contradicts developmental aims, especially with regard to projects in least developed countries (LLDC) and basic needs strategies, and this is the more true on occasions when financial co-operation begins to stagnate and mixed financing to increase because the room for manoeuvre becomes even more restricted when working with countries where the export of capital goods is usually ineffective.

5.2   Domestic Co-ordination

In general terms, the (West) German cabinet has never really developed into a collective decision-making body that is in effective control of government policy. In the area of foreign economic policy, for example, co-ordination is mainly the prerogative of a number of interministerial committees which have proliferated over the years (Karl, 1980, pp. 413-4). The question is therefore whether or not in this particular field this is a beneficial factor. Within the ranks of the ministerial bureaucracy, the committee for export guarantees is recognised as being highly routinised, independent and efficient, and in comparison to other elements in the ministerial bureaucracy it seems to perform fairly well. Official government circles often point to three features that help to explain such a positive evaluation: first of all, it is a very specialised body; second, it can rely on a well-established apparatus for the technical processing of applications and, lastly, the constant lead given by the Ministry of Economics provides the committee with a good degree of backing in the cabinet and facilitates good contacts with business (Prior, 1968, p. 151). In terms of the overall picture of domestic policy co-ordination, however, these features create negative co-ordination (Mayntz and Scharpf, 1975, p. 147), since participating ministries other than that of the Ministry of Economics only appear to make a significant impact when their own self-interests are at stake. Indeed, it is only well-established interests that are fully involved in maintaining enduring exchange relationships between government departments and private economic interests, a point illustrated by the composition of the advisory board, as shown in Table 5.1. All its members are leading representatives of banking and industry (Pollmann, 1993, p. 23).

Strictly speaking, the formal regulations in the German Budget Law are quite rigid, in so far as they only mention two possibilities for the extension of guarantees: either exports must fulfil the requirement of 'eligibility for support', or there should be a 'particular state interest' which they are helping to realise. But the interpretation of terms and decisions in specific cases rests with the interministerial committee, and thus leaves considerable room for discretion in support of the main goal of export credit insurance, which is essential for the promotion of the export interests of business as a whole. As part of the overall evaluation process as to whether an export business is eligible for supportive measures, the interministerial committee examines the type of products to be exported, the prospective buyer and the country of destination. The committee applies a series of criteria which refer either to so-called 'critical countries' who have difficulties in repaying credits and are accordingly registered as such by the Ministry of Economics, or to groups of goods which require official export approval because they could also be used for military purposes (dual use) or alternatively because they were ordered directly by an army institution. Any combination of these factors will lead to a classification as sensitive business and creates exceptions in otherwise routine application procedures (Stolzenburg and Moltrecht, 1991).

Table 5.1   German external advisers 1993

Member	Company
Hartmut Emans	Elpro
Hans Helmut Giersch	MAN
Hans W. Nolting	Metallgesellschaft
Harald Peipers	Hochtief
Carl Friedrich Petersen	MPC Münchmeyer-Petersen
Karl Schwiegelshohn	Liebherr Holding
Klaus Sturnay	Uhde
Hans-Jürgen Zechlin	Deutscher Maschinen- u. Anlagenbau
Christoph von Hammerstein-Loxten	Berliner Bank
Arno Puhlmann	Bayerische Vereinsbank
Louis Graf von Zech	BHF-Bank
Eberhard Zinn	Bayerische Landesbank –Girozentrale

Source: Fues (1993).

In the history of the committee there have, of course, been cases where the co-ordination process has not worked as smoothly as hoped by its technical operators. Between 1973 and 1974, for example, a controversy developed over whether or not the government should subsidise interest rates for long-term export credits, as had been requested by the Soviet Union, with the interministerial conflict taking place between the Chancellery on the one side, and the Ministries of Economics and Finance on the other. Whereas the former supported the idea for foreign policy reasons, the latter argued that the measure was totally inappropriate given the huge surplus in trade with the Eastern Bloc: the Economic Ministry raised objections related to reasons of *Ordnungspolitik*, while the Ministry of Finance opposed the move on budgetary grounds. With both interest groups and government divided in this way, the status quo option prevailed. However, when export demand slackened under the impact of the recession, interest groups in the export sector immediately seized the opportunity to propose a general revision of export finance and credit guarantee terms, and within three months the relevant interministerial committee had decided upon a revision of guarantee conditions (Kreile, 1978, p. 208).

The above episode already gives some indication of how changes in overall economic conditions can have repercussion for the exercise and use of discretion on the part of the spending authorities, but it also demonstrates that in the German context insurance activities are more open to political influence than those of finance. In the case of finance, the domestic co-ordination mechanism can only effect the interest definition of banks indirectly by means of adjustments in the availability conditions of loan guarantees, whereby the interministerial committee can hope to stimulate (or discourage) the commercial interest of German banks in entire areas of economic transactions, especially in relation to contracts with particular countries (Spindler, 1984, p. 30).

As has been mentioned above, the German case is one of negative co-ordination where - as a rule - the whole procedure is under the control and responsibility of the Ministry of Economics (Bellers, 1990, pp. 435-46). Though each decision requires explicit approval from the Ministry of Finance, it is sufficient for the Foreign Office and the Ministry for Economic Co-operation to give only a less formal agreement, but in practice such a system permits extensive rights of veto which, if exercised at all levels of the co-ordination process between ministries, could only be overridden by a full cabinet decision under the auspices of the Chancellor. However, these latter kinds of decisions more usually take the form of general guidelines, as happened in 1983, when the cabinet recommended a flexible approach to the management of the export guarantee system in order to take account of employment factors or to fulfil the need to keep involved in highly contested markets, even if the country concerned displays difficulties making repayments. Whenever export business is in principle eligible for official cover, considerations as to the inherent risks being run can still pose strong obstacles (Schwab, 1989). The close correlation between eligibility and risk can be expressed - as a rule of thumb - in terms of a linear relationship: the higher the risks, the stricter the requirements of eligibility. Nevertheless, in practice, non-risk related criteria such as the importance of the export contract to the individual firm, the employment situation, the structural position of the firm within a specific industry, the technological relevance of a project, different aspects of foreign and development policy as well as environmental policy considerations, can all influence the weighing up of a decision to an extent which can distort the establishment of an exactly linear relationship. To sum up, this process thus illustrates fairly well how a pro-subsidy argument expressed in terms of *Ordnungspolitik* does not actually match with the decision-making criteria being used.

The institutionalisation of the domestic co-ordination process obviously allows interest groups to pressure governments into adopting favourable policies, while at the same time politicians are able to pursue their own goals by considering these demands from a different perspective. As a means of safeguarding against an excessive instrumentalisation of the promotion system, there have been suggestions to place stricter regulations on the granting of export guarantees in the form of Federal legislation (Deutscher Bundestag, 1994), along with some detailed proposals for ensuring that officially backed business does not violate ecological standards, criteria for sustainable development or human rights. Moreover, it was also argued that an independent study should develop procedures for allowing these sorts of considerations to enter the routine decision-making process and that the introduction of ecological and social criteria into the examination of projects be left to the Ministries for Economic Co-operation and the Environment to jointly determine appropriate legal measures.

A Green Party (*Die Grünen/Bündnis 90*) initiative in precisely this respect explicitly acknowledged the need to modify the relevant institutional provisions. To begin with, a more balanced examination of eligibility for support would require placing the Ministries for Economic Co-operation and the Environment on an equal footing with the other participating ministries; in addition, an expanded advisory committee would than have to include nine representatives from non-governmental organisations (four appointed by the Ministry for Economic Co-operation and five by the Ministry for the Environment) in order to provide an adequate counterweight to the representatives of industry, banking and trade appointed by the Ministry of Economics. But these demands for positive co-ordination have been rejected by the government, who take the view that export guarantees are primarily an instrument for the promotion of exports rather than a way of contributing to the economic development of other nations. Whilst the broad area of discretion given to the interministerial committee allows for non-trade related factors to be taken into account, the government claims that there is no room for a more systematic and formalised analysis of such criteria.

5.3   The Interests of Firms

The unequal influence of interests on the domestic co-ordination process does not in the end produce results that can be said to demonstrate fixed state objectives or capacities. Instead, a number of changes over time can only be expected as an outcome of the interaction between firms and government, and when economic conditions are difficult and many firms are looking around for additional markets, the pressure on official agencies to reward business with special concessions will increase commensurately. Figure 5.1 shows how the official insurance agencies in Britain, France and Germany have reacted to these pressures by neglecting self-financing requirements and increasing deficits. As a consequence and, similarly to other European agencies, the German Hermes could not strike a positive balance between premium income, claim payments and recoveries for most of the period between 1982 and 1992. Only for a brief period in the first half of the 1980s it seemed as if in all three countries official export credit insurance could develop into a competitively neutral policy instrument. For most of the time, however, all three countries continued to diverge and accepted demands from export industries to distribute subsidies in the form of credit insurance.

In the German context up until 1982, the granting of cover was generally congruent with commercial criteria, without operating costs exceeding the income from premiums and repayments. That changed with the onset of the international debt crises. In 1992 the yearly deficit, calculated in SDR exchange rates at the end of each period, was more than four times as high than the 1983 level, and in 1993 the estimated deficit amounted to more than 2.53 billion SDR, while the overall cumulative deficit totalled more than 6 billion SDR. Table 5.2 also indicates that export credit insurance over the last ten years has developed into a subsidy instrument working very much to the advantage of exporters.

Table 5.2   German official export credit insurance[a]

	Premium income	Claims paid	Recoveries	Total
1983	212.4	535.8	78.4	- 245.0
1984	186.1	676.1	102.0	- 388.0
1985	252.3	646.6	135.3	- 259.0
1986	209.0	792.0	204.0	- 379.0
1987	131.5	972.2	171.7	- 669.0
1988	176.9	950.5	105.6	- 668.0
1989	191.2	1116.0	117.8	- 807.0
1990	183.4	1524.0	117.6	- 1223.0
1991	349.5	1338.0	112.5	- 876.0
1992	352.7	1514.0	125.3	- 1036.0

[a]SDR millions.

Source: Hermes (1993a) and own calculations.

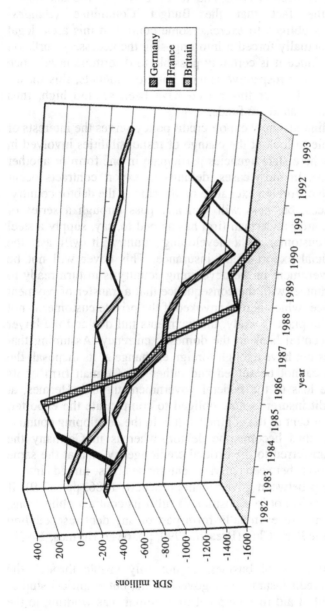

Figure 5.1   Deficits of official export credit insurance agencies
Source: Coface (1982-1992), ECGD (1992-1994), Hermes (1993a) and own calculations.

Although it could hardly be justified under the heading of correction of market failures, the respective costs had to be borne by the tax payer, because, despite the fact that the Budget Committee (*Bundes-haushaltsausschuß*) is obliged to exercise some control in this area, legal provisions have not actually forced it into imposing the necessary curbs on spending behaviour. Since it is certainly possible to determine in advance the upper restrictions on prospective annual liability amounts, this means that the maximum levels over this period have been set too high, thus giving a blank cheque to hand out funds.

In order to underline just how export credit policy serves the interests of business, it is possible to look at the change of responsibilities involved in export transactions where state agencies participate in one form or another (Fues, 1993, pp. 4-5). In most cases, defaults in export contracts occur because of a shortage of foreign exchange on the side of the debtor country. In these circumstances, business will typically pass through a series of stages. For example, after a German firm has agreed to, say, supply a steel plant to a private customer in a developing country, it will ask the government for official export credit insurance. This cover will not be given before the government in the developing country is in turn ready to produce a state guarantee, with the consequence that a transfer of payment obligations takes place, which is then invoked if the private customer is not able to pay. When the plant is ready, the payments fall due and the buyer makes these to the central bank in the domestic currency. Assuming that the central bank does not have enough foreign exchange at its disposal, the outstanding amount cannot be settled and either the German firm or its bank will report the loss to the Federal government through Hermes, at which point the credit insurer is now obliged to compensate the exporter, usually at up to 90 per cent of the contract value. In the developing country, the government has thus become the debtor, whereas in Germany the claims have been transferred to the official credit agency, and at the same time, a credit relation between private enterprises has turned into a debenture relationship between governments (Hichert, 1986, pp. 37-9). If the developing country is not in a position to fulfil its contract obligations, the remaining amount will eventually form part of any debt rescheduling negotiations within the Paris Club (Breach, 1990, pp. 68-9; Hermes, 1993b, p. 23).

The privileged position of business is not only visible through the provision of export credit insurance by governments, but empirical studies dealing with the field of aid finance point to a similar bias working to the detriment of both the recipient countries and of the economy of the donor country as a whole. At the bilateral level, financial co-operation is by far the more important in comparison to the other two co-ordinating instruments of technical co-operation and mixed financing, with resources most often going into the financing of single investment projects located in the machine building, construction and electro-technical sectors. As Table 5.3 indicates, these same sectors are also among the main recipients of single transaction cover from Hermes. Through the use of both promotion instruments, considerable amounts also went into shipping and transport systems; the recipient countries themselves are very much oriented towards the supply expectations in the donor country, and in most cases of contracts being given to German firms these were already clear at the outset, when the application for financing from German developmental aid was made. From 1973 onwards, the formal tying of aid to procurement was given up almost completely, though it remained a particularly important exception to the 'free choice' principle in sensitive areas such as shipping, transport systems, atomic power plants and consulting services (Cassen et al., 1994, p. 207). The basic approach was instead centred more around intergovernmental negotiations, in which attempts were made to arrive at a kind of self-binding agreement by developing countries to purchase products from the creditor country.

Table 5.3   German single transaction cover by sector[a]

	Plants	Machinery/ Transport	Aerospace/ Shipping	Construction work	Total[b]
1984	23.3	43.1	11.7	9.4	5342
1985	24.5	46.0	11.2	10.4	5337
1986	21.8	58.7	1.4	9.9	4235
1987	20.5	47.3	20.0	6.5	4659
1988	29.0	46.1	14.3	4.7	4563
1989	22.7	46.3	21.1	2.6	5287
1990	12.3	60.5	16.5	1.7	6023
1991	21.7	51.4	8.0	3.8	11349
1992	21.0	58.4	5.0	2.3	12188

[a]per cent of contract value;
[b]SDR millions, including other sectors with 12.5 per cent of contract value in 1984 (1985: 7.9, 1986: 8.2, 1987: 5.6, 1988: 5.9, 1989: 7.3, 1990: 9.1, 1991: 15.2, 1992: 13.3).

Source: Hermes (1993a) and own calculations.

With a change in government in 1982, the newly declared policy focus became 'employment effectiveness' and virtually the whole economy became a sensitive sector; in addition, the guidelines then adopted and modified no longer required international invitations for tender. However, neither the strategy of openly demanding a tying to national procurement nor that of resorting to more extensively covered forms of self-binding make much sense from a purely economic point of view. A study carried out by the *Deutsches Institut für Wirtschaftsforschung* (DIW) concluded that the demand for German goods and services financed through multilateral assistance, given under the auspices of international organisations or other OECD countries, is significantly higher than that generated by Germany's own bilateral aid system (DIW, 1987). Thus, the example of the employment argument per se is misplaced, if seen from a broader perspective than a purely project oriented view.

Table 5.4   Official and private export finance to developing countries[a]

	1985	1986	1987	1988	1989	1990	85-90[d]
Germany							
Official credits[b]	664	869	728	753	998	855	811
Private credits	1000	1512	3117	3345	3376	4390	2790
Total	1663	2381	3844	4099	4374	5245	3601
Official/Private[c]	39.9	36.5	18.9	18.4	22.8	16.3	25.5
France							
Official credits[b]	-	-	-	967	787	961	452
Private credits	6181	804	-	-	-	77	1177
Total	6181	804	-		787	1038	1629
Official/Private[c]	-	-	-	100	100	92.6	48.8
Britain							
Official credits[b]	3	193	74	97	81	-	75
Private credits	2980	3438	3402	1937	8655	-	3402
Total	2983	3632	3476	2034	8736	-	3477
Official/Private[c]	0.1	5.3	2.1	4.7	0.9	-	2.2

[a] credits in US dollar millions, including mixed credits and excluding other forms of tied aid;
[b] official export finance: aid credits and grant element in mixed credits + official credits to private national exporters + official credits to developing countries, figures rounded;
[c] per cent;
[d] average.

Source: Onida (1993).

The flow of finance to developing countries rose considerably in 1992, and a further rise was again in evidence the following year. Table 5.4 illustrates how, in the German case, this development was mainly due to the growth in private finance. A considerable shift in the proportions of private and official funds has emerged in recent years, most noticeably in the sphere of net transfers (i.e. loans minus interest and redemption payments) which were strongly negative for private lending in the second half of the 1980s, on account of the high level of debt service; hence the overall outflow of funds from the developing countries in this area. Since 1992, the private net transfer has returned positive, as new lending reached a higher level (Kreditanstalt für Wiederaufbau, 1994, p. 47).

Table 5.5   Availability of extraordinary support

	1989	1990	1991	1992
Germany				
Mixed/Tied aid credits	2.0	2.0	2.0	3.0
Foreign content support	2.0	2.5	2.5	2.5
Local cost support	2.0	2.0	2.5	2.5
France				
Mixed/Tied aid credits	3.0	3.0	2.0	2.5
Foreign content support	2.5	2.5	2.5	2.5
Local cost support	2.0	2.0	2.0	2.0
Britain				
Mixed/Tied aid credits	2.5	1.5	1.5	1.5
Foreign content support	2.5	2.5	2.5	2.5
Local cost support	2.0	2.0	2.0	2.0

0 - not available;
1 - used only in special circumstances (e.g. to match competition);
2 - an available, moderately used program;
3 - an extensively used program.

Source: Export-Import Bank of the United States (1993, p. 20).

Once more, this trend refutes the arguments which justify subsidies on the basis that they act as substitutes for the reluctance of private capital markets to cover long-term risks, and instead confirms the hypothesis that official support has actually been used to open up new markets. Table 5.5 suggests that the pattern has also been reinforced by a stronger recourse to extraordinary support measures in recent years.

As is true of any symbiotic relationship, both the Federal government and exporters benefit from the division of labour between the interministerial committee and business representatives. Whilst formal decisions on the granting of official support rest with the ministerial bureaucracy, these will be based on the recommendations put forward by the group of external advisers. Therefore, only specific contracts showing a clear foreign policy dimension or of vital importance to individual firms will enter the negotiation process between ministries. Private firms thus gain from the availability of comprehensive commercial advice given in strict confidence, which would be unlikely to be forthcoming from other officials, whilst the government saves on costs that it would otherwise have to pay for the creation of an institution with comparable expertise in all fields related to the insurance of export contracts. This is not simply a question of the purely technical advice offered to the committee on the part of private actors, but also an example of their participation in the administrative process or even in the independent execution of tasks traditionally associated with state agencies. That this happens is largely a matter of practical necessity: applications are made by private enterprises, whose processing automatically requires a detailed investigation into the commercial situation of the applicants, and to expect the state bureaucracy to forsake its neutrality and fulfil the same task would not only provoke an increase in costs, it would simultaneously run the risk of the interests of business and government colliding (Prior, 1968, p. 152).

Despite the arguments in favour of greater administrative separation (albeit somewhat artificial), the core fact remains that some parties benefit more than others. There is a built-in tendency for large firms to gain substantially more from official export credit insurance than small and medium-sized enterprises, which was precisely the type of criticism made by the five new German states, who argued that official guarantees would mainly end up supporting large West German firms via their subsidiaries in the East. And there have indeed been ample resources for boosting this kind of hidden support, because a special post-reunification budget for East German exports to the new independent states of the former Soviet Union (CIS) of about 1.7 billion SDR has been created, and while Hermes never usually covers more than 5 to 6 per cent of German exports as a whole, it does so at a rate of more than 50 per cent in the new Länder.

More general explanations for the overall bias can be found in the fact that large firms posses much better information on private insurance facilities and on the whole tend to prefer official insurance only in the case of very risky exports. The ever expanding capacity of financial markets works along very similar lines, as they exercise quite a different kind of influence on the overall decline in available cover (depending on the size of the firm). Likewise, a relative scarcity of capital resources can lead to a rise in interest rates, thanks to an increase in the availability of finance for what were formerly considered to be 'bad risks' and this will damage enterprises with comparatively little liquidity much more than others. Moreover, small enterprises participate to a lesser extent on the interministerial committee, just as they enjoy only very slight influence over the actual formation of cover arrangements. Given the balance of membership composition, it is of little use that discussions about modifications are held under the leadership of business interest groups if the smaller and medium-sized firms are felt to be under-represented among them.

5.4 The Political Dimension

Recent statements by the Minister for Foreign Affairs have indicated that providing a stimulus to the domestic economy via the development of foreign markets is a central aim of foreign policy, and other official statements from the government have announced the intention to make an exhaustive use of existing foreign economic policy instruments in the near future in order to promote export interests and, if need be, to improve promotion instruments still further (Schumann, 1994, p. 158; Nahrendorf, 1995, p. 51). As part of the new foreign economic policy strategy, decision-makers are obliged to actively support the economic interests of German industry. As such a policy has to date been inadequately applied, it is now necessary for state agencies and export industries to join together in developing a common export strategy. The social-democratic opposition favours a joint foreign export initiative between government and industry very much in that vein, and more specifically urges a further extension of the various Hermes instruments in order to create a more comprehensive promotion tool that also encompasses trade finance. Particularly in relation to the availability of foreign content support, they stressed that the granting of such cover should be restricted to contracts in which approximately 90 per cent of the value added pertains to the national territory.

However, it is difficult to imagine how these demands can simultaneously be reconciled with the existing support for a liberal world trading system and the reduction of protectionism. Equally, non-governmental organisations have already begun to complain that the focus of development policy on poverty is consistently undermined by foreign policy interests and export guarantee policy (Randel and German, 1993). The ministerial bureaucracy maintains that the boundaries between development policy and foreign economic policy are fluid, and that the former does not merely imply the fight against poverty, but the integration of developing countries into the world market as well. Hence, there have been a number of suggestions to the effect that the long-term goal of a uniform foreign economic policy would be better served by a merger between the Foreign Office and the Ministry for Economic Co-operation (Nahrendorf, 1995, p. 50).

These broad demands for institutional reform also reflect a certain dissatisfaction with the present use of promotion instruments for political ends. In the case of standard trade credits, for example, the underlying political motivation is to help projects that will produce a proportion of their output for the German economy, e.g. in the form of raw materials. In this particular area, however, banking and foreign economic policy interests only coincide to a very limited extent. The availability of official guarantees is only one of many factors which private banks have to take into account when making decisions on whether or not to extend financing. It is thus the indirect mechanism of the guarantee system alone that can induce the financial sector to serve as a subsidiary agent for the foreign policy objectives of government (Spindler, 1984, p. 14).

The creeping (and much criticised) politicisation of the promotion measures themselves was already pre-determined by the legal form given to the policy instruments. According to Paragraph 8 (1) of the Budget Law, the granting of cover is also permissible in cases where a specific state interest is at stake, thereby assuming a clearly recognisable political quality (Sickenberger, 1992, p. 109). One of the advantages of the distribution of labour within the interministerial committee is that the Federal government is able to keep a certain distance from the handling of guarantee business, and thus gains a politically important degree of room for manoeuvre. As several problematic foreign policy situations have demonstrated, this enables government to hold on to business contacts while at the same time not appearing to be directly involved, and historical experience indicates that even in times of crisis new guarantees can be extended to politically undesirable but economically advantageous trading partners.

Obviously, it is better for everyone involved if both trade interests and political interests go hand in hand, as happened with the decision of the Federal government to temporarily apply preferential conditions to official cover for existing contracts between East German firms and buyers in Central and Eastern Europe. Contrary to customary procedure, the authorities refrained from making pre- and interim payments and instead advanced the full amount of the contract value. In addition, credit periods could be extended up to a maximum of ten years, including a repayment-free period of up to three years, which the Ministry of Economics believed would avoid producing competitive distortions owing to the fact that these special conditions would only be valid for the continuation of business already involved in trading contracts.

That notwithstanding, the process of politicisation in practice is strongly manifested in the market distribution of unrecovered claims and amounts at risk (cf. Table 5.6). Furthermore, the regional distribution of maximum liability totals given in Table 5.7 shows that changes in the definition of political interests have influenced the willingness to provide cover for other countries. In the case of trade transactions with Africa and South America, annual cover ceilings reveal a declining propensity to distribute official support between 1990 and 1992.

Table 5.6　Hermes exposure 'Top Ten Markets' 1992[a]

Country	Exposure
CIS	16562
Brazil	7602
Iran	5318
Iraq	3742
Argentina	3702
Indonesia	3363
South Africa	3225
Turkey	3105
Algeria	2736
Saudi-Arabia	2622
Subtotal	51977
Total (all markets)	93314

[a]SDR millions.

Source: Hermes (1993a) and own calculations.

Table 5.7　Relative composition of maximum liability amounts[a]

	1990	1991	1992
Developing countries[b]			
Asia/Pacific	31.9	30.9	31.8
Africa	18.5	16.0	14.6
Latin America	15.9	14.5	13.9
Europe	5.5	5.3	5.4
Subtotal	71.8	66.7	65.8
Central/Eastern Europe	12.4	18.9	20.2
Industrial countries	6.3	5.8	5.7
Others	9.5	8.6	8.3

[a]per cent;
[b]by region and including OPEC countries.

Source: Hermes (1993a).

As a result of rising deficits, a new procedural regulation concerning decisions over cover for the CIS has been introduced, an exceptional measure implemented by a committee of State Secretaries from the Ministry of Economics, Ministry of Finance, Foreign Office and Chancellery, which has been justified on the grounds that the 'particular state interest' should be the responsibility of political officials, and not of the technocrats who deal with matters on a practical level. At the same time, a regular meeting between Chancellery officials and the heads of offices of the East German Chief Ministers (Ludewig Round), considered *inter alia* export guarantees as an instrument to support economic development after unification (Czada, 1996, p. 102). For this reason, there can be few illusions as to the main motivation at work, namely the Federal government's desire to keep the export industry in the five new *Länder* alive. This is contrary to it being a question of allowing the CIS to benefit from special aid or 'to demonstrate political and economic support' for other countries which were undergoing the transition to market economies (Davis and Dombrowski, 1997, p. 13).

The practice of deviating from the standard, procedurally fixed export promotion rules when politically desirable has a long tradition in the history of the Federal Republic (Dean, 1974, p. 68). During the 1960s, export finance, development aid and guarantees were deliberately exploited as a policy instrument for implementing the Hallstein doctrine, according to which West Germany alone was felt to be entitled to speak in the name of Germany as a whole (Weis, 1990; Brown and O'Connor, 1996, p. 96). The method of distributing credits became public knowledge in 1962, when the consequences of a pipeline embargo against the Soviet Union led to the introduction of a special risk category into the guarantee schemes, and in the similar context of another pipeline deal with the Soviet Union, the predetermined length of credit periods were extended with government approval. In 1975, a German-Brazilian nuclear agreement likewise amounted to a breaking of international agreements, after Hermes retrospectively covered the rapidly increasing construction costs.

Modifications in distribution criteria have occasionally induced limitations in official expenditure (cf. Section 5.2), which is what occurred in the case of the introduction of special conduct rules for German exporters doing business with South Africa. Still more restrictive consequences followed upon the Gulf War, when tighter control mechanisms were introduced with regard to so-called 'sensitive goods', according to which the exporting firms are themselves obliged to provide evidence that their exports will only be used for civilian purposes. By way of contrast, human rights considerations played a central role in 1989, with the repercussions of the Tienanmen Square massacre provoking the complete removal of the People's Republic of China from eligibility for cover. More often, however, the pursuit of foreign policy goals is advanced by modifications that increase the amount of money pumped into promotion efforts. During the Iran-Iraq War, additional guarantees were taken on in 1980, whereby increased claims would be covered even after the signing of the original contracts. Later on, the reform process in Poland was supported by extending the guarantee schemes on preferential terms, and the most recent example is provided by the Chinese Canton underground project, where the Federal government made available a soft loan with a repayment period of forty years.

Faced with a situation of still mounting deficits at the end of 1993, a more rigid application procedure was then introduced for guarantees relating to export contracts with Russia. The Minister of Economics argued that, aside from purely legal reasons this action also represented a tactical signal to Russia that it could not expect to count on further support from Hermes guarantees without meeting repayment obligations stemming from previous rescheduling agreements, even though over the same period, an exception was permitted to help the export of transport systems from former East German industries. Another example of how the instrument is used to squeeze concessions from trading partners is the granting of medium and long-term export guarantees to Vietnam. Here, this issue was linked to the question of whether Vietnamese residents living in Germany would receive permission to return to their home country, whilst the Federal government was simultaneously influenced by demands from industry to back their efforts to gain a foothold in an important Asian market.

These kinds of politically motivated cover decisions can hardly be evaluated in purely economic terms. Political aims such as the giving of assistance to developing countries or the consolidation of trends towards democracy can be more effectively realised by other instruments, like direct transfer payments or debt remission, so on balance it is the compensatory function, i.e. the evening out of the competitive distortions that derive from foreign export credit insurance systems and which work to the detriment of domestic exporters, that possess the greatest importance and make the range of instruments appear tenable in terms of *Ordnungspolitik* (Halfen, 1991, p. 182). The Ministry of Economics claims that the range of promotion instruments can be defended, because the neutralisation of competitive distortions would have a higher chance of success than attempts to eliminate their actual causes: a unilateral reduction in national cover arrangements is hardly likely to encourage the governments of major competitors to do the same in their own systems; on the contrary, efforts in that direction would represent the loss of a security in any future negotiations on the reduction of state aids.

The increasing politicisation of Hermes cover has already corrupted the nature of official export credit insurance because of its misuse for purposes which it was not originally designed to fulfil. In particular, it is widely feared that only limited resources will be available in the future for the original task of risk-oriented security, if cover policies continue to pursue aims which are not appropriate to the system, i.e. if excessive demands are put on Hermes cover through its exploitation as an instrument of structural and employment policy.

In fact the Federal government had to put up with similar criticism as early as 1957, when it was accused of trying to circumvent the obligations that it had entered into with developing countries for reasons of a political motivation connected to the export guarantee business (Weis, 1991). Precisely the same sorts of warnings were repeated at the start of the 1990s, against a background of ongoing export relations between East German firms and their partners in the former Soviet Union. The industrial sector foresaw additional financial burdens resulting from politically motivated single covers or the provision of guarantee frames at high risk, which potentially could have had negative repercussions for the cover policy of the Federal government as a whole and seriously affect ordinary business that was in need of support. One suggested solution was to separate cover given for political reasons from guarantees that are obliged to follow commercial criteria, to which end a specific instrument would have to be created whereby more sophisticated accounting procedures would help to differentiate between political and commercial aims and between safeguards against high financial losses and other types of expenditure.

5.5   Reform

Discussion of reform in Germany is largely focused on the field of export credit insurance because, having been a self-supporting mechanism for a number of years, it has now become an instrument for providing subsidies, thus running up increasingly large deficits and placing a heavy burden on the Federal Budget. More recently, the general discussion about the direction of the Federal Republic's future as an industrial location has also influenced the debate on the reform of Hermes instruments.

Against the background of world wide recession in the early 1990s, the prospects for improving the German position in foreign markets were not very promising, given that such an export-dependent economy is so strongly influenced by reductions in international demands for industrial products. Up to 1994, most sectors showed a decreasing number of new export orders, and, as was noted above, this was especially true for regions in the former German Democratic Republic (GDR) because of a complete breakdown in the East European markets. Even for many West German firms it proved impossible to maintain trading relations with these areas because of the lack of availability of Hermes cover to the necessary degree. The industrial sector therefore put forward criticism that the official handling of the situation was unsuited to current economic requirements. Given these circumstances, some additional doubts were raised as to whether European Community plans to introduce changes in the premium systems would be an appropriate measure, not least for the fact that any subsequent reform of the national system would make Hermes services even more expensive (Peipers, 1993, p. 10).

In relation to the reform of premium rates, however, it should be recognised that the Federal Republic operates with a system which could no longer be justified in technical, legal or political insurance terms and had only been introduced in the first place for practical reasons and because it was accepted by its respective trading partners (Gehring, 1993, p. 21). On the whole, the system's chief advantage was that it made it possible to avoid some of the pressure likely to arise from countries dissatisfied with their classification in a specific risk category.

By anticipating some of the relevant attempts at reform on the part of the EC, Germany finally abolished the traditional flat rate system in 1994, and in a way similar to other European countries, world markets are now divided into five risk categories with corresponding differentials in premium rates (Hermes, 1994). Category I includes countries without any particular risk involvement, i.e. mainly the OECD bloc, but also some of the newly industrialised countries such as South Korea, Taiwan and Singapore. Countries with relatively low political risks are to be found in category II: contract relations with countries like China, the Czech Republic, Saudi Arabia and Israel have been characterised by good payment records for some time, and are not therefore considered likely to present difficulties in fulfilling future obligations. Category III comprises countries which were traditionally covered by Hermes political risk insurance, and in particular refers to developing countries which do not show immediate signs of repayment difficulties, e.g. Turkey, Hungary, India, Indonesia and Mexico. In the fourth grouping there come increasingly risky markets such as Argentina, Brazil, Bulgaria and Algeria, places where considerable repayment difficulties have already occurred in the past: all these countries have had to enter into rescheduling arrangements and their internal economic performance to date does not indicate a capacity to deal with future debt problems. Finally, the fifth category deals with markets involving highly increased credit risks. As a rule, medium and long-term business tends to fall into this category and some countries in this group already have been removed from cover because no further risk was acceptable (examples of such countries include Egypt, White Russia, Ukraine, Vietnam, Cameroon, Zambia and Sudan).

Prior to this reform, the majority of business would have come under category III, and the new premium system has thus been constructed around this band through the creation of two lower (cheap) and two higher (expensive) rates. However, a strong concentration of risks within a particular country can also produce a classification in the next highest category. Be that as it may, the differentiation achieved by the new categories is unlikely to lead to any fundamental relief in the financial burdens incurred by the Federal Budget. A hypothetical calculation for the years between 1988 and 1991, for example, gives an average improvement of seven per cent in premium income, far too little to counter-balance existing deficits (Deutscher Bundestag, 1994, p. 4).

Official government representatives have argued that it would make more sense for the premium structure to reflect actual risks as they arise from individual contracts in particular countries, and therefore favour the development of a system more or less congruent with the EC proposal to introduce five risk categories of risk-laden countries; at the same time, they would prefer a system oriented towards the needs of the Western industrial nations, whilst leaving some room for flexibility as regards historical traditions and country relationships. Once again though, the fear of diplomatic repercussions and protests by countries dissatisfied with their classification meant that the new country list has yet to be published. In public, of course, great efforts are made to give the impression that these categories do not constitute final decisions and that actual risk assessments are under constant revision.

In 1992, leading German interest groups such as the *Deutscher Industrie- und Handelstag* (DIHT, Federation of Industry and Trade), the *Bundesverband Deutscher Banken* (BDB, Confederation of German Banks), the *Bundesverband des Deutschen Groß- und Außenhandels* (BDGA, Confederation of German Wholesale- and Export Trade) and the *Bund der Deutschen Industrie* (BDI, Confederation of German Industry), acknowledged that the traditional flat rate system had to be abandoned in line with European harmonisation, yet at the same time, they expressed reservations against a unilateral introduction of this reform without a simultaneous improvement in cover instruments. Unless that happened, they argued that there would be an adverse effect on the competitiveness of domestic firms since other countries offer much more favourable financing packages through officially supported credits.

In concrete terms, the industrial associations demanded a 5 per cent reduction in internal fees, efforts to avoid imposing a country specific increase in fee rates, a shortening of waiting periods to three months, provision of cover for interest rates after maturity and, in general, the creation of greater flexibility in dealing with the needs of the economy. In addition, the necessity was stressed of following the categorisation of buyer countries into five risk groups, using an objective rating procedure founded on the basis of economic data, and in this respect, governmental decisions motivated by foreign or economic policy considerations should not be allowed to influence the method of classification (being restricted instead to the formulation of cover policy). Finally, the industrialists asserted that it should be possible to differentiate premiums by making deductions within single risk guarantees, and to qualify for these preferential rates a contract would either have to be additionally covered by private bank guarantees, provide extra securities on behalf of the recipient side, or include parties holding a positive standing in relation to loans from the World Bank or the European Bank for Reconstruction and Development (EBRD).

The following year, in the midst of recession and structural adjustment problems, the same associations recommended complete abstention from any cost-increasing changes until all national systems are harmonised within the framework of the European Community. In the case of countries located in the middle category, the intended reform would have led to a rise in costs of up to 25 per cent, and in the fifth country category, part of the amount to be paid would have more than doubled. The interest groups viewed it as absolutely imperative to ensure that the European harmonisation of national cover systems was accompanied by similar adjustments in other competition distorting measures in the field of risk protection and financing. In terms of average costs for credit insurance, and compared to other EC countries, Germany now already occupies a position at the top end of the scale and recent experiences in internationally contested large-scale projects have demonstrated how current protection and financing disadvantages can lead to the loss of employment intensive contracts. It is, for example, almost impossible for German exporters to match officially subsidised fixed interest rates within the US dollar range.

Within Germany, the chances of being able to solve competition problems within an EC setting seem to have been considered to be quite low. In 1994, the Budget Committee of the German *Bundestag* decided on the introduction of a new Federal guarantee, the so-called 'development aid financing facility for infrastructure projects' which amounted to more than 500 million DM. The guarantee is envisaged as a protection of resources from the capital market and will be used within the framework of development co-operation to finance large-scale projects in upper-middle income countries. The Budget Committee has authorised the Ministry of Finance to take over all sureties and guarantees concerning credits which contribute to the financing of bilateral co-operation projects that deserve aid, thus opening up the way for the introduction of a 'development-financing infrastructure'. While the entire sum of development aid has so far been provided by resources from the Federal Budget, this new guarantee for the first time mobilises additional aid finance from the capital markets. By means of this modification, the government brought itself into step with most other industrialised countries. The credits include a 5 per cent fixed interest rate, a credit length of 20 years and a repayment-free period of five years, with the setting of interest rates below actual market levels being attained by mixing resources from the private market with official financial co-operation money, to which conditions of the International Development Agency (IDA) with an interest rate of 0.75 per cent apply (Bundesverband der Deutchen Industrie, 1993). Consequently, the extension of official cover has been mirrored by reform within the financing sector: the Federal Budget Committee decided in 1994 to reduce the proportion of multilateral co-operation in the total of development aid to 30 per cent in the medium term.

Domestic interest groups have since estimated the effects on their interests in terms of the expected gains and losses from specific policies; for the representatives of industry, it was clear that any policy deriving from an international agreement would make it more costly to benefit from official support. The most effected groups thus had strong incentives for articulating their opposition, but governmental decision-makers deflected these criticisms by paying more attention to their own foreign policy considerations. However, the dissatisfaction of the industrial sector with the Hermes reform has to some extent been moderated by provision of the new facility in the financing sector and various other initiatives to give more active backing for exports to developing countries with promising markets (Kessler, 1996, p. 36). Moreover, in contrast to the original draft legislation, which stipulated a general extension of preferential credits without tying them to national exports, the final version renounced that clause and actually further extended the list of potential target countries. Thus, in terms of empirically observable preference articulation, Germany's internal reforms moved in the direction of a domestically managed solution to external trade relations.

PART III
EUROPEAN
AND
INTERNATIONAL
INSTITUTIONS

6 Institutional Choice in the European Community

Only the briefest glance at the dominant practice in the field of export credits and export credit insurance within the European Community's trade policy is sufficient to grasp the essentials of a somewhat surprising and contradictory situation. Despite several court rulings relating to the Community's claim to exclusive competence in matters of international trade (Stein, 1990, pp. 157-62), the fact remains that so far no truly European policy instrument has been developed that goes beyond the incorporation of export finance agreements drawn up within the institutional framework of the Organisation for Economic Co-operation and Development (OECD). Research in the field of jurisprudence has defined the situation as constituting a unique case in the history of the Community because of the incompatibility between the formally existing rules and those rules which are actually observed in practice (Ernst and Beseler, 1983, p. 1955; Bourgeois 1991; Houbé-Masse, 1992). Two directives were approved by the Council of Ministers, dealing with the two major aspects of export credit insurance, namely the harmonisation of the basic provisions for guarantees on short-term transactions and the adoption of a common credit insurance policy for medium and long-term transactions, but neither of them came into effect (Council of the European Communities, 1970a; 1970b; 1971).

In order to try and resolve this contradiction, most political economists would probably point to the role played by the different interests held by the leading actors in EC politics, i.e. those of the individual nation-states, Community institutions such as the Council, Court of Justice, Parliament and last, but by no means least, the Commission. In the case of the latter, it seems reasonable to assume that the Commission would be *a priori* in favour of a common export policy, whereas a similar kind of assumption regarding the member states would be at best problematic. One substantial problem in this respect is the parallel continuation of national programmes aimed either at protecting domestic production or opening up foreign markets for the benefit of national industries. However, it cannot be supposed that there will automatically be a straightforward divergence of interests: depending on who the major trading competitors are, or the nature of the export market, it is possible for there to be a coincidence of interests between European firms, for example as when bidding against American or Japanese companies to try and secure a large contract to export capital goods to a developing country.

In terms of co-ordination there is therefore a clear need to find some type of agreement that will prevent ruinous competition but without more extensive support measures or financial resources. However, in terms of market liberalisation and free competition this would not only have to be achieved between the members of the European Community, it would have to apply to countries which pursue an active export promotion policy: as long as any agreement failed to include as a minimum all the major industrial powers and some of the Asian developing countries, the damaging race for preferential conditions would simply continue, albeit between major trading blocs rather than individual states.

As a result, the Community institutions are faced with the following dilemma: on the one hand, they are obliged by their Treaties to implement measures for the co-ordination and harmonisation of regulations as agreed by the member states; on the other hand, this kind of action will only help to avoid distortions to competition within the sphere of the common market. In the final analysis, regulations determined solely by the institutional framework of the EC are not adequate for the task at hand, and any initiative taken by the Community would thus require the same kind of co-ordination and consultation with the above mentioned group of countries as takes place when equivalent measures are being formulated among the member states of the Community (Seidl-Hohenveldern, 1977, p. 37).

This chapter examines in greater detail the process of co-ordination and the activities of the EC's common institutions. Section 6.1 presents the historical background to the regulatory framework that forms the subject of Section 6.2. Section 6.3 questions the Commission's ability to act as a neutral arbiter, while Section 6.4 explores the varying degree to which expertise impinges on reform efforts. Finally, the chapter concludes by presenting a tentative assessment of the role export promotion can play as an instrument of the Common Foreign and Security Policy (CFSP).

6.1   A Complex Legacy

From an historical perspective, a number of exceptional features can be discerned in the various attempts to make export credits and export credit insurance part of a common European policy. The working group of the

Council of Ministers, which was first established in 1960, had as its direct precursor a technical committee that was created by the official export credit agencies of the six original member states to fulfil certain 'co-ordination tasks'. At this point in time, the most striking aspect of the new set-up was its lack of any substantial legal foundation, but this obstacle was overcome by interpreting the formation of the working group and related decisions of the Council as *acta sui generis,* which recognised the existence of an overlap between national and Community competencies. Aside from the harmonisation of export aids according to Article 112 of the Treaty of Rome, a special emphasis was also put on the links to the potential granting of development aid as a related policy area which already had a clear foundation in Community law (Council of the European Communities, 1960). Thus, by emphasising the relationship between these two policy areas it became possible to incorporate an informal decision-making process into the institutional structure of the Community (Houbé-Masse, 1992, pp. 61-4).

Right from the outset, the Policy Co-ordination Committee for Export Credit Insurance, Guarantees and Financial Credits was much more than just a talking-shop for the exchange of opinions. Co-ordination was intended to keep the export financing and insurance policies of the member states under constant review, through the provision of further information or the use of increased consultation whenever member states had questions to raise concerning a proposed action. Moreover, it soon became compulsory to give notice of infringements of Community rules, and in cases where objections were voiced against a particular state practice but dispelled to the satisfaction of fellow EC countries, the procedure was such that all other EC members were permitted to remain competitive by being enabled to match the terms of credits or credit insurance offered in support of a specific export contract (Council of the European Communities, 1960; 1973; 1976). The matching procedure used by the OECD was taken as an obvious blueprint for implementing the same underlying logic, i.e. that the threat of retaliatory measures by other member states would prevent deviations from firmly agreed rules (Houbé-Masse, 1992, pp. 211-21). In practice, these rules took the form of minimum interest rates established by the OECD Trade Directorate and from the early 1970s onwards, were formally incorporated into EC policy through decisions taken by the Council of Ministers. The output of the Community's internal co-ordination process thus heavily relied on mechanisms agreed upon in a different institutional context. In turn, these mechanisms could serve as a basis from which Community institutions could gradually develop their own regulatory framework and follow the integrationist path towards an independent agency.

Therefore, the Community did not limit itself simply to the provision of an institutional structure designed to facilitate the exchange of information and thus enable member states to better co-ordinate their export support measures, it also pursued the more ambitious aim of changing national rules in such a way as to achieve a competitive neutrality among the official export credit agencies and, in addition, then strove to develop a truly common trade policy based on that new framework. When the Commission realised in the late 1970s that the programme harmonisation envisaged as the second stage of the strategy was being obstructed both by the diversity of legal and financial traditions in the member states and their considerable institutional differences, the project of a European Export Bank (EEB) was first mooted (European Parliament, 1977a; 1977b; Lainé, 1982, p. 189). Although the main idea was to establish a body only fulfilling tasks that were complementary to those of the official agencies, from a strategic point of view it was assumed that it would, to some extent, be possible to by-pass much of the harmonisation phase in the process. It was felt that at least in the field of export financing, the successful operations by American and Japanese companies carried out on the back of their ability to offer comprehensive contract terms in a single currency and at fixed rates, could be emulated through institutional innovation.

In comparison to the early work undertaken within the Community framework towards the creation of an Economic and Monetary Union (EMU), the proposal for a European Export Bank nevertheless appeared to be a relatively small enterprise. The idea was to substitute the existing, separate banking facilities in the export sectors of member states with a single financing system (unlike the already established European Investment Bank, EIB, the capital and management of the EEB would not have been under the control of national bodies). In order to distribute resources in a manner consistent with the objectives of a common EC export programme, it would have been made mandatory to channel all existing export assistance funds through the new bank. A few encouraging signals came from the UNICE (*Union des Confédérations de l'Industries et des Employeurs d'Europe*) and export-oriented banking groups, but in practice the proposal for a regulation to set up the institution got little further than budget requests to the Commission, and a general move back towards programme harmonisation rather than unification became evident when some amendments to the original EEB proposal only referred to a new EIB department, wherein its exact role was left rather unclear (Rallo, 1983, pp. 169-70).

Very similar ideas had already been put forward in 1973, even if only in an unofficial capacity (Glibert, 1983, pp. 271-6), although at the same time, reservations were expressed as to the advisability of creating a separate

European institution dealing directly with exporters and bankers, principally because of the practical difficulties in clearly defining the nature of the activities involved and due to the possibility of exporters creating unhealthy competition between European and national institutions. According to one expert opinion, it would have been more fruitful to restrict the European entity's responsibilities to those of reinsuring national credit insurers, thus rebalancing the portfolios of private insurers and inter-credit insurers' contracts. In this respect, Glibert (1983) suggested three potential activities: (1) mandatory reinsurance, linked to the creation of a fund limited to reinsuring special kinds of business, i.e. those involving credit periods of five or more years; (2) voluntary reinsurance, in order to allow national insurers to rebalance their portfolios particularly in cases where they have already reached their direct insurance ceilings and also to enable the partial resolution of problems relating to the incorporation of foreign goods and services, as opposed to those of EC origin; (3) mandatory reinsurance for non-EC incorporations, provided that the national insurer would be prepared to co-operate. In consequence, the new body would have tried to encourage the harmonisation of EC insurance conditions and policies in relation to third countries by determining the extent of divergences between national systems, as well as attempting to facilitate reinsurance decisions in what is a limited field by drawing up a third country policy to deal with the amount of risks and length of credit. This was considered a necessary preliminary step towards the centralisation of risk appraisal, thereby reducing the potential to duplicate administrative costs incurred by member states. However, the Commission did not choose to follow this proposal, but instead opted for a more ambitious project which somewhat predictably foundered on the shores of member states' opposition (Wielemans, 1985, p. 39).

With hindsight the early attempts to make export insurance and financing part of a common trade policy show the reliance on a *functionalist strategy*. Though the output of the Community's co-ordination process in the form of directives and decisions as well as its subsequent reliance on different co-ordination mechanisms sometimes ignores the interest constellation of the member states, it is flexible enough to maintain direction towards an integrated solution. This becomes even more evident through an analysis of the relevant Treaty provisions and their interpretation by the European Court of Justice.

6.2   Community Law and its Interpretation

The existence of a group of major industrialised countries in the world helps create an incentive for producing separate agreements between single member states and non-Community members such as the United States and Japan. From a legal perspective, this raises the question of whether these kinds of bilateral or international agreements actually contradict the provisions of the EEC Treaty. For this reason, the European Court became active in the area in order to prevent a situation from arising in which EC members are tied to arrangements with third countries under rules of international law that simultaneously contravene Community law.

With reference to the second subparagraph of Article 228 (1) of the EEC Treaty, the Court had to decide in one particular case on the legality of a draft 'understanding on a local cost standard' that had been drawn up under the auspices of the OECD, but which took account of EEC Treaty provisions. In this instance, the specific question was whether the Community had the power to conclude such an agreement, and if so, whether that power was an exclusive one.

Comparatively little attention was paid to the formal structure of the agreement that was being fixed under international law: its status within the context of other OECD activities was not considered to be of 'decisive importance'. Instead, the greatest emphasis was put on Articles 112 and 113 of the EEC Treaty, in so far as they empower the Community not only to adopt internal rules, but also to conclude agreements with third countries. The former of these two articles clearly refers to official export credit schemes as constituting a part of state aids:

> Member States shall, before the end of the transitional period, progressively harmonize the systems whereby they grant aid for exports to third countries, to the extent necessary to ensure that competition between undertakings of the Community is not distorted.

Paragraphs 1 and 2 of the second article states that, '... the common commercial policy shall be based on uniform principles, particularly in regard to ... export policy'. Taken both together, the two articles led the Court to come to a fairly flexible and far-reaching interpretation (Court of the European Communities, 1975, p. 22):

> A commercial policy is in fact made up by the combination and interaction of internal and external measures, without priority being taken by one over the others. Sometimes agreements are concluded in execution of a policy fixed in advance, sometimes that policy is defined by the agreements themselves.

This amounts to a generalisation that goes far beyond the original intention of the OECD's Understanding on Local Costs as basically being a co-ordination device. The Court's insistence that the implementation of an export policy be pursued within the framework of a common commercial policy not only implies the adoption of general rules of internal or Community law, but also means that the terms of international agreements be taken into account, in order to arrive at some uniform principles. By ignoring the formal status of the OECD negotiations, the Court was able to demonstrate their potential for the EC's own integration purposes, essentially because the common commercial policy was defined as being the ultimate outcome of a *progressive development* that was founded upon specific measures which might occasionally refer to autonomous and external aspects of that policy. In other words, the favoured strategy was to produce a *gradual combination* of internal and external rules in order to develop a much larger body of regulations, because this was considered to be an essential requirement for a truly common commercial policy in the future.

Moreover, the co-ordinating intention of the negotiations taking place within the OECD context became completely distorted when giving an affirmative answer to the question as to the range of exclusive Community powers. On the one hand, the need for a gradual development was conceded, whilst on the other, a clear-cut ranking system was established according to which national interests would have to adapt to Community policies. The opinion of the Court was such that the conception of a common commercial policy was believed to be incompatible with the freedom to which single member states could lay claim by means of invoking the authority of competing, alternative powers. In addition, the Court did not acknowledge the existence of potentially different interests within the Community institutions, but simply treated them as a homogeneous whole, on the basis that to adopt any other position in relations with third countries would only serve to disrupt the institutional framework, call into question the bonds of mutual trust within the Community and prevent the latter from fulfilling its role of protecting the common interest. Finally, some member states objected that the obligations and financial burdens concomitant upon the implementation of the judgement would be borne directly by them, to which the Court reacted by stating that (Court of Justice of the European Communities, 1975, p. 3):

> The 'internal' and 'external' measures adopted by the Community within the framework of the common commercial policy do not necessarily involve, in order to ensure their compatibility with the Treaty, a transfer to the Community of the obligations and financial burdens which they may involve: such

measures are solely concerned to substitute for the unilateral action of the Member States, in the field under consideration, a common action based upon uniform principles on behalf of the whole of the Community.

The news of the Court's judgement was greeted with strong resistance on the part of the member states, who were all too aware of the potential consequences of its being rigorously enforced, as it would no longer be deemed sufficient to harmonise national regulations concerning export credit insurance and simply confine these efforts to some of the competing elements in the different systems. As a matter of fact, however, even harmonised rules are in practice open to a broad interpretation, and this becomes particularly relevant in cases of political risk insurance, where there is a wide use of uncertain legal terms and discretionary decision-making. Ultimately, therefore, it is virtually impossible to prove whether or not national exporters have actually gained an advantage from the workings of the domestic system, with the consequence that it would seem logical to transfer decision-making and distribution procedures to Community institutions *en bloc*. Any serious attempt to create equal opportunities for competition tends to make the idea of complementary national and European activities appear unsatisfactory, and it is thus more realistic to think in terms of a supervisory function being performed by the Commission in order to ensure the implementation of a common trade policy following uniform principles, even though the carrying out of the latter would still be the job of national agencies. When seen from this perspective, the judgement by the Court primarily constituted a request to begin with a new round of negotiations aimed at delineating more precisely the content of those principles in the area of non-commercial risks.

In the case of the firm *Tubemeuse*, a steel pipe and tube manufacturer, the European Court of Justice was obliged to deliberate for the first time as to whether aid granted to an enterprise exporting by far the greatest part (approximately 90 per cent) of its production outside the Community amounted to unfair competition within the Community. In this instance, the Commission authorised the Belgian government to grant a series of aid measures, which were earmarked for an investment programme designed to secure the firm's future in relation to two medium-to-long-term contracts concluded with the Soviet Union. This was accompanied by a general reorganisation of the firm's product line structure, in order to improve its profit margins, but the anticipated effects of these combined measures failed to materialise and the government found itself in the position of continuing to supply aid support in a way that ran contrary to stipulations laid down in Article 93 (3) of the EEC Treaty. In reaching its decision, the Court rejected the possible interpretation according to which the activities of the Belgian state could be compared to the behaviour of a private investor, and instead argued that some additional loans which had been made by an international banking consortium pointed to a different conclusion (Court of Justice of the European Communities, 1990, p. 999):

> With regard to the finance which Tubemeuse obtained from the banks, the decisive factor ... is that such investments were in fact covered by a guarantee provided by the Belgian State, which thereby assumed the risks inherent in such transactions.

According to the Commission, the outcome of this situation for *Tubemeuse* was that it was now in a position to gain a larger share of the market within the Community itself and was thus able to increase its production capacity at a time when nearly all its competitors were having to make major cutbacks and create redundancies. Hence the initial question regarding state aid perforce could only be answered as follows (Court of Justice of the European Communities, 1990, p. 1013):

> Regardless of whether the aid may be regarded as export aid, Article 112, which concerns the harmonization of national export aid in the context of the common commercial policy, does not exclude the application of Articles 92 to 94. It is not impossible for export aid to affect intra-community trade.

Both court rulings therefore clearly tended towards an integrated solution and can entail future legal action before the Court of Justice. At the same time, in the field of export credit insurance, the Court had decided against the demands raised by private insurance companies to hold the Community liable for the delay in adopting 'measures of co-ordination' concerning their competitive standing towards public export credit insurance operations (Court of Justice of the European Communities, 1991, p.1802). Instead the judgement emphasised that 'the competent Community institutions must be recognized as enjoying a discretion in relation to the stages in which harmonization is to take place' (Court of Justice of the European Communities, 1991, p. 1799). While from a legal perceptive this ruling provided another example of the indeterminacy of the co-ordination concept in the context of the Community, it also signalled to member states the need to take precautionary steps through modifications in their promotion systems to maintain export credit insurance as a national policy instrument.

Rather than relying on the inefficiencies in the EC bureaucracy and its cumbersome negotiation procedures, it became now more convincing for the member states to recognise the importance of the fact that all the legal regulations referring to official export credit insurance systems have basically been a part of the EEC Treaty since it first came into force. From this point of view, the Single European Act did not entail any new developments, apart from the declared intention of the Commission to implement Treaty provisions more rigorously, and in this respect, two groupings of regulations are of particular interest (Dörr, 1993): those dealing with trade policy and those dealing with questions of competition, and each will be looked at in turn.

In the first grouping, Article 113 of the EEC Treaty represents the basic provision concerning the common trade policy, central to which are exports to third countries and the related issue of export promotion measures (manifested in the form of official export credit insurance). The provision lays down that the common trade policy should be conducted along uniform lines and in addition establishes a foundation for the co-ordination of trade policies between the member states, as well as for their representation by the EC Commission in international negotiations such as those of the OECD Consensus.

A second important regulation is given in EEC Treaty Article 112, which has the harmonisation of state aids as its main object. When referring specifically to the question of export credit insurance systems, the latter has been a highly contested issue - no member state is fond of having its own agency's activities characterised as a subsidy or as an aid to industry and reference is usually made to the GATT code in support of the national position, because that only rules out official promotion schemes which are inadequate to cover their long-term operating costs and losses (cf. Section 7.6, below).

The Commission, however, has taken a different approach. With the backing of the European Court of Justice, a much broader perspective on the whole matter tends to prevail in Community circles, with all measures which give firms an economic or financial advantage without their having to provide something in return being defined as aid. Applying this principle to the case of state guarantees could in theory lead to the conclusion that even a system with no or only very slight losses still amounts to a system of state aids, if - as the Commission assumes - state cover does indeed have a positive influence on the availability of and conditions attached to credits; whether or not the costs of premiums and fees would be enough to counterbalance this advantage is open to doubt. An alternative interpretation would be to accept that official export credit insurers can actually offer cover at much lower costs than those which would arise on the private market, whilst recognising that Article 112 in this regard implies a gradual harmonisation where that is necessary for the removal of distortions to competition.

Finally, the last regulation in the first grouping - Article 110 of the EEC Treaty - provides for the gradual dismantling of international barriers to trade. Although the main focus is on tariffs, here the Commission concludes that a further reduction in subsidies is necessary, including those measures to be used in international trade transactions and which are under the control of the member states. However, export credit insurance would certainly fall into this category.

In the second group of rules concerning competition, Articles 92 to 94 are the relevant ones. In order for Article 92 to apply, three requirements have to be fulfilled: firstly, there has to be involved some kind of state aid, in the sense that has been discussed above; secondly, this aid must actually cause a distortion of competition between exporters, and according to the European Court of Justice, this may also apply to an abstract possibility of unfair competition, in cases where certain firms receive state cover and others not; lastly there is the question of negative influence on trade between member states. In the Court's restrictive interpretation, the mere fact that certain measures can potentially facilitate exports is sufficient proof of this, with the consequence that all state subsidies have to be notified to the Commission, even if not all the measures in this category are always considered to be incompatible with the common market. A few exceptions are made in the ship-building sector or in the case of projects with a greater community interest, the most prominent example of the latter being the Airbus industry. In general, state aids will be permissible if the Council of Ministers is advised by the Commission to declare their compatibility with the common market, and any intervention by the Council is thus dependent upon a relevant proposal being made by the Commission. In the field of export credit insurance, however, the Commission has decided not to make any exceptions to the rule, so a negative decision on compatibility with the common market will accordingly be accompanied by a demand for the return of any subsidy, and in this respect, Article 92 is comparatively more extensive than Article 112. Both regulations can nevertheless be applied simultaneously, one with reference to foreign trade, the other to the common market.

In addition, Article 90 also falls within this second grouping and deals with the role of public enterprises or enterprises in a monopolistic position. The activities of public enterprises are expected to concur with the terms of the EEC Treaty, and when taken in conjunction with Article 92 this implies the prevention of unfair competition between public enterprises and private companies which are active in the same market area. Moreover, public enterprises are further subject to a non-discrimination requirement, as laid down in Article 6 of the EEC Treaty (Article 7 EC Treaty). In the context of export credit insurance, this raises the question of whether cover should be provided for foreign exporters as well, though to date no clear-cut EC position on the matter has been developed.

The examples presented in this section have indicated how Community law offers several routes to pursue the integration goal in a specific policy area. Despite this indeterminacy Court rulings have so far supported the position of the Commission concerning state aids. It comes as no surprise, therefore, that the member states have tried to anticipate potential activities of the Commission in the area of official financing and state guarantees. With a reliance on legal instruments at the EC level the need for co-ordination between the member states and its external trading partners does not disappear. However, the findings of this section suggested that the Commission will not behave as a neutral actor in this co-ordination process. Therefore, we expect further evidence in support of this hypothesis by concentrating on various institutional modifications proposed to provide for a better cohesion between the Community's internal and external commercial policy.

6.3   The Commission as Co-ordinator?

In one particular case, concerning an intention by the French government to grant special exchange risk cover to exporters in regard to a tender for the construction of a power station in Greece, the Commission was already obliged to decide whether export aids relating to intra-community trade were compatible with the aims of the common market within the meaning of Article 92 (1) of the EEC Treaty (Commission of the European Communities, 1984, pp. 25-7). Aside from France, Germany and Britain were also in contention for the award of this contract and they had to make some provision in their respective offers to cover themselves against risks stemming from the inflation rate of the currency in which the offer was estimated and a potential devaluation of the Greek currency against their own. From this point of view, it is noteworthy that the requirements under EC laws are much stronger than those of the equivalent procedure in the OECD Arrangement. The Commission maintained that exchange rate cover constituted a type of aid outside the scope of any of the exceptions laid down in Article 92 (3) of the EEC Treaty. Because firstly, general state support was ruled out generally and secondly, the private insurance market did not provide adequate cover, the resultant disadvantages for Community firms thus became obvious when undertakings were obliged to face potential losses themselves in cases of defaults. The immediate consequence of this situation was that the prices of their offers had to increase. However, the use of co-ordination would have instead implied the granting of cover on equal terms to the competing companies, i.e. the co-ordination of the modalities under which the national export credit insurance agencies operate.

In 1984, the European Parliament pointed out that, with regard to export credit subsidies and the OECD agreement, there were still some problems which remained unsolved, particularly in the fields of mixed credits, the inclusion of subsidies on agricultural products, aviation and nuclear power plants. In short, the Parliament paid more attention to a whole range of closely related export promotion policies. In the *Delorozoy Report* of the Committee on External Economic Relations the Parliament renewed its call for the Commission to draw up an inventory of the existing situation, in order to ensure greater harmonisation of the member states' various export subsidy systems (European Parliament, 1984a). The timetable envisaged provided for a first stage during which new national measures would be introduced, but with a strictly compulsory consultation procedure. Then in the second and final stage, all measures in this field would become the responsibility of Community institutions. In addition, the Parliament recommended the undertaking of new research into the possibility of a European Export Bank, which would also be intended to facilitate wider use of the ECU. This was thought to be the best overall response to the problems encountered in financing multinational projects.

As a general conclusion, it was acknowledged that, since the confirmation of the Commission's competence in the area of export aids by the Court of Justice, no satisfactory progress had been made in the intervening years towards the effective integration of national policies. Even more damning were the remarks made about the workings of the Council in relation to export subsidies, as expressed in a draft resolution by the Parliament, which argued that the Council had failed to come to terms with the situation in the international capital market by not making joint preparations for the world economic summit and by not properly implementing agreements adopted at the Venice Summit of the European Council, according to which the capital market was not to be unnecessarily distorted by subsidised export credits. When seen in the light of the provision of unilateral subsidies to exporters by means of special credit systems, it seemed more than reasonable to question the extent of solidarity among the EC partners and the strength of their common belief in a free market economy. In contrast to the Parliament's insistence on the creation of an independent agency, the Committee on Economic and Monetary Affairs adopted a more moderate position and suggested following a principle of commonality (European Parliament, 1984a, p. 16):

> There should be a commonality in the basis and level of export subsidies provided by member states so that unfair advantage between different community enterprises is obviated.

To this end, the Committee proposed that the Commission should be more attentive to the problem of ensuring fair play and full transparency, given the variety and number of overt and covert ways in which export advantage can be promoted by governments. One pragmatic step in this direction would have been to establish a common method for measuring the benefits gained by the distribution of subsidies, for example by allowing officially supported export credits, but only in ECUs and at the appropriate ECU interest rates. However, the establishment of such mechanism never became a central concern in the deliberations concerning a common trade policy.

More recent efforts in this area have focused on the establishment of joint guarantees for contracts involving one or more subcontractors in one or more member states of the Community (Council of the European Communities, 1984). The respective Council directive recognised that the supply of insurance and finance for exports can influence international trade flows and as such constitutes a powerful instrument of commercial policy. After a 1982 decision, in which national export credit insurance agencies were allowed to insure supplies from other member states up to a limit of 40 per cent of the total value of a contract, the Council then took the logical next step in dealing with the increasing interdependence of the European economies by encouraging a growing trend towards the undertaking of export operations on a co-operative basis among a number of enterprises in different member states. This kind of co-operation was seen as a major, even a decisive, factor for the competitiveness of EC exports in third country markets, and it seemed to be similarly useful in intra-community trade, in spite of the apparent differences in national guarantee and finance systems.

Yet, seen from the perspective of national firms these activities are less attractive. Due to the limitation of joint guarantees to the field of subcontracting, preference is given to a method in which the so-called principal insurer becomes the sole manager of the entire risk, including the subcontracted elements. As a consequence such contracts become more expensive since the previous possibility of risk sharing is excluded. At the same time, the innovation of leaving the settlement of disputed cases to an arbitration board, composed of two members appointed by the litigating parties and a third judge appointed by the President of the European Court of Justice, was still in the position of having to fall back upon proceedings governed by the rules of conciliation and arbitration of the International

Chamber of Commerce (ICC). Thus the only change introduced by placing this mechanism in a Community context was the participation of a Community official in the arbitration process on the same terms as representatives of the member states.

By the early 1980s, it had become clear that an integrative solution to the problems within the export credit field was out of reach, e.g. in terms of a European export credit agency along the lines of the Export-Import Bank in the United States. Those original, much more comprehensive ideas have been narrowed down more and more: a 1985 White Paper, for example, merely emphasised the importance of an environment favouring the development of co-operation between firms throughout the Community. On the other hand, it was more feasible to envisage the consequences of a growing demand for multi-sourcing, including export credit insurance, especially for those companies involved either in capital intensive high-technology projects or in the search for new markets in competition with other industrialised nations. Hence a European Export Credit Insurance Facility (EECIF) was now seen as an additional instrument for making progress towards the ultimate objective of a real internal market by 1992 and was defined in abstract terms as (Commission of the European Communities, 1987, p. 1):

> an administrative entity to be set up to manage a common credit insurance policy which, under defined conditions, could be issued when exports originate from more than one member-state.

And this at the same time as the failure of previous attempts was admitted (Commission of the European Communities, 1987, p. 2):

> Despite many years of trying, it has not proved possible to harmonize the insurance cover they provide, so that there are significant variations of detail, such as the proportion of credit covered, the risks covered and premium rates. The use of different export credit insurance agencies thus also complicates the arrangement of finance which is generally linked to the export credit insurance provided.

In this respect, finance consortia, such as Airbus, were cited as particularly instructive examples. Here, the availability of finance and the export credit insurance on which it is based are factors of major importance, to the extent that they often override the choice of source of supply, which would otherwise be made on grounds of quality and production costs. In turn, exporting companies and financial institutions have themselves widely acknowledged the existence of two main problems:

firstly, in the case of projects like the building of mass transport systems or power stations, which frequently require the supply of equipment and engineering contractors from more than one country, too many sub-optimal 'Community' bids were being made in third markets; secondly, transnational companies found it necessary to redirect production to different locations within their group, or alternatively, have been offered preferential cover on condition that they transfer production from one member state to another.

In contrast to earlier efforts, the EC could at this point only offer an alternative option if it were to act as a catalyst for co-operation between public and private European export credit insurers rather than through simply enabling the direct provision of finance and insurance services. The idea behind the EECIF was to set up a pooling operation between national export credit agencies, which would then act as a co-ordinating device. To this end, one particularly promising segment of the market, namely that dealing with medium-term contracts, was selected as a target for the operation. Both the one-off kind of large export contract for a complex product requiring a combination of materials and technology from different countries, and the more diverse export contract for manufactured products whose parts are assembled in several member states, would then be expected to grow larger in number as industries adapted to the reality of a common market.

A number of rough plans as to how the pool should function were drawn up, and these reveal that some of the earlier ambitions were not renounced entirely. On the basis of a common policy to be elaborated in consultation with national agencies, it was envisaged that the EECIF would be responsible for 'co-ordinating the issue of policies to insure credit for multisource export contracts' (Commission of the European Communities, 1987, p. 6). Yet the same time, there was to be no setting of an independent country policy, with the pool in this respect still being regarded as dependent upon the export consortium leader, as well as the leading national export credit agency. The same was to be valid for most cases of default (Commission of the European Communities, 1987, p. 7):

> With regard to the question as to who should pursue claims as they arise, the Commission considers that either the lead national export credit agency should do so, or the Facility.

The main role of the Facility would be restricted to the arrangement of direct cover, i.e. it would not be involved with the financing of exports, which would quite definitely be left to the more traditional official support for interest rates (Commission of the European Communities, 1987, p. 10):

in order to avoid disadvantaging high interest rate currencies participating in a contract with multicurrency financing, companies insured through the Facility should have access to the existing mechanism for subsidising interest rates in the countries from which exports are sourced. This would enable exporters with high interest rate currencies to compete on an equal footing.

Equally, there was no question that the need remained to achieve greater uniformity through a Community-wide set of credit insurance policy regulations. In relation to medium-term business, it was suggested that premium rates could be fixed using a weighted average of existing national levels, whilst taking into account the actual structure of the export market. Once again, the principal difficulty lies in the nature of the business in these markets: contrary to the assumption made by the European Parliament, it quite often becomes necessary to withhold cover or to carry out an investigation into the credit-worthiness of the importing countries, e.g. in cases where they are already 'off-cover' for economic or political reasons at the level of the national agencies. In practice, it is hard to think of an institutional design which is capable of fulfilling the task of co-ordination in a neutral and efficient way, because of the dependence on exclusive expertise when forging close operational links with their national counterparts. This is a point which came particularly to the fore in the proposal for the formal structure of the EECIF board. The suggested composition of members drawn from each Community country *plus* a Commission official, together with the requirement for majority decision-making in relation to each request received, is nothing other than a perfect recipe for complex negotiations and delays in an area where fast decisions have become vital. Moreover, the document also downplays the need for financial support for the EECIF. In a market situation where the smallest of price differentials can determine the success or failure of a bid, it is unlikely that the creation of additional operating costs either in the form of a percentage of premiums, the paying of a commission or a direct administrative charge would be welcomed by the national agencies.

The discussion around the EECIF did not mark an end to the search for feasible institutional innovations in the area of trade policy. Again, the move to even smaller segments of that policy indicate the reliance on incremental changes rather than comprehensive solutions. Although many in Community circles - with the exception of the Parliament's Committee on Legal Affairs and Citizens' Rights - have tried to avoid making any explicit connection between the EECIF and proposals for the establishment of a reinsurance pool for export credits to Central and Eastern Europe, the latter can undoubtedly be regarded as a watered-down version of the former. It will be shown below how further problems with an already curtailed project eventually persuaded the Community to introduce a credit guarantee for exports of agricultural products and foodstuffs from the Community to the Soviet Union. At present, and especially within the European Parliament, the ongoing discussion tends only to focus on the creation of an additional reinsurance pool that would be available to the national export credit insurers, and can basically be characterised as an attempt to understand the technicalities of the issue rather than its political implications.

A new draft Council Regulation concerning the establishment of a reinsurance pool for export credits to Central and Eastern European Countries was made in 1990, Article 2 of which states (Commission of the European Communities, 1990):

> In cases where an export credit insurance agency grants insurance or reinsurance or provides guarantees for export credits with a duration longer than two years concerning contracts for exports of goods or services; and the insurance or reinsurance of the provision of guarantees is carried out on behalf of the member state or with its support; 40 % of all risks resulting from such operations for the agency shall be redistributed proportionally to such agencies in all member states according to a formula to be established in accordance with the procedure laid down in Article 5 (3) and shall be reinsured jointly by all these agencies.

It was felt that this would make it possible to achieve a better spread of risk exposure within each national budget, enable the co-ordination of national cover policies, and extend insurance cover to consortia formed by Community exporters from different member states. The co-ordination procedure set out for reinsurance applications indicates that the main role would be played by the Commission, which could turn down any request within 15 working days if there were serious doubts about as to its compatibility with the EC's common trade policy or sound insurance principles. As far as the reasons behind this go, the official statement ran as follows (European Parliament, 1991, p. 8):

> With its present proposal ... the Commission is confining itself to what it deems feasible, so as to achieve the desired aim of helping to stimulate exports and capital flow into eastern and central Europe swiftly.

The European Parliament then suggested several modifications and amendments to the Commission, among which one in particular is significant for our purposes (European Parliament, 1991, p. 4). In changing recital 8 to:

Whereas such a pool should be operated by the Commission in close cooperation with such credit insurance agencies in the Member States and should be a first step towards harmonizing export credit insurance in the Community, leading to the creation of a uniform export credit insurance scheme at Community level.

and deleting Article 5 (3) which stated that,

The representative of the Commission shall submit to the committee a draft of the measures to be taken. The committee shall deliver its opinion on the draft within a time limit which the chairman may lay down according to the urgency of the matter. The opinion shall be delivered by the majority laid down in Article 148 (2) of the Treaty in the case of decisions which the Council is required to adopt on a proposal from the Commission. The votes of the representatives of the Member States within the committee shall be weighted in the manner set out in that Article. The chairman shall not vote.

The Commission shall adopt the measures envisaged if they are in accordance with the opinion of the committee.

If the measures envisaged are not in accordance with the opinion of the committee, or if no opinion of the committee is delivered, the Commission shall, without delay, submit to the Council a proposal relating to the measures to be taken. The Council shall act by a qualified majority.

If, on the expiry of a period of three months from the date of referral to the Council, the Council has not acted, the proposed measure shall be adopted by the Commission,

the Parliament was trying to clarify the motivation behind the Commission's seemingly more self-interested intentions, and thus attempting to prevent the establishment of what would have been an extremely cumbersome procedure, especially in export credit terms (European Parliament, 1991, p. 6). An additional criticism from a financial perspective was that the idea of reinsurance at a Community level would only be convincing if the requisite amount of funds were to be made available from the Community budget: an effective solidarity in the promotion of exports to countries in Central and Eastern Europe via export credit insurance could only be achieved if the Community's and its member states' reinsurance capacity is financially strengthened. But while these demands for modifications put some limits on the future role played by the Commission, the overall aim of a uniform export credit insurance scheme at Community level was reconfirmed.

More technical - though no less serious - deficiencies were discovered by the Committee on Legal Affairs and Citizens' Rights (European Parliament, 1991, p. 19), who brought to light the worrying lack of accuracy shown when incorrectly defining the subject matter as a credit insurance pool and not as a reinsurance pool. Obviously, there was a need for a precise definition of the term 'export credit reinsurance' in order to stress the fact that the reinsurance provided by the pool was to be a third tier in a series of successive insurance arrangements that built on the insurance and reinsurance already provided by the member states. By the same token, Article 2 of the Council's draft regulation stipulated that all the risks should be distributed proportionately, but without making this notion of proportionality any more explicit by specifying its scope. Even more worrying was the content of Article 3, Paragraph 2 of which states that the Commission can notify the agency concerned that its application raises serious doubts as to its compatibility with the Community's common commercial policy or sound insurance principles. Unfortunately, however, the precise way in which these principles are to be applied is not entirely clear, with the powers of judgement of the Commission and the putative committee seemingly allowed free reign. Also according to Article 3, an agency whose application for reinsurance has not been granted would have to refrain from insuring, reinsuring or guaranteeing the proportion of risks that have not been accepted. If that really was the intention of the Commission proposal, then it effectively nullified its own main objective, because it would ultimately have reduced the overall amount of risk cover, seeing as those agencies whose applications for reinsurance were rejected would not even have been allowed to provide first degree insurance cover for such risks. Again it follows that the motivation of the Commission's efforts concerning an insurance pool were different to those of a neutral arbitrator.

Since the foundation of a European Export Bank has been removed from the immediate agenda, official EC policy finally had to make it part of a long-term strategy which in the short run relies on a broadening of the private market. On the basis of the principle of mutual recognition, export credit insurance companies can currently carry on their business in all member states. But even though some private companies have recently introduced 'European' insurance policies, they will nonetheless mainly deal with short-term contracts (of 2-3 years) rather than with medium or long-term transactions, and in the latter case mutual recognition is in fact something of an empty casket because of the mismatch between demands from internationally operating companies and the supply provided by the few (mainly Anglo-American) insurers with the capacity to cover long-term risks. Hence, it is also unreasonable to expect the semi-automatic creation of a mechanism whereby the need for reassurance capacity will increase and gradually lead to an institutional response at the Community level.

What is more, this co-ordination mechanism cannot level out existing asymmetries in the national distribution of costs and benefits as a consequence of the support given to particular export industries. Though economists could make a convincing argument about the advantages of risk pooling in cases where several member states are jointly involved in an export contract (Kunreuther and Kleindorfer, 1983, p. 252), the individual national preferences in relation to industrial policy pose a clear obstacle to the necessary resource transfers for the funding of such an institution. Even if an agency with an independent budget would be viable in the long run, the industrial system of the member states remain highly fragmented with regard to firm size and foreign markets; and therefore it would be quite likely that in terms of the actual distribution of any additional risk cover the main beneficiaries would primarily be found among the bigger exporting firms (Onida, 1993, p. 38). In this respect, it is significant that even now there is already an observable tendency within the national systems for the credit finance terms that are offered by state or semi-state agencies to barely fit into the internal calculation systems of small or medium-sized firms. The non-neutrality of the co-ordination mechanism can be expected to aggravate rather than ameliorate the original policy problem at the national level.

In a proposal for a Council Decision, the Commission asked for a closer parallelism between the international obligations of the Community and its internal rules (Commission of the European Communities, 1991c). Yet, when analysing the actual policy formation process these differences continue to persist. As writings on policy entrepreneurship suggest organisations such as the Community have an institutional self-interest to pursue which favours the provision of externally non-comparable services. While competition with other international organisations is ruled out, it is initiated internally as a dispute between and within Community institutions (Ehlermann, 1995, p. 1222).

The procedural considerations as to how to implement a new policy in the export credit field are a case in point (Sie Dhian Ho and Werkhorst, 1995, pp. 457-8). DG I of the Commission, which is responsible for external affairs, is more in favour of rules taking the form of a directive, whose content would thus not apply directly to individuals or companies with it, instead being incumbent upon member states to modify their national laws. On the other hand, DG IV, which oversees questions of competition would prefer to see a solution in the shape of a communication to the member states. Whereas the latter is a unilateral act on the part of the Commission, the former necessitates a process of negotiation within the Council and would certainly provoke more direct state influence. Finally, the Committee on Economic and Monetary Affairs and Industrial Policy

(European Parliament, 1991, p. 15) suggested that the Commission should instead propose a new Council decision, which would be directed towards all official export credit insurance agencies rather than pursuing the line of the Commission's original proposal which was targeted at a restricted category of recipients and was not necessarily generally applicable.

As pointed out above, the general problem that is underlined by these discussions has to do with the difference between internal EC competition and external competition with non-members. Due to the almost complete failure of integration attempts in the early years of the Community, the Commission from then on favoured a more piecemeal approach, though this nevertheless aims at the realisation of a common trade policy. But in doing so, Community institutions generally fail to put the export credit problem in its proper context. An obvious solution to the difficulty would be to '*support programmes or programmes to coordinate national measures,* as opposed to harmonization of laws', while at the same time 'achieving the objectives set out in the Treaty through *international agreements* rather than via an internal instrument' - in short, by applying the principle of subsidiarity (Commission of the European Communities, 1992, p. 14). Yet, leaving further juridical reservations to one side, such a remedy is already precluded by the existence of exclusive Community powers in the field of the common commercial policy and with regard to the general rules on competition (Dehousse, 1992; Eeckhout, 1994, p. 351). In conclusion, Community institutions can thus be seen to complicate problems of policy co-ordination as they simply constitute an additional party to the conflict rather than acting as a neutral arbiter with the task of finding new co-ordinated solutions. This then leads on to another question, namely whether experts can help to defuse the interest constellation through the provision of consensual knowledge.

6.4   The Changing Role of Expertise

So far the analysis has concentrated on the output of the Community's co-ordination process to describe the Commission's reliance on incremental changes as a response to the resistance of the member states to follow the integrationist path towards a common trade policy. Since the institutional framework will shape the direction expert advice takes, the observed incrementalism can be seen as the consequence of a particular organisational incentive structure. This section, therefore, focuses on the role expert knowledge plays in the formulation of a co-ordinated policy. Under the respective direction of representatives from the Belgian, German and French official export insurance agency three reports have been drafted each suggesting different methods to achieve the aims of the single market in the export credit field. It is argued that because some experts arrived at findings unfavourable to the Commission's view of the matter, their positions were successfully discarded from further deliberations in the Group for Co-ordination of Export Credit Policies.

The first report by an European expert committee on export credit insurance (the Single Market Group) defined marketable risks as commercial risks up to a maximum period of three years in the case of exports to OECD and non-OECD countries. The report argued that in this 'zone of competition', private and public agencies should be permitted to be active according to the same conditions, and also that the monopoly that enables certain insurance agencies to cover economic and political risks in combination with each other should be abolished (Callut, 1991).

In response to widespread criticisms from the member states, the UNICE and the International Credit Insurance Association (ICIA), the Commission felt obliged to look again at the question of marketable risks. By way of contrast to the recommendations by the group of experts, the Commission's first draft of a communication gave preference to a definition which referred only to commercial risks up to a maximum period of two years and which was geographically restricted to OECD countries (with the exception of Turkey). Commercial risks were defined with reference to the inability to pay, non-payment, refusal to accept goods and the arbitrary rejection of contract obligations on the part of private debtors and guarantors (Commission of the European Communities, 1991d).

The Commission thus decided to deal separately with the insurance of marketable risks for exports to non-OECD third countries and non-marketable risks. The Commission argued in the latter case that the situation would be treated differently and 'that the resulting problem would not be directly connected with the internal market'. According to the Commission, this problem should be dealt with on the basis of Article 113 of the EEC Treaty with the ultimate aim of harmonising the regulations for export credit insurance and introducing common principles for the cover of countries. However, in terms of giving more consideration to the programmes of non-EC countries without undermining the competitive standing of Community exporters, Article 92 and 93 of the EEC Treaty was now seen by the Commission as constituting a much better legal basis with regard to the insurance of marketable risks within the OECD, and the only possible legal basis in relation to the Community's internal trade policies. This runs contrary to the arguments presented in the *Tubemeuse-decision*, since the Commission further differentiates between third countries in terms of their relevance for internal competition within the common market (cf. Section 6.2, above).

In 1993 the Commission began to send communications to the member states containing details of its planned policy in the export credit field. Now, member states were requested to change their export credit insurance systems in the field of marketable risks according to Article 93 (1) of the EEC Treaty within one year after publication of the Commission's final communication. In general, the Commission formulated its policy towards potential distortions of competition along the following lines (Commission of the European Communities, 1993, pp. 11-2):

- state guarantees for insurance agencies have to be abolished and changed into reassurance arrangements.
- reinsurance systems of the state in the field of marketable risks have to be open for interested private insurers.
- insurance agencies under the control of the state will be obliged to create adequate reserves.
- exemptions of official export credit agencies from taxes and similar charges have to be repealed in so far as they insure marketable risks.
- for official insurance agencies, the provision of capital and other forms of financing on the balance account of marketable risks can only be made under conditions that were under normal market conditions considered as acceptable by a private investor.
- if private export credit insurance companies do not get free access to the existing infrastructures at the state level, those possibilities may not be offered to the official insurance agencies in the future. The same applies to the free access to special information centres, e.g. the involvement of embassies to obtain information on debtors.
- official and officially supported export credit insurance agencies shall be subject to the same supervisory rules as private insurance agencies. Public enterprises can still insure marketable and non-marketable risks as long as they provide for separate accounting of both areas.

The ambiguity between free competition within the common market and the desire for a competitive edge over third countries is also reflected in some of the UNICE comments on future community rules applying to short-term export credit insurance. In principle, European exporters resorting to short-term export credit insurance should not be subject to distortions of competition within the Community, nor should they be disadvantaged with respect to competitors from third countries who benefit from more favourable export credit insurance mechanisms. However, since there are no internationally binding rules in the field of short-term export credit insurance, the UNICE argued that the proposed rules should either tend towards the most efficient system or should at least provide for more flexible solutions, in order to allow Community insurance agencies to match the better offers from non-communitarian agencies (UNICE, 1992a).

The UNICE reckons the capacity of the private insurance and reinsurance market to be not always sufficient to provide cover for both commercial and political risks, especially with regard to non-OECD countries. Therefore, it still considers that government support for the commercial side of combined risks is necessary when the market capacity is inadequate, and generally speaking favours the use of flexible rules which permit a frequent reassessment of the concept of marketable risks. Hence its request for, firstly, an escape clause which would allow national insurance companies to increase their cover capacity if there were no risk cover available at pure market conditions and, secondly, the establishment of a Committee composed of representatives from member states and the private sector (insurers, reinsurers and exporters), in order to assist the Commission in the implementation and adaptation of the envisaged regulations (UNICE, 1992b).

Moreover, representatives of the private insurance market themselves doubt the feasibility of continually more far-reaching Community plans, on the basis that within the EC political as well as economic risks should not just be left to official insurance agencies. Until now, political risks as a rule cannot be, or are not, insured by private export credit insurance companies (Ruloff, 1987, p. 268; Meyer, 1993, p. 46). This refers primarily to the loss of claims because of transfer, convertibility and payment prohibition or a moratorium, but the same holds true for currency risks. Likewise, no cover can be offered for insolvencies as a result of *force majeure* or politically rooted damages such as war, revolution and strikes. In addition, there are still considerable risks in the conduct of business with public buyers within the area of the European Community. The main weakness in the Community's plans is the capacity of the private market to provide for reinsurance, because private export credit insurance companies are simply unable to offer the kind of comprehensive cover envisaged by the Commission. They mainly cover short-term exports of up to twelve months, or a maximum of two years if the risk of production is included; in other words, it is only the economic risks of exports to OECD and other industrialised countries which are covered.

As has already been mentioned, any still existing political risks - e.g. in the case of business with public buyers in the European Community - can hardly be insured, and there are even more problems with regard to reinsurance. The market for reinsurance is at present dominated by two companies which do not even want to address this topic, and although there are some private credit insurance companies which provide cover for these risks, they have yet to be confronted with the payment of large claims. If the EC institutions were to be able to push through their ideas, that would almost certainly lead to considerable distortions in competition.

In the area of medium and long-term business, an initial report was presented in 1992 under the guidance of a representative from the German official insurance agency, Hermes, which predicted that the repercussions of free choice in places of production and the free movement of services after the abolishment of national borders in the Community would encourage export firms to shift their interests to the best qualified area of production (Stolzenburg, 1992). When taken together with industrial diversification, a greater division of labour and the growth in co-operation between European producers and service industries, the tying of official export cover to the countries from which the goods actually originate would therefore become increasingly problematic.

Particularly due to the by now standard flexibility of financing institutions and markets, it has become necessary for the official export instruments to try and keep pace with the altered financing modalities of European export business. This is the more true in relation to export financing by one agency in one currency, which previously caused difficulties when the other supplies and services were based in different member countries and had to be treated as an exception. As long as stricter international regulation are lacking, the internal dimension to a common EC policy in the financing field will be severely constrained, and member states will attempt to dodge restrictions that do not apply to non-EC competitors. Before doing anything else, a common internal policy therefore has to ensure that an effective response to non-EC subsidies remains possible (Abraham, Couwenberg and Dewit, 1993, pp. 400-3).

Two proposals are worth consideration in this respect. First of all, the *consistency approach* implies that the Commission is fully responsible for the approval of financing conditions on export contracts with a value above a well-defined threshold level. In the case of distorted competition between EC firms, it has to specify what are the admissible export financing conditions or to refuse official financing all together, with the consequence that in cases where contracts actually break specified conditions, exporting firms are obliged to pay additional insurance premiums or to make further interest payments. Secondly, the *non-discrimination approach* demands from official agencies the extension of their financing conditions for domestic firms to exporters of other EC countries competing for the same contract. Here, it is assumed that official export financing agencies are more likely to attract firms from other EC countries when offering more favourable export financing conditions than are available elsewhere in the Community. Possible objections to the use of the first approach can be found in the delays to be expected from a decision procedure that is actually very similar to those already applied in the area of industrial subsidies and merger controls, and also in the difficulty to find suitable evaluative standards in each specific case. Arguments against the second proposal chiefly rest with its built-in propensity to provide the largest subsidies to the most competitive EC firm. Not only can this be seen as objectionable on industrial policy grounds, but it is also likely to provoke resistance when resources from national budgets are continuously used to support the already strong export sectors of other countries.

Both approaches could only seem viable if the strategic motives for export financing were removed through the replacement of the *cost to the government principle* by the *benefit to the firm principle*. As in the export insurance sector, it should be the case that firms should derive no special benefits from official export financing that is not available on the private market, but crucially, financing by private banks depends on the availability of risk cover and the conditions under which that cover is given. If taken together, the strict adherence to the private market in these two interrelated policy areas at the Community level and a reluctance on the part of major competitors at the international level to do likewise, will inevitably damage the position of European industries.

Ultimately, the overall consensus of expert opinion was that there is no need for immediate action, and according to the second group of experts, the development of extended and improved co-ordination techniques would be sufficient for the foreseeable future. These could in fact be strengthened considerably if the member states were to show a greater willingness to modify and more actively apply supplier and co-insurance agreements, to accept parallel and reinsurance, or to employ the principle of mutual recognition instead of harmonisation. The delegations from the member states, who participated in the writing of the report repeatedly expressed the opinion that the most important and competitively relevant differences lay in the political sphere. This dimension is most clearly manifested in firstly, the field of cover policy, where governments decide on country categories, the type of cover and its costs; secondly, in the basic attitudes towards export promotion, especially in certain fringe areas such as tied aid financing, credits to East European countries, agricultural exports, high technology and sectoral aid; in the field of export finance mechanisms, and finally, in the field of export influencing devices such as compensation, joint ventures or other types of co-operation, and as leasing, forfeiting, untied credits and import prepayments.

Another of the tasks entrusted to the group of experts was to evaluate the position of the Commission with regard to its duties deriving from

Community law, and here it was open to some major criticism (Stolzenburg, 1992):

First, the Commission had announced its aim of improving the distribution of resources in the common market and introducing a *level playing field* by means of a strict and systematic application of Treaty provisions with regard to state aids and public subsidies to export credits and export credit insurance. Yet it was left open to what extent the planned insurance pool for Eastern Europe should constitute the first exemplary application of harmonisation or a common trade policy.

Secondly, no reference whatsoever has been made to Article 16 of the GATT or its requirement for national insurance systems to cover long-term operating costs. On the basis of this regulation, it could be concluded that it is not really possible to speak about state aids and/or distortions to competition as long as systematically commercial criteria are used to ensure the cover of operating costs. A connection can thus be created between terms such as subsidy, distortion to competition and cover of long-term operating costs (as well as their effects on the need to harmonise national systems and which leads on to additional questions not addressed by the Commission, e.g. whether a common trade policy is capable of sustaining self-financing systems organised according to commercial principals). Ultimately, therefore, the Commission had not defined the type of institutional form that it was trying to aim at through its interpretation of the Treaty.

Thirdly, there are a number of possible alternatives with regard to the consequences of the non-discrimination requirement of Article 90 and its connection to Article 6 of the EEC Treaty (Article 7 EC Treaty), because, unlike with short-term business, in the medium and long-term sectors it is not really feasible to make a similar distinction between public and private credit insurers. That also leaves open the question of the treatment of supplies from non-member countries and of additional supplies originating from within the Community.

Fourthly, no answer has been forthcoming in relation to the fundamental issue of to what extent - if at all - state subsidies are permissible in order to match competition from outside the EC. Furthermore, the notion of the national interest, which is inherent in the systems of all the member states, is ignored altogether, as are the consequent interpretations of national sovereignty. In particular, there is no meaningful consideration of whether, or how, political interests (in terms of development aid, employment and technology policy) should be evaluated in cases where export efficiency is only of secondary concern.

Fifthly, the Commission had concluded on the basis of the anti-protectionist tendency of Article 110 of the EEC Treaty that the process of the harmonisation of export subsidies should simultaneously be concerned with their overall reduction, in the interest of fairer competition. This then raises the question of its relevance in relation to co-operation between community firms, which is usually undertaken precisely in order to increase the competitive standing of export financing or insurance by exploiting and concentrating on the capacities of individual national systems, with the result that co-operation always amounts to more than the sum of its single, purely national parts. Moreover, the same impact would be achieved if co-operation were to take the form of a pool or consortium, which would likewise contradict the Commission's interpretation of Article 110 EEC Treaty.

Finally, the Commission failed to differentiate between short-, medium- and long-term risks, even though it is not possible to deal with all three in the same way, due to the fact that from a medium and long-term perspective, the private market is primarily composed of banks and private finance houses rather than private credit insurance companies. Again, this is a situation that has its roots in the lack of an adequate reinsurance market, be it in the area of commercial or political credit risks. In short, there is simply no private business that operates on a parallel with the official agencies, and hence almost no competition from the private insurance market. It therefore seems necessary to take account of other considerations in addition to those articulated exclusively in terms of the common market and free competition, if state support for export goods by means of medium- and long-term export credits for countries outside the EC is to continue to be feasible and worthwhile.

At the end of 1993, the group of experts' mandate culminated in the presentation of a third report. Although the group generally strived to come up with commonly agreed proposals, a unanimous consensus was hard to come by and a single common technical majority view had to prevail over most of the issues under discussion, meaning that a number of serious reservations on a variety of issues on the part of certain experts had to be overlooked in favour of guaranteeing a set of presentable results. A degree of (self-interested) unanimity was nonetheless achieved in the common proposal to extend the mandate of the working group to involve further technical research. While the suggestion was in this respect dependent upon the eventual outcome of deliberations in the Policy Co-ordination Group, it was stressed that the group of experts were not proposing any change in the underlying principles behind their recommendations. Here it is important to recall the terms of reference under which the group had operated (Tuffraut-Barriant, 1993, p. 4):

To facilitate the achievement of the Single Market aims in the export credit field, the Group for Co-ordination of Export Credit Policies has decided to set up an experts group chaired by Ms. Tuffraut (Coface). This group will examine: - the main constituents of guarantees; - systems for setting premiums; - guiding principles for cover policy, with a view to formulating common principles applying to the three above-mentioned areas. In this respect, the Single Market Group will make operational proposals to be submitted to the Plenary Group for assessment and decision for implementation.

On the one hand, all the experts were able to agree that one of the above aims was to create a level playing field for those insured, whilst on the other, it should be recognised that this interpretation has failed to produce a unanimous agreement on premium systems and rates or cover policy principles, which would ensure both the same availability of cover for exports to third countries for each EC exporter (independent of nationality) and the same cost of export credit insurance cover for a given export transaction, irrespective of the location of the issuing export credit agency in the Community.

In the particular area of premium setting, a few experts strongly opposed the setting of guidelines on premiums if its main result would only be to privilege the point of view of those insured which is certainly what the concept of the *level playing field* implies. Instead, they argued that the calculation of premium rates should also take into account the financial obligations of export credit agencies to operate on a break-even basis, if not at all times (though that might be necessary in some cases), then at least in accordance with the GATT rule that requires solvency in the long run and on a global level over their whole portfolio. Premium rates should thus be fixed at levels appropriate to the potential realisation of the financial *break-even objective* of export credit agencies.

However, the majority of specialists countered with the argument that by giving weight to such considerations, there would inevitably be an adverse impact on the objective of the level playing field. Partly because of differences in the way each official export credit insurance system is organised, and also because of variations in portfolios and the concentration of risks (both of which directly influence the financial results of export credit agencies), it was felt that the continual assessment of factors specific to each agency would inevitably lead to great divergences in premium rates, thus endangering the *main objective of harmonisation* as stipulated in the original mandate. Therefore, no final decision was made regarding specific proposal in relation to the financial break-even objective.

In the field of country cover policy, the building of a consensus was complicated by three connected factors of an essentially political nature.

Firstly, risk concentration and the spreading of risks are influenced above all by the framework of industry in the respective country and need to be considered along with the traditional trade relationships and foreign policy goals of each individual government *vis-à-vis* third countries. Secondly, the overall amount of new cover which an export credit agency is able to offer depends on political decisions concerning national budget priorities. So long as credit and insurance schemes continue to be funded by public money, support will as a rule not be provided for anything other than national exports and it was not therefore possible to form a majority opinion based upon a Council Decision concerning the 'rules applicable in the fields of export guarantee and finance for export, to certain subcontracts with parties in other Member States in the European Communities and in non-member countries' (Council of the European Communities, 1982). Finally, a common baseline was ensured by the establishment of principles to ensure the transparency of individual cover policies and to measure the coherence of official agency practice when compared with a methodological assessment of country risks. A minority proposal to partially level out cover capacities between agencies through the use of reinsurance mechanisms or the exchange of risks did not receive any further attention.

Although the experts group mainly incorporated into its report the opinions that found a majority among its members, it did not go so far as to resort to compromise formulas or to ultimately leave decisions to the Policy Co-ordination Group, a point perhaps most evident in the common principles for setting premium rates. It was recommended that the fees to be paid in export transactions considered to involve political risks should only be set as *minimum rates* for each country category, whilst commercial risks were accommodated by a set of simple *reference rates*, after the failure of other attempts to find a technically feasible solution to the problem of providing more definitive guidelines than those merely assessing the buyer risk. A similar tendency is observable in the proposal for a country classification designed to include six categories ranging from one to six from the lowest to the highest risks. The final report refrained from making concrete recommendations relating to the specific classification of individual countries, as it was not possible to extensively test the whole model against a complete scale, and it was in any case stressed that in the end no amount of quantitative modelling could totally replace the judgement of policy specialists who are able to analyse the data input and assess the political situation in a way not encapsulated by mathematical measurement. Likewise, a third and final set of principles corresponding to the 'main constituents of guarantee' were not drafted with a view to forming a legally binding text as such but were intended as recommendations which could at a certain stage be incorporated into individual agency policies, in accordance with the corresponding legal system.

In many ways, the *Tuffraut report* can be interpreted as a rejection of the results of its precursor, the *Stolzenburg report*, although neither of the two can be said to successfully conceal the basically political character of their efforts. Where the two differ most fundamentally is over the question as to at which *political* decision-making level any future export credit policy should be situated: where the former clearly favoured a co-operative solution, the latter concluded that the entire series of common principles constituted a sound basis for the harmonisation of medium and long-term export credit insurance. Notwithstanding the fact that this fell short of demanding the creation of a new Community institution, the role implicitly assigned to the Policy Co-ordination Group suggests that there exists a nucleus for an integrated trade policy. Fairly logically, if a unified policy-making instrument is to prove efficient and administratively convenient, then this is something best handled by a central authority, otherwise there is precious little to justify the duplication of parallel efforts at the domestic and international level.

6.5   Export Promotion as an Instrument of the CFSP

Given that the role of credit and insurance can be interpreted as being analogous to a foreign policy instrument within the national context (Hill, 1994, pp. 120-1), it is easy to understand the motivations behind comparable Community efforts organised under the heading of a common commercial or development policy (European Parliament, 1993): The granting of export cover or preferential financing conditions, renouncing claims and classifying countries into risk categories do indeed constitute formidable instruments for exercising influence over third countries. But most of these expectations take it for granted that the instrument would be exclusively in the hands of an independent Community institution with control over its own resources, and hence assume that, at this level, interventions are both permissible and desirable. However, I would argue that the marginal steps taken in this direction can only work to the detriment of the CFSP because the decision-making process is time consuming and will create inconsistencies with national policies. In other words, preliminary steps towards a common export credit policy will not necessarily enhance the development of a common foreign policy as such (Walzenbach, 1994). Three clear examples demonstrate this point:

Firstly, for the first time in the history of US-EC relations, the Community in August 1982 submitted a formal written note to the US concerning a pipeline dispute against the background of the crises in Poland. The document expressed the reservations of the member states with regard to the American embargo and made it clear that they would nevertheless continue to honour their export contracts. American requests to limit the extent of financing and guarantee conditions in East-West trade were also refused. What is mainly of interest here is the fact that the Commission only took on an active role in reaction to a unique coincidence of interests between member states, and not the other way round. As one observer has remarked (Lowet, 1984, p. 148):

> In doing so, the EC did not limit the sovereignty of the member states tout court, but enriched it. By performing a protective function, it not only gave the individual European Countries greater room for manouvre under this coverage, but it also allowed them to refer to the Community position when necessary. The EC action functioned as an umbrella under which they could find shelter and to which they could refer. The Commission accordingly protected the business community in the EC and at the same time its Common Commercial Policy).

The second example refers to the Commission's running of aid programmes to support the economies of Eastern Europe and Russia, under the heading of PHARE and which has also involved export credit packages on the part of twenty-four OECD countries. Two factors are of importance. First, the form taken by the aid measures 'is not always immune from considerations of self-interest', as almost all the exports are EC-products (Nello, 1991, p. 68). Exceptions to this rule were made, but it took quite some time until it became at least formally possible to extend credit and cover to the sale of East European agricultural products to the former Soviet Union (Commission of the European Communities, 1991a; 1991b). Second, a number of serious doubts exist as to whether the lengthy and elaborated application procedures make any sense from an economic point of view. The costs of making appropriate project proposals considerably outweigh the potential benefits in terms of the resources actually available in the case of a positive decision (Frankfurter Allgemeine Zeitung, 1993a, p. 12).

Lastly, the Airbus consortium is an often cited example when complaints are made about the lack of an integrated European export institution. It is frequently claimed that if more favourable finance and insurance conditions were to be provided, the project - which is of major political importance because it demonstrates the technical capability to meet the potential requirements of a future common security policy - would be far more successful on foreign markets. There are two major weaknesses in this argument. To begin with, private banks working in the multi-sourcing business have themselves emphasised the advantages of precisely these types of contract: they have, for example, become quite common even in the case of the consortium's leading competitor, Boeing. In the second place, right from its very inception, the Airbus consortium has had to deal with an organisational problem, namely that its main task is to sell aeroplanes, not to produce them, which is the job of Airbus Industries, i.e. of four different European aircraft constructors (Dasa, Aérospatiale, British Aerospace, Casa). In consequence, a situation arises in which the consortium, on the one hand, has to make relatively cheap supply contracts in order to maximise profits on behalf of these firms, while on the other, the aforementioned companies maintain a strong interest in selling their parts at the highest possible price, with the upshot that the additional costs of this practice are estimated to amount to up to ten per cent of total sales.

In all three examples, export credits and guarantees have been involved in one way or another in Community policy-making that deals with its own 'third country' relations, and in particular, they give a good illustration of how problematic their actual role has been at this level. Be that as it may, it is still the case that individual export promotion measures have not been shown to be independent, proactive instruments for furthering the 'Community interest'. Rather than being precedents for, or the major ingredients of, a common foreign policy, they have up until now only achieved a certain degree of practical relevance through their assertion, concealment and protection of the pre-existing individual interests of the member states.

Throughout this chapter, it has been argued that Community institutions, above all the Commission and the Court, complicate co-ordination problems. This last section, which focused on limited attempts to employ export finance and insurance as a foreign policy instrument under the existing mechanisms of the Community, further supports this conclusion. Broadly speaking, the continuous efforts to install something like an independent agency can be attributed to the ultimate goal of the integration of the European Community, but in the final analysis, this is also the reason why it will be impossible to attain the benefits of an efficient and effective co-ordination under a tighter institutional structure.

7 Institutional Choice in the OECD

The main rationale behind international agreements reached within the framework of the OECD is to be found in their domestic context: by means of negotiating a set of international rules designed to encourage the use of market interest rates by official agencies, governments have been trying to solve their own problems with export finance. If all governments experience similar degrees of budgetary restraint and a sharp rise in borrowing costs, then the move towards institutional settlements could well prove to be the most sensible solution (Duff, 1981, p. 894), as the following chapter discusses in detail. At the same time, it is essential to be quite clear about the whole range of motivational factors lying behind the search for a consensus. Although certain technical co-ordination mechanisms may in practice meet the approval of all interested parties, their nesting within a concrete institutional form primarily constitutes a reflection of an overriding concern with essentially political factors. In other words, governments will rarely tie themselves down to the extent that their own freedom for strategic action is severely constrained.

Economists and policy-makers alike have always been aware of the outright waste of resources that accompanies competitive subsidisation. If one country's subsidy is matched by a subsidy from a competitor, both end up losing the cost of the respective subsidy while gaining nothing overall, since their relative competitive positions will have remained the same. In addition, the risk of an officially sponsored export credit race between supplier countries through such means as the lowering of rates of interest, the lengthening of repayment periods or the relation of other credit terms, means that the effective working of the credit system is potentially undermined. In such circumstances, the system's function of reflecting the opportunity costs of capital, supplying information to borrowers and investors and thus directing scarce resources towards their greatest productive potential, cannot be properly fulfilled, with the logical implication that both parties to the original credit contract will suffer losses due to a lowering of their long run productive output. It is probably only the existence of commercially realistic terms for export credits that could actually lead to an improvement in factor allocation among recipient countries and to a sustained period of growth (Ray, 1986, p. 296). But hypotheses such as these are only of limited help, given that the post-war period presents such a mixed record in terms of the defensive and aggressive use of export promotion tools. Once again, it can be assumed that political motivations could account for the general acceptance of the substantial and often unpredictable costs involved in the whole process, instead of trying to apply self-restraint in the sense of only attempting to match the competitor's offer.

The underlying assumption behind successive agreements concluded within the framework of the OECD Trade Committee was always somewhat ambitious, namely that export subsidies should be abolished as soon as possible, which would necessitate that the participants adopt a longer term perspective and evaluate the potential long-term benefits in terms of trade volume to be greater than the short-term costs. In practice, however, and as one former chairman of the organisation's export credit group has readily admitted, the overall strategy tended to be that of a gradual step-by-step process wherein the speed of adjustments was still heavily influenced by the overall trade climate and the generally diverging attitudes towards subsidisation held by the member states (Wallén, 1986, p. 270). Because each government employs a different combination of instruments from the range of available export promotion tools in a way that best corresponds to its particular economic system, financial institutions and trade patterns, the impact of apparently formally identical subsidies will vary considerably from one country to another. Moreover, as the section below on the historical background to the negotiations will show, the 'political climate' also proved to be a significant factor. Taken together, all these factors suggest that the fundamental problem in the OECD context is constituted by the question of how to devise 'rules that do not appear to favour one country more than another' (Pearce, 1980, p. 41; Majnoni, 1981, p. 101).

The OECD's appeal as the primary forum for discussion derives from a number of reasons, above all because most of the funds committed to subsidisation are distributed through the agencies of the industrialised nations. In addition, as most standard formulations of collective action issues tend to argue, unilateral action is not a viable option for the prevention of, for example, a credit race in which countries compete on the basis of who grants the most favourable financial terms. The utility to exporting countries of having an institutional brake on this kind of destructive competition is fairly self-evident, whilst the same benefits apply to importing countries as well, especially those at a lower stage of economic development, and a sufficiently skilfully devised mechanism should be capable of achieving a proper control of the volume of credit and dealing with the associated problem of debt accumulation. On the other hand, some of the OECD arrangements may be more ambiguous in their implications. In many parts of the western world, any similar kinds of agreement entered into by private financial institutions would almost certainly violate domestic antitrust laws and lead to legal proceedings. In the international arena, however, the exclusive membership of the OECD allows for cartel-like behaviour to be possible, to the extent that such limits on competition such as floor rate fixing are actually rewarded rather than censured.

This type of co-ordination problem arises from the simple fact that several different states are pursuing separate policies of trade promotion. When seen from the standpoint of political economy, however, the story becomes slightly more complex: official export credits, guarantees and development aid can all be interpreted as 'tools of statecraft' for achieving broader foreign policy goals, which can either be employed as 'leverage to extract concessions from a potential borrower' or can be suspended in order 'to signal displeasure with the borrower's political behaviour' (Crawford, 1987; Spaulding, 1991). In short, they can act as instruments which introduce some form of political conditionality, with the consequence that the potential area within which interests might collide increases. For example, state A may be in a position where it has to improve its trade balance, whereas state B's major concern is to see a change in the political conduct of some recipient country C; in this particular situation, the possibility actually arises that C simply opts for the more convenient trading partner A, thus neutralising the effectiveness of B's policy strategy.

This chapter will address the question of how a comparatively less tight institutional arrangement goes about performing its co-ordination function, e.g. is a neutral mechanism both a viable and sufficient response to the 'economic' and 'political' type of co-ordination problem? Who takes greater advantage of whom? How effective is the performance of the OECD in its role as a co-ordinator? And is the result of the type of institutional choice the development of a pro-active, anticipatory policy, rather than an ex-post rationalisation of what is already happening anyway? The chapter is divided into five analytical parts, beginning with a look at the historical background, in order to emphasise the importance of a contextual interpretation. Section 7.2 then moves on to describe the overall regulatory framework and examines the institutional response to the demand for co-ordination mechanisms, while Section 7.3 provides an evaluation thereof. The significance of expertise and its role in persistent reform efforts form the subject of Section 7.4, and finally, the conclusion discusses the external aspects of these findings.

7.1   Institutional Development

The existence of conflicts between nations in the kind of foreign trade policy that we are interested in is well documented from at least the 1930s, when virtually all the industrialised countries attempted to safeguard their own markets in the wake of international economic depression. In the post-war period, the issue took on much greater significance because the United States assigned to its most important financing institution, the Export-Import Bank, the mission of pushing back the spread of socialism. The majority of trade promotion efforts thus became linked to explicitly political considerations, and support for less developed countries by means of cheap supplier credits was designed as much to prevent their passing under 'communist domination' as to integrate them into trading relations with the rest of the world (Marer, 1975).

Initially, the post-war activities of international institutions in the export promotion field grew out of the necessity to build trade relations back up again after the complete breakdown of the international transport infrastructure and information channels. In a situation of great uncertainty as regards the possibility of exchanging goods and services, the case for an institutional arrangement between governments was especially strong, and up until the 1950's it was also relatively easy to secure agreements since official involvement primarily concentrated on the provision of short-term insurance for political risks. It was only gradually that the role of government expanded to include the coverage of commercial risks and the provision of unconditional bank guarantees.

In 1955, the Organisation for European Economic Co-operation and Development (OEEC) for the first time adopted a set of rules governing measures designed to subsidise exports, whose classic formulation prohibited 'the charging of premiums at rates that are manifestly inadequate to cover the long-term operating costs and losses of the credit insurance institutions'. Three years later, the list of prohibited measures underwent expansion, and now explicitly included the financing of export credits by bodies wholly or partly dependent on public authorities. What is particularly striking here is the relevance of these stipulations to the present situation. Firstly, the ban on the setting of export credits at rates below those which official agencies have to pay in order to obtain the funds employed to that end, and secondly the acceptance of all or part of the costs incurred by exporters in obtaining credits, were both seen as a natural corollary to the ban on insurance policies. Furthermore, the organisation recommended 'that the government of each member country shall communicate, confidentially and subject to reciprocal treatment, to the government of any other member country which so requests, the financial results of export risk insurance operations practised either by the government or by institutions controlled by it' (Ray, 1986, p. 297). However, the governments concerned were reluctant to see the backdoor closed in this way, and when the OEEC was transformed into the OECD, the obligations relating to export subsidies had to be transferred to the GATT organisation.

In itself, the OEEC was only a second-best solution, as an examination of the alternative promotion instrument of aid finance shows. For domestic reasons, the industrialised nations had initially opted for a bilateral system of supporting economic development (Hveem, 1992, p. 13), with a move towards international efforts to co-ordinate budgetary flows first arising in the 1960s. In trying to explain this change, Prout (1976, p. 361) stressed the role of American foreign policy goals over more ideational factors such as a desire to bring a greater sense of justice in the system, and it was in fact within the framework of NATO where the notion of burden-sharing was first launched. The Americans felt that if the Europeans conformed to and benefited from the organisation's overall objectives, then it was also their duty to contribute as much to its costs as their partners in the alliance, and in a way similar, though not identical, to military expenditure, external financing was considered an additional means of fostering the same political aims. When viewed from this angle, the initial US attempt to use the defence organisation as a forum for the co-ordination of aid expenditures was not without a certain logic, although in instrumental terms, it could not of course provide any substantial mechanism for dealing with the technical issues involved in aid financing, in which respect the OECD promised to be a much better solution.

At the same time, a number of changes in the constellation of interests on the demand side of the equation helped produce pressure for an institutional solution from the opposite direction. At a point when the Export-Import Bank remained bound by restrictive legislation regarding the distribution of its resources, European credit facilities were going through a sustained period of growth. Many OECD members, notably France, Britain and West Germany, started off by supplying tied aid as soon as the number of new and independent recipient states increased. The founding of the Development Assistance Committee (DAC) within the OECD thus reflected a parallel concern to that of the earlier attempts already mentioned in this section, and its central aim soon became that of trying to strike a balance between a steady increase in development assistance and manageable debt-servicing obligations for Third World countries. The various attempts to construct suitable co-ordination mechanisms were complicated by the fact that the latter's indebtedness was also due to the activities of official export credit institutions, whose unfettered growth during the 1960s exacerbated the problems of financial instability, especially in less developed countries (LDC). Even though they fully acknowledged the problem, the DAC ultimately gave up on the attempt to construct a regulatory framework, because it considered the commercial element in export financing contracts to be beyond the control of its member states.

In the meantime, competition to sell capital goods to developing countries by using the support of official credit institutions continued apace. In the decade between 1960 and 1970, for example, the contract value of officially backed long-term export credits rose sharply from just under one billion to approximately eight billion SDR. Particularly in the case of credit maturities, the content of the financial package involved now became a central element in the making of a contract, a situation which allowed the institutional solution put forward by the OECD Trade Committee in 1963 to slowly gain momentum. By bringing together representatives both from national treasuries and export agencies, a high level group of officials concerned with export credits and export credit guarantees (ECG) was able to begin formulating its aim of identifying, mitigating and even preventing destructive promotion policies.

Since the group's terms of reference were directly concerned with co-ordinating export credit policy, it was obliged to make recourse to the general institutional mechanisms of the organisation within which it was nested. However, instead of producing substantive solutions in the form of common guidelines, the discussions got bogged down in procedural questions relating to prior notification and consultation for individual transactions. The difficulty in making progress, especially in the field of soft long-term credits, eventually convinced the group to renounce all-encompassing approaches in favour of more limited, piecemeal attempts at regulating specific commodities rather than capital equipment as a whole. In this respect, it was Working Party 6 of the OECD that first made some headway in negotiating the regulation of subsidies in the ship-building industry, and in 1969, thirteen of the main ship-exporting countries formulated a prototype export credit arrangement, in which they jointly agreed on credit length maximums, interest rate minimums and a weaker version of what later became to be known as the matching mechanism (Wallén, 1984, p. 261). Following on from this lead, the ECG succeeded in setting up an informal *Exchange of Information System* in 1972, through which all participating members could request from one another details of long-term export credits that they were prepared to offer for a particular transaction. Nevertheless, the lack of political will to go any further and accept genuine mandatory limits reinforces the impression that for most of this period, the preservation of an overall market growth for capital goods exports was 'a far more important collective interest than (the) ironing out of any trade distortions that might result from an individual nation autonomously cutting the price of its own credit' (Prout, 1976, p. 383).

In retrospect, it is possible to see that the apparent unwillingness of governments to establish a regime with real authority to monitor maturity and interest rate changes was in fact accompanied by a more tacit form of co-ordination, because all exporting countries in practice agreed on the lengthening of maturities. By the early 1970s, even the US government was willing to join in the further easing of trade restrictions as part of its new strategy of *détente* towards the Soviet Union, even if the situation in American domestic politics or more precisely, contrary voting by Congress, was to counteract those plans. The founding charter of the Export-Import Bank had already prohibited lending to communist nations without prior presidential approval that a proposed loan was in the 'national interest', and from 1974 onwards a series of further amendments demanded congressional consent in the case of each individual project (Crawford, 1987, p. 441). Faced with such tight domestic restrictions, the government was continually obliged to take a tough stand in international negotiations. Although the OECD group was principally formed to avoid damaging trade competition, the American intention behind this particular institutional choice was now to reduce the *volume* of official support going to the Soviet Union and its satellites.

A complementary, albeit incomplete, explanation as to the timing of this regime creation has been proposed by Moravcsik, who also argues that it was essentially the US that assumed the leadership in the negotiations for an export finance agreement. However, Moravcsik's (1989, p. 201) own account is ambiguous as to whether it was less a case of America's hegemonic position in world affairs and more a matter of its relative decline that was the real motivation for seeking an international arrangement, seeing as it was above all the 'persistence of American power in one aspect of international finance (long-term bonds)' that was able to guarantee the installation of a regime, despite 'the simultaneous decline of confidence in American financial markets'. Be that as it may, when looking for economic explanations for the problem, another strong incentive in establishing internationally co-ordinated action undoubtedly derived from the effects of the first oil crises. A massive rise in prices between 1973 and 1974 led to enormous balance of payments deficits in western countries, a change in economic climate which was expected to encourage the major trading states to try and maintain their own positions by means of a return to mercantilism, a new round of protectionism did indeed seem to be on the policy agenda at that time.

The OECD thus offered the ideal intergovernmental forum for dealing with these concerns and a joint declaration by the member states specifically agreed to avoid the artificial stimulation of exports, as well as aiming for 'appropriate co-operative actions to this effect in the immediate future'. In addition, they explicitly asserted a desire to make use of the organisation's general consultation mechanism, when in 1975 the Trade Pledge was renewed. The two legal analysts Hahn and Weber (1976, p. 223) have both stressed the informal nature of the obligations resulting from that agreement, arguing that it had no foundation in international law but that the content of the standstill agreement was clear in terms of economic policy and would gain in influence thanks to its unanimous acceptance. Moreover, it also had the side-effect of reviving the search for all-encompassing, rather than incremental, solutions in that its request for common policy guidelines made specific reference to the original goals of the ECG, i.e. the aim to achieve discipline and transparency across the whole policy field rather than in limited sectors.

The Seven Power Summit of 1976 gave further impetus to the project, once the OECD had inquired among its member states about how to regulate subsidised export credit. In the end, the resulting statement, the Consensus on Converging Export Credit Policies, was little more than a collection of individual replies: a succession of separate, unilateral declarations with a similar wording that were made at different points in time by the major industrialised countries, each of which was thus susceptible to individual interpretation. Although the label of 'Gentlemen's Agreement' could justifiably be attached to this document, all of its signatories had at least agreed on the fixing of a matrix with standardised interest rates along three country categories (relatively rich, intermediate, relatively poor), as well as with reference to short, medium and long-term repayment periods. Other important factors were left out altogether: for example, the Consensus made no mention of the conditions and terms of insurance or guarantees - only the conditions and terms of the export credits that benefit from such insurance or guarantees (Ray, 1986, p. 301). It was particularly in this last respect where the agreement differed markedly from the former rules of the OEEC, as well as those of the subsequent GATT Code on Subsidies and Countervailing Duties. Furthermore, certain noticeable institutional features developed in the period shortly after the Summit, including the fact that the G-7 governments formed a small *ad hoc* group which began to hold regular meetings over the export credit issue. Technically, this Participants Group (PG) was not officially an OECD body, i.e. it was not subject to organisational rules requiring its actions to be approved by the OECD Council, even if it could nevertheless anticipate important procedural issues such as the exclusion of non-OECD members or the exclusion of export credits from the multilateral trade negotiations of the GATT (Blair, 1992, pp. 45-6).

Two years later, in 1978, the Arrangement on Guidelines for Officially Supported Export Credits was finally concluded. Despite still being referred to in internal administrative parlance as the 'Consensus', it undoubtedly represented a significant advance on the previous agreement. It consisted of a single, uniform document with comprehensive and much more precise provisions, to which all the members of the ECG subscribed from the outset, and contained the first systematic attempt at dealing with the various elements distorting the competitive use of trade finance. To begin with, the Arrangement codified terms relating to interest rates, repayment periods, down payments, local costs, cost-escalation insurance and exchange-rate guarantees, and in addition, some of its new regulations were intended to limit the use of development aid in commercial contracts. Lastly, but not least, it attempted to strengthen the exchange of information between official agencies in order to ensure that their individual support measures were not based on false assumptions about the bids of other major competitors. The underlying idea was therefore a relatively simple one, namely that if some of the participants failed to conform with the agreed guidelines, they would be obliged to notify the other members, who could then have recourse to appropriate countermeasures.

A set of regular refinements and modifications to the Arrangement were, however, soon accompanied by questions regarding the formal status of its provisions, and the respective opinions among the member countries were reflected in the divergence of academic writing on the issue. Pearce (1980, p. 49), for example, claimed that 'although it was not a formal OECD agreement, because one of the signatories (the EEC) was not a member of the OECD, the Arrangement was a binding agreement'. In a study by the Rand Corporation (Kohler, 1985, p. 2), a proponent of the opposite view remarked:

> Western governments provide loans to eastern bloc purchasers of their exports at interest rates that are often lower than what the Western governments themselves have to pay for the money they borrow. The OECD tries to limit this practice by setting guidelines regarding the minimum rates governments should charge for export loans. However, these so-called consensus rates are not binding; the OECD member governments may ignore this gentlemen's agreement if they want to.

The following sections of this chapter attempt to come to terms with this dispute, not least for the fact that, somewhat erroneously, practitioners in the field tend to regard the whole discussion as redundant. The first problem that has been addressed here was the growth of regulations under economic conditions that appeared to be inhospitable to co-operative efforts. In tracing the historical development of these interrelated regulations devised by various international organisations, this section has tried to present some arguments against one of the more important elements in the standard regime-type explanation. Indeed, any account which concluded that 'the Arrangement was formed outside the established framework of the GATT and hence did not benefit from a preexisting, highly developed institutional milieu', would be extremely misleading (Moravcsik, 1989, p. 174).

On the contrary, export promotion policies are a particularly instructive example of how international institutions, or better some of their co-ordination mechanisms, have managed to survive, even though their surrounding environment has changed completely. In the post-war period, the initial need for the continuous provision of financing resources through official institutions gradually disappeared, and the rapid recovery of the financial markets was able to cover the gap in resources for trade transactions. Although this development should in theory have made official involvement obsolete, governments soon rediscovered their utility as policy instruments for manipulating trade flows. In this respect, another of the central claims of regime theory relating to the effectiveness of international arrangements begins to look rather dubious, given that it is actually necessary to undertake a much more detailed analysis as to whether governments are really restricted in their domestic subsidies to particularly vulnerable industries with high surplus capacities. Before turning to the broader issue of evaluation, it is worth taking a closer look at the rules and mechanisms of the Arrangement in their current form.

7.2   Rules and Mechanisms

The introductory chapters detailing the theoretical foundation for a case study have underlined the need to provide for neutral mechanisms by means of international institutions. Again, the hypothesis put forward by Moravcsik (1989, p. 198) is of interest here, because he argues that the OECD, 'under whose aegis the regime functions, seems to have had little effect on the negotiations', and instead merely became the institutional home of the regime, 'largely because it offered a neutral forum'. Moravcsik goes on to suggest that the OECD contributed neither a set of meta-norms nor opportunities for issue linkage, since the arrangement remains an *ad hoc* institution, existing in an anarchic environment outside of 'the context of other regimes'. Crawford's (1987, p. 433) application of regime theory, on the other hand, provides an alternative interpretation, with her account proposing that any analysis would have to begin with NATO's policy co-ordination efforts in East-West trade. Starting with the Co-ordinating Committee for Multilateral Export Controls (COCOM), the rise of new trade issues such as countertrade, energy dependence, and finance, eventually led to demands for institutional changes in order to better manage their consequences, which left the newly expanded regime being 'nested chiefly within the OECD'.

In this instance, the fundamentally different interpretations once more reveal a number of problems with the theoretical framework employed by the two authors, but rather than passing over the relevance of these arguments, their cogency can be tested against a set of follow-up questions. For example, if the GATT does actually have an institutional design that threatens to impede co-operation in this area, how does that affect the viability of vertical co-ordination between the two structures? And if linkage strategies were not observable at the level of OECD negotiations, is it likely that they took place at 'lower levels', nested inside the broader international structure? Or if the Trade Directorate is merely an opportunity for treasury and credit agency officials to continue what they are already doing, how can this be reconciled with the image of an essentially forward-looking organisation? These questions can be addressed by looking first of all at the co-ordination mechanisms as manifested in the regulations of the Arrangement (OECD, 1992).

As has already been mentioned, all the provisions in the Arrangement do not formally count as acts of the OECD Council and thus cannot be regarded as a full legal instrument of the OECD (Abraham, 1990, p. 6). Nevertheless, the guidelines upon which several co-ordination mechanisms have been based would seem to hold out the promise of bringing to an end a rather uneven history of co-operation, despite the significant amount of autonomy and flexibility they leave to the participating governments. Technically, these informal rules encourage participants to accept restrictions on the repayment of any export credits that are officially supported by means of direct credit, refinancing, or the possibility of an interest subsidy, guarantee or insurance. The general principle which the guidelines try to put into everyday action can be summarised as follows (OECD, 1991, p. 2):

> OECD Members' export credit and tied aid credit policies should be complementary; those for export credits should be based upon competition and the free play of market forces; those for tied aid credits should provide needed external resources to countries, sectors or projects with little or no access to

market financing, ensure best value for money, minimise trade distortion and contribute to developmentally effective use of these resources.

To this end, three basic types of regulation can be devised: (1) those which place certain limits on the conditions - interest rates, term to maturity, down payment, repayment schedules - under which credits may be granted; (2) those which provide automatic adjustments to changes in domestic capital markets and international exchange rates; and (3) those concerning the mandatory exchange of information on credit practices, which are best described in terms of the key requirements of discipline, automaticity and transparency. For much of the time, the participants in the Arrangement have tried to establish a modified minimum interest rate matrix below which members are not allowed to provide subsidies, whenever the market rates are *above* the matrix, and this general emphasis has gradually shifted in order to cope with problems relating to tied and partially untied aid financing and the preparation of new sector agreements. The following paragraphs will show that each of the OECD's main co-ordination mechanisms suffers from inherent deficiencies leading to results (*bias effects*) that leave the neutrality assumption of regime theory wanting.

To begin with, it is fairly artificial to try and distinguish budgetary loans from publicly-funded or insured commercial loans, given that both are tied categories, are government supervised and create identical problems: both provoke the borrower into a heavier external debt-servicing burden, and both induce the same response, namely pressure for more credit on softer terms. However, if the focus of attention is primarily on institutional solutions, then the two are recognisably distinct and the respective differences were also regarded as of importance by the developing countries themselves. When funds are allocated from a particular budget, the domestic political process intervenes to constrain their availability, as well as the terms upon which they are distributed. In the absence of a pure market solution for the softening and equalising of terms, negotiations within the framework of the OECD essentially rely on political pressure to lower interest rates or lengthen maturities in a uniform manner. In contrast, the cost of commercial credit - be it from a public or private source - is influenced to a much larger extent by the balance between supply and demand factors relating to financial resources in the international capital goods markets. In this respect, it was the *matching procedure* which seemed to contain the greatest potential for subjecting such pressures to some kind of control, because ideally, it should ensure the orderly and equitable softening of terms between both lender and borrower, and between the lenders themselves.

The Arrangement establishes minimum interest rates, in a form known as a matrix, and which is subject to change every January and July, in accordance with the workings of an *automatic mechanism*. Changes in the matrix interest rates follow the weighted average of government bond yields for the five currencies that go to make up the IMF's special drawing rights (SDR), and the rates vary depending on the groups of countries to which the export credits are destined. If the commercial interest rates for the currency of one participant fall below these minimums, any other participant is allowed to provide loans in that currency at a commercial interest reference rate. Behind this regulation, which permits deviation from the matrix rates, lies a desire to remove the possibility that credit market financing in countries with low interest rates becomes more attractive than official export financing, and for this reason, any of the participants can offer export credits in the currency with the lower interest rate. However, a bias effect enters into the situation because of the use of the SDR as a currency basket, as it is only the respective interest rates of the US dollar, German mark, Japanese yen, French franc and pound sterling that are included in the calculation of the matrix rates. A second bias follows from the fact that the Arrangement defines export credits as subsidies whenever they are financed at an interest rate below the borrowing costs of the government agencies from precisely these five countries. Hence, subsidies are allowed to the extent that the market interest rate, which would otherwise have to be paid in the absence of official export credits, remains above the Arrangement minimum rate.

In addition, the current system introduces a third bias in that it discriminates against countries with low interest rates (Abraham, 1990, p. 12), due to the fact that the official agency is only obliged to finance exporters at a rate that reflects actual market conditions (the commercial interest reference rate, CIRR) when the national interest rate is below the matrix rate. Thus, the maximum interest subsidy allowed will always be higher for export firms in countries with high market interest rates, which creates an incentive for driving up interest rates in order to enlarge the potential for official support measures, and it is at this point that microeconomic considerations combine with macroeconomic strategies, e.g. to correct current account deficits or to maintain a stable exchange rate. Yet, if the government itself is prepared to pay a higher interest rate, and assuming that the money would have to be borrowed on the private capital markets, then even state-funded export credits at - or close to - the matrix interest rates will be expensive in terms of the costs they incur for the domestic budget.

The hard construction of interest rate adjustments to market conditions is embedded in several different soft co-ordination mechanisms, amongst which the procedure of adapting to the contract conditions of other competitors has perhaps the longest tradition. As Prout (1976, p. 383) remarked around the time of its inception:

> The beauty of the matching mechanism in its limited 'reprisal' form, was that it achieved softening with the minimum amount of distortion: because one member was entitled, automatically to 'level down' to, or 'match' the terms of another. It provided in effect a *surrogate market mechanism* whereby price changes by one supplier were transmitted smoothly to another, accommodating economic realities to the requirements of free market dogma that rates and terms had to be uniform (emphasis added).

Historically, a free market in the export trade sector has of course never existed, nor is it likely that it was ever meant to. There was in fact a rather different motivating force behind the co-ordination efforts of official agencies, whose institutional self-interest forced them to try and obtain reliable information regarding the details of the terms being offered by partner organisations in other countries (and in this respect, it is certainly better to rely on the information of those actually supplying the resources than of those who merely wish to benefit from them). Paragraph 16 of the Arrangement confers the right to match credit terms and conditions offered by participants or non-participants, with the restriction that the validity of a matching commitment does not exceed the counterpart offer's termination date, although this does not necessarily imply that other provisions will become invalid since it is expected that the agencies will achieve a match 'by offering terms that comply with this arrangement unless the initiating offer does not comply with this arrangement' (Paragraph 11). Once a participant decides to react to the non-conforming practices of a competitor, the regulations establish certain time limits in order to give the latter the chance to withdraw; otherwise, the former has the right to support terms and conditions which include an 'identical non-conforming element'.

These represent only the most important elements in a procedure to which the Arrangement devotes considerable space, but despite the equally substantial attention this particular mechanism has attracted in academic literature, its practical relevance - as OECD officials have stressed - has steadily declined. Other co-ordination devices have since occupied the prominent position it once maintained. In particular, the four complementary instruments of consultation, notification, information exchange and annual review have become much more significant, practically amounting to regular *mini-negotiations* between government representatives.

The change in emphasis as regards procedures was also accompanied by a change in substance. Particularly in the field of aid financing, the participants tried to give greater weight to the Arrangement, and although it continues to allow tied or partially untied aid financing, a few regulations were passed in order to increase what is known as the concessionality level, i.e. the subsidy element within an aid package (Paragraph 8). Credits with a concessionality level of under 35 per cent are considered as going towards improving the competitive standing of what is basically a commercial transaction, in order that the same conditions apply as those in purely commercial export credits. Through the use of *consultations,* any participant is able to ask for clarification about the likely trade motivation for a tied, or partially untied, aid credit and may, for example, request that a full Aid Quality Assessment be undertaken. Consultations are especially recommended in cases where mixed credits are given to projects with a contract value larger than 50 million SDR and with a concessionality level of less than 80 per cent, with the intention being to find out whether it is in fact realistic to expect that financial resources will be made available at market rates, or at least within the limits laid down by the Arrangement. The job of subsequently notifying all members about the progress and results of the consultations is the responsibility of the Secretariat. However, it is still possible for a credit supplier to proceed with a project despite a lack of substantial support from other members, in which case the protagonist has to write to the Secretary-General of the OECD in accordance with Paragraph 14(a) 3 of the Arrangement outlining the results of the consultations and explaining the 'over-riding non-trade related national interest' that determines such an action.

The Arrangement specifies limits on the terms and conditions for export credits with a duration of two years or more, but even that cannot entirely prevent a number of infringements of the rules or deviations from what is considered to be normal practice. All that the relevant stipulations require is for any such intentions to be notified early enough in advance in order to allow the matching and consultation procedures to function adequately. In this area, the OECD guidelines identify various degrees of non-compliance: outright infringement, infringement justified by a prior commitment or by the need to match, permissible infringements, and finally, transgressions where a participant is required to notify the others. The *notification procedure* differentiates only between infringements and deviations: the former can entail a more detailed discussion if requested by one of the other members in response to planned actions which do not conform to the rules, whereas the latter does not necessitate such extended communication, instead referring only to support credits with specific repayment terms, unconventional payment practices or to credits which direct resources towards sectors excluded from the general arrangement.

There have of course been complaints from the private sector to the effect that some of the participating agencies have not properly followed the notification procedures as detailed in Paragraph 15 of the Arrangement. In order to work smoothly, the mechanisms require an exact knowledge of what credit offers involve, and hence, are open to various forms of manipulation, e.g. by only giving incomplete information, by providing information after some delay, or by simply suppressing its supply altogether. As a matter of fact, administrations are rarely that bothered if financing resources have actually circumvented some of the official channels or not, and this kind of ex-post opportunism will not be detected either, since such occurrences are not subject to the notification procedure (Lessard, 1986, p. 258). Clearly, an administrative process which attempts to regulate export finance will not always share the main concerns of bankers and industrialists, who are essentially interested in winning orders.

In asking why actors accept norms with seemingly little scope for infringements or opportunities of cheating, functional regime theory emphasises the transparency provisions of the regulatory framework. However, the part of the argument relating to the provision of reliable, and therefore highly valued, information is less straightforward than it seems, and a closer look at the *framework for information exchange* and its *common line procedure* (as presented in Annex VI of the Arrangement) will enable us to qualify that proposition.

In general, credits, guarantees and aid transactions can become the subject of an enquiry addressed by one participant to another, the actual content of which may refer to three types of questions. Firstly, the initiator of an enquiry may be interested in learning the attitude a particular agency takes in respect of a third country, an institution in its home country or a particular method of doing business. Secondly, by responding to an application for official support, the initiator might ask another official agency about the most favourable credit terms that it would be willing to support. Thirdly, the actor may want to verify allegations that another participant has offered official support which infringes on the guidelines of the Arrangement, and the addressee would then have to respond within a given time limit, presenting all the information that is available and indicating the likely decision to be taken.

What is perhaps most striking is the explicit acknowledgement that this type of information exchange and the resulting face-to-face consultations can sometimes lead to a proposal, which 'may contain terms and conditions that are more or less favourable than the terms and conditions allowed under the Arrangement' (OECD, 1992, p. 56). The rules of the so-called *common line* can on occasion actually go beyond the OECD guidelines, thus making it seem as if the acceptance of the regime is just as much about the reduction of information asymmetries in order to protect exporters against deception and exploitation, as it is about building up the competitive standing of its membership, even though this is a point which undermines the Arrangement's overall aim of keeping export credits competitively neutral. Strictly speaking, it should be noted that such agreements only apply to specific projects. Yet even here, it is possible to discern the hint of a fourth bias in the system, in the propensity to favour a project-oriented, rather than a more general, disciplining approach - a point to which we can return in the next section.

One final co-ordination mechanism within the Arrangement, and indeed of the OECD as a whole, is the *annual review*. By undertaking an examination of the working and implementation of its various procedures, an attempt is made to ensure their complementary functioning (Paragraph 21). But the review process often raises questions which have not yet been internalised by the regulatory process. Discussion of subsidising practices for agricultural commodities is a good case in point, as is the question of the acceptance of new participants to the agreement; likewise, even the 'hard' co-ordination mechanisms are open to modifications, although the incremental changes in the calculating techniques of the SDR based rates have not to date challenged any of the bias effects mentioned in the preceding paragraphs. From this point of view, it can perhaps be conjectured whether the participants have not taken too literally their own desire to see that 'the objectives of the Arrangement and the prevailing economic and monetary situation' is properly respected by the review process.

7.3   The OECD as Co-ordinator?

The following section evaluates how the OECD as an institution has carried out the role of co-ordinator. In relation to trade finance agreements, the organisation has played a fairly modest part in exerting influence over bargaining outcomes and state compliance, serving the industrial countries as a convenient forum for the major suppliers of credits whilst excluding their principal recipients. This was after all the primary reason for the issue being negotiated within a restricted 'Atlantic' context rather than in the GATT, and given the frequent battles between trading states, the possibility of conducting ongoing negotiations within the various subgroups of the

Table 7.1   Official export credits with over five year repayment period[a]

	1982	1983	1984	1985	1986	1987	1988	1989[b]	1990[b]	1991[b]	1992[c]
United States	2,008	1,165	1,542	899	1,210	773	548	1,227	1,183	3,203	3,992
Canada[d]	1,489	526	903	418	366	455	479	646	283	275	275
Britain	2,539	1,663	645	504	747	783	575	970	627	489	555
France	4,465	4,911	4,321	3,032	2,694	1,545	4,132	1,778	1,012	1,433	2,592
Germany	2,035	2,515	745	786	240	789	872	614	802	2,382	3,407
Italy	630	54	513	163	452	263	1,415	1,600	654	825	2,074
Japan	3,112	1,988	728	801	1,067	669	382	807	1,216	1,370	1,489
Total G-7	16,278	12,790	9,397	6,603	6,776	5,277	8,403	7,642	5,777	9,977	14,384
All OECD	18,792	15,855	10,783	8,268	7,965	6,427	9,666	9,224	7,470	11,486	15,480

[a] data reported to the OECD; SDR millions, credit value; SDR were used to minimise the effect of US dollar fluctuations;
[b] revised, March 1993;
[c] preliminary, May 1993;
[d] estimated for 1992, Canadian activity not reported to OECD as of May, 1993.

Source: Export-Import Bank of the United States (1993, p. 8).

Trade Committee fulfilled a residual function of keeping the wider discussion alive.

Most evaluations of the performance of the OECD have usually been quite positive (Hufbauer and Shelton Erb, 1984, p. 76; Blair, 1992, p. 57), and in comparison with other international regimes, the Arrangement is considered to constitute a strong regulatory framework because it refers to several different industrial sectors across a large group of countries. More specifically, Cheney (1985) views the automatic adjustments of interest rates to market levels as an important breakthrough in negotiations. Pearce (1980, p. 50) suggests some qualifications to the overall assessment, in so far as the situation is very likely to vary according to the position of the different participants, and between officials and exporters within countries. Pearce nevertheless basically comes out in favour of the agreement, firstly because of the very fact of its existence and because the countries concerned widely support its continuation; secondly, and more importantly, because 'there is general agreement that the Arrangement has stabilised competition in export credit, and made it fairer', but also because in the official opinion of the system's administrators, the guidelines actually work.

As Table 7.1 shows, the co-ordination system has not really achieved its main objective of neutralising official export credit as a competitive element within capital goods exports: the overall volume of long-term credit in the G-7 began to increase again after a period of decline between 1982 and 1987. Most striking of all are the cases of the United States, Germany and Italy, where the total credit value reached in the 1990s amounts to a figure even higher than those piled up during the debt crises of the early 1980s. On this issue, the economic analysis by Abraham (1990; 1993), which focuses particularly on the potential of interest rate support, comes to a similar conclusion to an earlier observation made by Wallén (1984) and Duff (1981, p. 984) when assessing 'Consensus' performance:

> Even those governments who had not earlier subsidized interest rates, or who had not done so extensively, felt pressured by the general acceptance of the agreements to provide their exporters the opportunity to export at the minimum rates contained in the guidelines. Thus, in practice, overall interest rate subsidization was increased by the mere introduction of the Consensus.

At the same time, the problem-solving capacity of the revised regulatory framework is relatively low, within its own limited area. Moreover, even a positive compliance record over a certain period of time can be undermined by developments taking place in other, closely related areas of the same policy space. The various threats that were made towards competitive subsidisation tended to originate in practices which were left out of the rules, rather than a lack of respect for the rules themselves. Indeed, as the previous section has shown, the rules do in fact allow member states to make adjustments in line with changes in the international economy, and the OECD system was only accepted in the first place because it tries to reconcile opposing and contradictory aims. After all, there is not a single cartel in the world of business which is created purely for reasons of internal competition, rather than trying to increase profits by driving up prices. Similarly, each member state is basically interested in a system that has an interpretative dimension allowing for discretion whenever their own export industries might be at an advantage. In the words of Strange (1986, p. 33):

> Closely related to the creditors' club question was the management of competition among industrial exporting countries in the tying of aid and the subsidization of credit and insurance for export contracts. The two policies were close substitutes for each other. If a government provided tied aid, it was offering vouchers redeemable only with its own exports. If it subsidized an agency that gave export credit insurance on easy terms to its national exporters it was offering a discount to the importer on deals done with them as opposed to deals done with others.

To take the point further, we can turn first of all to the issue of *export credit insurance*. Here, the Arrangement does not cover the terms and conditions of insurance and guarantees provided by official agencies and thus does not govern the provision relating to implicit subsidies through the premium structure (OECD, 1992, p. 5), meaning that the two support instruments are not directly connected. It is the official agency which decides whether the contracts eligible for cover also have to conform with the repayment periods established by international regulations. The data presented in Table 7.2 elucidates on the basis of three indicators why it has been practically impossible to include national export guarantee systems into a uniform regulatory framework. The country ranking shows considerable variations depending on whether we compare their financial results in absolute terms, their financial balance as a ratio between premium income and indemnity payments or their relevance for the domestic export sector. A comparison between these different categories shows that Britain, France and Germany do not even remain in the same relative order to each other. Hence the difficulty of devising commonly acceptable criteria which, on top of that, have to be brought into congruence with the limits imposed on export finance.

Table 7.2 Ranking of major OECD countries

	Country	Export guarantees[a]	Country	Premia/Indemnity payments[b]	Country	Guaranteed/ Total exports[c]
1	Japan	-1,992	Canada	2.20	Japan	46.5
2	France	-1,570	Portugal	2.04	France	26.7
3	Germany	-1,299	United States	0.60	Austria	18.8
4	Italy	-943	Netherlands	0.43	Britain	13.6
5	Britain	-483	Austria	0.36	Spain	13.4
6	Spain	-367	Finland	0.32	Italy	10.2
7	Australia	-272	Germany	0.29	Portugal	7.3
8	Austria	-205	Belgium	0.28	Finland	6.8
9	Finland	-22	Sweden	0.28	Australia	6.3
10	Belgium	-21	Spain	0.19	Germany	5.5
11	Norway	-12	Britain	0.16	Belgium	4.1
12	Sweden	0	France	0.14	Canada	3.5
13	Portugal	3	Switzerland	0.13	United States	2.5
14	Switzerland	11	Japan	0.10	Switzerland	2.2
15	United States	20	Norway	0.09	Sweden	2.0
16	Canada	26	Italy	0.09	Norway	1.8
17	Netherlands	101	Australia	0.06	Netherlands	-

[a]US dollar millions, 1992 financial results, 1991 figures for Japan, France, Spain, Australia, US and Canada;
[b]ratio, 1991 figures;
[c]per cent, 1991 figures.

Source: Rambousek, W.H. and Siegrist, M. (1993).

Be that as it may, the middle column of Table 7.2 also indicates that in the early 1990s - with the exception of Portugal and Canada - the ratio between premiums income and indemnity payments is less than one, i.e. none of the systems were self-financing. One remarkable feature is the high ranking achieved by Germany in export guarantee deficits (first column) when it is considered how low a profile this type of business has in terms of percentage of total exports (third column), which provides a good indication that the resources were primarily directed towards high risk markets. By contrast, in the top ranks of column one, we find France and Japan, which is much as to be expected because their high deficits correlate with the large volume of exports they support (third column). These two countries show again the problem of combining the regulation of export finance and credit insurance in one arrangement. Their particular domestic institutional setting favour certain forms of interventions in the economy: France takes a prominent position in finance and guarantees, whereas the Japanese model concentrates much more on the latter version of export promotion (cf. Table 7.1, above).

This empirical evidence is very much a reflection of changes which had already started in the second half of the 1980s, when official agencies extended and refined their instruments in line with the regulatory cycle. A set of new insurance services were offered in order to protect exporters against inflation, cost escalation and fluctuations in exchange rates and several insurers increased the range of risks eligible for cover, introduced guarantees for foreign currency operations and revised their country lists to include economies which were previously off cover. Yet the most important innovation was the introduction of new procedural requirements stipulating a distribution of resources on a *case by case* basis (Brau and Puckahtikom, 1985), and it was this feature which was also incorporated into the Arrangement framework, thus leaving more room for manoeuvre in negotiations between governments. In consequence, there is a lessening of the possibility of exercising international control on auxiliary forms of protection to domestic firms, i.e. those which tend to blur the distinction between insurance and direct financial assistance. A similar effect is produced by the 'nature' of the export insurance business as a whole, since it is first and foremost an area of short-term considerations. The standard time period between the start and the end of a bit is between two and four weeks, and it is extremely difficult to imagine how such short time spans can be accommodated by the conventional mechanisms and usual delays of the bureaucratic process.

Let us now turn to a second area in this policy space. In Section 7.2 above, it was noted that the preoccupation of participants with the question of interest rates gradually shifted towards the issue of *mixed credits*

(Wallén, 1987, p. 102). By combining conventional export credit with development aid funds, it becomes possible to offer a 'blended' interest rate which undercuts the Arrangement matrix. This provides a clear incentive to expand the use of development aid for competition purposes, with this strategy being supported by the rules governing tied aid credit operations and the mixed financing to which they give rise. The aim here is no longer to reduce or eliminate subsidies; on the contrary, the Arrangement actually has the effect of increasing them. In practice, levels of concessionality below 35 per cent are prohibited in all cases, and they must reach a proportion of at least 50 per cent if the destination country happens to be classified among the least developed countries. The notification system then confirms the general thrust of this approach: credit transactions whose level of concessionality is below 50 per cent are subject to prior notification, discussion and matching, whereas credit transactions whose concessionality level is over 50 per cent are not subject to prior discussion and are only reported ex post. Taken as a whole, the Arrangement therefore leads to a somewhat paradoxical situation, in that it aims to eliminate any subsidy on export credits proper, but imposes the use of subsidies on mixed financing. The negotiating positions behind this paradox are well known: certain countries believe that the higher the costs of credit to the lender, the less of it there will be. Equally, the countries most opposed to a hard line also find benefits in the current system because the increase in subsidies ultimately leads to a more generous aid policy.

Not one agency reported lower demand for export credit cover as a result of the increase in the minimum matrix interest rates or the abolition of the matrix rates for Category I countries. Although the basic purpose of the increase in the minimum grant element for mixed credits was to discourage their use, OECD data indicate that the volume of offers has in fact increased. More definitive data on new commitments are not available, and as there may be several competing offers for individual projects, it is difficult to form a proper assessment of the actual level of activity. Nonetheless, there is still a general perception that the increase in the required grant element has not yet led to a decline in mixed credits (Johnson, Fisher and Harris, 1990, p. 16).

The US tried to limit the use of mixed credits in order to gain commercial advantages (cheaper financing offers) over their competitors. They demanded an increase in the official grant element for this type of financing, i.e. an increase in the minimum element of financial or development aid in order to make the mixed credit offers for the supplier countries more expensive, in the hope that the resultant higher burdens for state budgets would prevent competitors from employing this kind of financing. Several agencies have noted that there is a significant number of countries, particularly in Asia, where competition between agencies means that mixed credits are virtually an unavoidable requirement for securing major export contracts. Concern was also expressed that, since there has been precious little increase in the aid budgets of most major industrial countries, the share of foreign aid going to support mixed credits has substantially increased, and in the process, some ODA resources may well have been diverted away from the non-creditworthy poorer countries to those - often middle-income - countries where export credit competition is at its strongest (Johnson, Fisher and Harris, 1990, p. 17; Kuhn et al., 1994, p. 41).

Finally, we can look at several different *sectors* which for one reason or another have not been included in the general agreement (Strange, 1996, p. 126). To begin with, there is the agreement on shipping, which has been accepted by the OECD Council and is therefore a legal instrument of the OECD, although the actual operation of this system is co-ordinated by a working party that functions as a separate body (Cafruny, 1987, pp. 280-1). During 1994, a new ban on subsidies in the ship-building industry was negotiated, including a price codex as well as regulations concerning export credits. More specifically, it requires that Japan renounce its preferential credit terms to their shipyards, that Korea calculate prices according to production costs and that the Europeans call a halt to official subsidies. However, an exception has been made in the case of the United States, who are still allowed to fulfil the conditions of the Jones Act, which demands that internal sea transport be undertaken exclusively on ships produced by their own industries.

In a general situation of surplus capacity, allied to the pressures of large investment decisions and 'superpower' relationships, a more managed solution would appear to be necessary. The agreement concluded between the United States, the European Union, Japan, Korea and the Nordic states is essentially intended to prevent a subsidy war. After the 1970s, Korea - like Japan before it - became one of the largest shipbuilders in the world, and when in 1994 a government decision abolished limitations on the extension and construction of new capacity, other competitors became concerned about their own prospects for further expansion. Above all, it is the European shipbuilders, with a market share of only 20 per cent, who can expect to be the main losers as a result of 'the capacity extension not justified by market reality'. Faced with this situation, the EU and Japan have tried to invoke the principles of solidarity, fairness and international responsibility, warning against a return to the aggressive strategy of *fait accompli* that held sway in the 1970s and 1980s, when crisis conditions provoked most shipbuilding nations into drastically reducing their capacities (with the exception of South Korea who simply took a free ride).

At the same time, the EU has had to delay giving its consent to the agreement, because one of its members, France, has chosen to internally link any decision in this regard to a further extension of subsidies to the steel sector. Yet that is only part of the problem. Even if the agreement does come into effect, a further intensification in competitive pressures is still to be expected, since important shipbuilding countries such as Poland, Romania and China, all of whom operate at extremely low price levels, are not signatories (Frankfurter Allgemeine Zeitung, 1994, p. 11). Despite several efforts undertaken in the national and international arena, to date it has not been possible to introduce effective restrictions.

Secondly, in the field of nuclear power plants and aircraft, the structure of the markets has again heavily influenced the viability of agreements. Here, the OECD Arrangement provides a general umbrella for two sectoral *understandings* that enjoy complementary status (Paragraph 9). Initially, negotiations focused on these industries primarily 'because they were perceived as the most critical areas in need of harmonization'. In the early years of the Airbus consortium, for example, a crucial precondition for its success was market penetration, with the result that European governments were only too willing to offer financing on highly concessionary terms. Likewise, the US was simultaneously experiencing a highly unfavourable trade balance and consequently it too favoured export support measures for its air industry. In the case of the new technology represented by nuclear power plants, the member states by way of contrast believed in the mid-1970s that special restrictions could be established before market conditions stabilised or a credit race began. Nevertheless, considerable difficulties arose because of the high contract values involved and the resulting need for long-term financing. On the one hand, the Europeans preferred credit periods not exceeding ten years, due to their comparatively smaller size of their capital markets, whilst on the other hand, the United States and Canada argued for a maximum repayment period of at least 15 years. At present, almost in the same way as in the case of shipbuilding the aircraft sector presents a bilateral scenario dominated by two main companies. Both Boeing, with a market share of 59.5 per cent and Airbus, with 31 per cent are way ahead of McDonnell Douglas, the second largest American producer. Again in a way analogous to ship-building, the threat of high unemployment and the need to make long-term investment decisions create strong incentives for supporting high-tech areas by stabilising market shares through international regulation.

Market structures, national and producer interests are also important factors in two other areas where there are no regulations in effect, the first example being agriculture. Though a new sectoral group has begun with negotiations, an agreement in this regard has only been formulated for exports below two years, and thus - if ever implemented - would in any case not apply to the grain trade, where credit periods of up to five years are involved. There is also a clear lack of symmetry between exporting nations because of the form in which the subsidies are given: whereas in Europe they take the form of direct price subsidies, the US instead provides support through export credits. Ironically, and in complete contradiction to the GATT negotiations of the Uruguay round, the Europeans are here the more in favour of having restrictive regulations applied within the OECD context. Much less optimistic is the outlook for achieving agreements to put some kind of limits on export subsidies to the arms trade. A recent proposal by the Swedish delegation was rejected out of hand by American negotiators because of its potential interference with national interests and security considerations. More generally, there would seem to be three main reasons as to why it always proves so difficult to make any progress in this area: first of all, few defence ministers take an active interest in seeing such products included within the scope of the guidelines; secondly, as long as the major weapons producers themselves show no propensity to agree, the whole enterprise is very likely to fail; lastly, there is the technical difficulty of mediating between the interests of arms traders who vary significantly in terms of country size.

From what has been said so far, Crawford's (1987, p. 448) conclusion that the regulatory regime 'has grown to be robust and effective in facilitating stable policy co-ordination' can at best only be endorsed in very narrow terms. In the comparatively limited field of interest rate subsidies, the co-ordination mechanisms of the OECD were to a certain extent and for a certain period of time largely self-enforcing. Beyond those limits, the idea that participants were for the most part conforming with rules, and that this had contributed to preventing an export credit race cannot really be reckoned to be a decisive factor - far more important is whether or not the overall amount of public resources going into promotion efforts has been reduced. As our examination of the entire policy space has shown, this is simply not the case: the necessary problem-solving has not taken place. The conclusion that aside from the initial period, policy co-ordination occurred without US dominance, would have to be qualified in so far as there are still several factors which help create a bias, despite the unanimity rule. There is, however, no reason for dissenting from the overall evaluation of the six main rounds of negotiation in the general export credit field, as presented by Blair (1992, p. 60):

> while the United states took the lead in setting the agenda, it did not consistently attain all of its objectives. In some rounds the US obtained most of what it was demanding, in others it gained only some concessions from other

parties, and in still others most of its demands were rejected. When the stated long-range objectives of the United States are examined, however, it appears that the US did obtain most of what it wanted, although it had a very difficult time doing so.

In addition to the historical and institutional factors which have been referred to in the preceding sections, there are two other important elements, which even the regime theorists themselves are obliged to recognise. Firstly, in the agenda setting phase of discussing new proposals, the US could regularly count on the support of Canada and Britain, while other members remained passive. Secondly, and more importantly the North-American capital markets have a much greater capacity for extending long-term credits than their European counterparts (Blair, 1992, p. 71; Moravcsik, 1989, p. 185). Firm evidence that this power resource has actually been put to good effect is provided simply by looking at the gradual development of repayment periods: in the 1970s a credit length of five years was regarded as exceptional, whereas in the 1990s, a period of more than 10 years is no longer thought of as unusual. In much the same way, the data presented in Table 7.3 indicates that it is the US which has experienced the strongest increase in share of developing country imports over a ten year period. This trend implies that demand for credit on the American markets is increasing faster than the overall pace of developing country import growth and that financing institutions such as the Export-Import Bank were able to supply these resources rather than their European competitors.

In the standard account offered by regime theory, the OECD mechanisms work well: despite ever-increasing conflict, the Arrangement has not collapsed and several compromise solutions have been achieved. Yet at the same time, there can be little doubt that this mainly has to be attributed to the fact that the co-ordination of *certain aspects* of official export credit policies have often been in conformity with the interests of other major exporting nations. When the analysis is expanded to take in the policy space developments in the field of insurance, mixed credits and sectoral arrangements, however, the most convincing conclusion is that the obvious increase in export credit volume has gone hand in hand with the competitive use of other promotion instruments. Moreover, neither the existence of official agencies nor the formal expansion of Arrangement rules (from the original 2 pages to 62 in its current form) fit very well with the free-market doctrines. Instead, policy co-ordination through an international institution such as the OECD has only served to multiply the number of opportunities for strategic bargaining between governments desirous to further the interests of their export industries.

Table 7.3   G-7 share of developing country imports[a]

	1983	1984	1985	1986	1987	1988	1989	1990	1991	1992[b]
United States	14.2	14.5	15.0	14.4	14.5	16.0	16.4	15.6	17.3	17.7
Canada	1.5	1.5	1.4	1.4	1.4	1.4	1.3	1.3	1.2	1.2
Britain	4.2	4.1	4.3	4.9	4.2	4.0	3.9	3.9	4.1	3.9
France	4.6	4.4	4.3	4.7	4.6	4.3	4.2	4.6	4.4	4.4
Germany	7.0	6.6	7.0	7.8	7.6	7.1	6.7	7.4	7.4	7.3
Italy	4.1	3.5	3.5	3.5	3.4	3.3	3.3	3.4	3.4	3.5
Japan	12.9	13.6	14.5	15.2	14.9	15.0	14.5	14.5	14.7	15.0
Industrial Countries[c]	59.0	59.1	61.1	62.6	62.7	62.3	61.5	62.0	63.0	63.2
Total Imports[d]	542	543	512	514	592	702	763	864	987	948

[a] per cent;
[b] estimated, April 1993;
[c] excludes former Soviet Union and other non-IMF member countries;
[d] US dollar billions.

Source: Export-Import Bank of the United States (1993, p. 5).

7.4 The Marginal Role of Expertise

According to Blair (1992, p. 70), the overall distribution of resources has not effectively determined either the outcome of negotiations or the impact of export credit agreements, since there has been no attempt to enforce agreements by the use of anything other than issue-specific power resources. Consequently, it can be expected that ideas, as manifested in the form of expert knowledge, play an important role in the whole process. By the same token, and as has been discussed in the previous section, if the matching of subsidy proportions has indeed become irrelevant, with mini-negotiations taking place in their stead, this can be seen as constituting an important change in attitude among the participating parties. On the other hand, the achievements of a system of face-to-face consultations might be the more exaggerated, precisely because it is essentially an ex-post device for bringing different perspectives into line by rationalising what has already happened. Nevertheless, as has been noted above, there has been an obvious shift in emphasis in the shape of paying greater attention to aid financing as a promotion tool.

Going back to the early 1960s, the DAC Secretariat did in fact emerge as an independent force at the same time as American interest in the aid issue was declining (Little and Clifford, 1965, pp. 251-3). By gradually building up expertise in the field of development policy, it managed to succeed in re-defining 'assistance' by means of a set of statistical measures which more accurately reflected the actual costs borne by members, as well as their individual motivations for distributing resources in that area. But, as Prout (1976, p. 365) has remarked, the statistical reformulation brought about 'a more realistic analysis of real burdens borne, but it could not compel nations to change their ways'. At this point, it is worth noting the relevance of *DAC reports* summing up the issue 25 years ago (Prout, 1976, p. 387):

> Donors in general tend to oppose any system of universal rationing or setting of ceilings for export credits, and are equally sceptical about the practicability of establishing general criteria governing the extension of such credits to developing countries, preferring to deal with the problem on a case by case basis.

Ever since then, different DAC definitions of tied, partially tied and untied aid have been rather difficult to put into practice. A recent OECD study estimates the average level of formal tying of total ODA from DAC countries to be approximately 40 per cent or just under, against an estimated figure of 50 per cent when no adjustments are made to incorporate multilateral assistance or to exclude partially untied aid (Jepma, 1991, p. 11). In terms of concrete measures, the DAC formulated some guiding principles in 1983 on the use of subsidies in association with export credits and other market funds, and on acceptable procurement practices in 1986, though neither was to have much effect in reducing the volume of subsidies directed either towards project financing or procurement practices under tied aid. In this respect, a *DAC report* on 25 years of development co-operation concluded (OECD, 1985, p. 241):

> Considering the relative orders of magnitude involved, it is improbable that aid tying provides significant macroeconomic benefits to any donor's domestic employment or bop-aggregates. The case for tying is essentially political rather than macroeconomic.

This section will present some additional examples of technical studies relating to the export credit field which have been conducted within the institutional framework of the OECD, and whose findings and practical implications support a more general criticism as regards deficiencies in the organisation's information base. In the light of these observations, the most recent Arrangement reforms will be discussed, in order to arrive at an overall assessment of the role played by expert knowledge.

A few studies carried out in the early 1980s were inspired by the problems East-West trade was causing to the partners in the Alliance. Both Europeans and Americans held a common belief that finding agreement on technical questions could settle otherwise controversial political disputes, yet the respective suggestions from each side neither supported the American intention to effectively reduce the volume of cheap credit going to the Soviet Union nor favoured European promotion practices. Instead, as a OECD ministerial communiqué recommended, 'credit flows should be guided by the indications of the market' and governments 'should exercise financial prudence without granting preferential treatment' (Crawford, 1987, p. 447). In other words, it was suggesting a greater regulation of the market in order to leave trade relations unaffected by state intervention.

In contrast with such general statements, the Secretariat on occasion proved influential, primarily by proposing compromise solutions when negotiations were deadlocked. After the Consensus was transformed into a formal agreement in 1978, the bulk of the member states remained dissatisfied with its outcome, and though a dispute about country categories was eventually settled by accepting World Bank GNP per capita figures, the setting of fixed interest rates for all currencies without any reference to changing market rates continued to be a matter of some controversy. Further research efforts were therefore directed towards studying the relationship between inflation rates, exchange rates and interest rates. The end result, known as the *Wallén report*, produced a conclusion which argued to the effect that exchange risks, inflation and market rates interacted in such a way that high inflation currencies tended to have high market interest rates and a low exchange risk. In combination with the matrix system of the Arrangement, countries with high inflation currencies and low exchange risks were thus permitted to subsidise to a greater extent than others. Two basic ideas were floated as a potential solution to this problem: either a *differentiated rate system* (DRS) could be introduced, in which a different minimum interest rate based on market rates would be established for each currency, or alternatively, preference could be given to a *uniform moving matrix* (UMM), where a single minimum interest rate for all currencies would adjust automatically according to changes in average market rates (Wallén, 1987, p. 100). The accuracy of this analysis of the problem was never seriously challenged, but only really succeeded in identifying the issues at stake instead of resolving them (Blair, 1992, p. 81). Indeed, it took almost ten years until a combination of the two proposals was introduced in 1987. For the richer (Category I) countries interest rates were to be no lower than market-related rates in the relevant currency, whilst for the intermediate (Category II) and poorest (Category III) countries, agencies could still use a fixed spread, using an SDR-weighted average of market-related rates in the relevant currency.

It seems that the technical studies stemming from the Secretariat tend to have more practical applications when they are focused on marginal technical problems, cases in point being the 1985 study on how to strengthen the transparency of mixed credits practices, or the 1987 proposal to introduce a differentiated discount rate in order to determine the subsidy element in a mixed credit package. In both instances, corresponding modifications to Arrangement rules have taken place in the same year.

By contrast, when experts direct their attention to fields which are central to the deficiencies of the Arrangement in its current form, the dependence on the consent of the member states clearly restricts their activities. As a reaction to the potential substitute effect triggered off by different premium rates in national export insurance systems, a new working group has been set up to clarify the meaning of the various concepts employed in this sector. According to the OECD Secretariat, a disciplining effect should in the first place be achieved by using cash flow questionnaires and analysing the premium setting process, and secondly, by increasing transparency through reporting on financial results and cover policy, thus bringing state behaviour into line with international obligations as expressed in the general GATT principle 'that the level of premia charged for export credit insurance should not be manifestly inadequate to cover long-term costs and losses' (Carmichael, 199, p. 348; OECD, 1991, p. 5). At the same time, the longer-term task of developing guiding principles can only be properly pursued once the OECD Council has approved the report of the working group. In the meantime, the member states remain divided as to whether the GATT *break-even principle* should be the over-riding concern, or if market rates should be used as benchmarks for setting premium levels (Fues, 1994).

Export credit insurance was only one of the areas identified as being in need of reform by one recent study completed under the auspices of the OECD's development centre (Raynauld, 1992). Another example was the interest rate matrix, where the idea was to abolish the differential treatment in country categories and to introduce instead the commercial interest reference rate for all contracts. This would mean that there would no longer be any need to impose maximum maturities, since the calculation of the reference rate would still be able to take into account different country risk premiums and variations in the duration of the loan. In fact, at the end of 1991 the participants in the Arrangement arrived at an agreement precisely along these lines, with an exception in the case of credits to least developed countries. Some of the other proposals in the *Raynauld study* are even more far-reaching. The report argues that official assistance (ODA) should in principle be distributed exclusively in the form of grants in order to eliminate distortions in aid and trade flows, and similarly, that it would be appropriate to prohibit altogether mixed credits which link ODA grants to export credits and make the former conditional upon acceptance of the latter. It also challenges some of those organisational features of the Arrangement that are based on decisions which have already been described in the section on institutional development. For example, since there are many new countries that are in a position to compete with the participants to the Arrangement, but without themselves being constrained by the application of common rules, it is suggested that the scope of the export credit guidelines should be extended to include new members. For similar reasons, the existing sectoral agreements and the currently excluded areas of agriculture and military supplies are considered to require incorporation into the general competition rules of the Arrangement.

As a general precondition for expertise to become influential in the policy process, reliable information first has to be provided by the member states and it is in this area where most problems still continue to exist. The statistics on export credits gathered by the Bank for International Settlements (BIS) and the OECD are compiled on the basis of reports received from commercial banks and export credit agencies. However, there are doubts as to whether the reporting system's use of pre-determined questionnaires adequately reflects business reality and hence, it is necessary to exercise a certain degree of caution when using these statistics for analytical purposes. Although transparency comprises one of the fundamental concepts for the successful working of the Arrangement, the present situation leaves much to be desired for a combination of the following reasons (Xafa, 1987; Johnson, Fisher and Harris, 1990; Johnson, 1991; Raynauld, 1992):

- In the case of bilateral transactions, confidentiality requirements make it virtually impossible to discover the details of export credit financing conditions, even for past operations which are now only of historical interest.
- Since the classification code employed by the OECD does not follow the Standard International Trade Classification (SITC), the available information only refers to the user industries, rather than the exact nature of the exported goods i.e. destination sectors of financing projects are given rather than their content.
- Because stock data are converted into US dollars using the exchange rates prevailing at the end of each period, the respective changes in outstanding debts reflect both the volume of net new lending and valuation changes resulting from exchange rate movements between the dollar and other currencies in which the debt has been contracted. This valuation effect tends to be stronger for officially supported credits, which are believed to contain a larger share of non-dollar currencies than is the case for non-guaranteed bank credits. However, the data fail to indicate the currency composition and in addition, several agencies give the value of their commitments as the size of their contingent liability, which may diverge from the actual value of the loan.
- The data series on the stock of commitments and the stock of supplied credits are affected by variations between agencies in their treatment of arrears and restructured credits. For example, neither France nor Britain, which together account for perhaps one third of all officially supported export credits, has included restructured credits in their reports to the OECD creditor reporting system as these are not the responsibility of the agencies. At the same time, refinanced credits are not reported by these agencies either, whilst other national agencies omit altogether countries that have not rescheduled their debts, or alternatively, file their claims under different categories once the overall responsibility is passed on to the respective government through the payment of indemnities. Thus, the data usually understate the original stock of supplied credits due to the fact that some loans will have been transferred to the official sector.

• All export credit agencies report the commercial component within mixed credits in their returns. Yet, the institutional arrangements for providing mixed credits vary considerably between creditor countries, and in the case of those countries which conduct the financing through combining concessional loans from their national aid agency with commercial export credits, the data on export credits only covers the commercial loans. By contrast, for those countries providing all of the financing in the form of commercial credit supported by cover from the export credit agency and giving additional interest rate support to the lender through their aid agency, the data on export credits covers the whole sum of the mixed credit.

All this begs the question of whether the most recent reform, in which certain facets of tied aid assumed greater prominence, has actually dealt effectively with the deficiencies of the Arrangement (OECD, 1991b, p. 451; Presse- und Informationsamt der Bundesregierung, 1990, p. 430). In November 1991, negotiators agreed on the *Helsinki Package,* which was specifically intended to limit especially the use of mixed credits by the major donors (OECD, 1991a; Jepma, 1994, pp. 129-53). In fact, this new agreement marked an end to traditional approaches which assumed that by driving up the concessionality level, the mixing of subsidy with other sources of finance would become too expensive to circumvent the discipline of the Arrangement. But while the concessionality level increased from 20 per cent to 25 per cent, then from 30 to 35 per cent and even up to 50 per cent in the case of LDC's, the terms for export credits became softer and softer, though without leading to changes in the overall amount of aid spending. Indeed, it was an unintended result that this strategy ended up robbing 'the poorest for the sake of the richer developing countries', because more and more development aid was spent to support attractive contracts with newly industrialising countries.

The new approach implied that 'tied and partially untied concessional or aid credits, except for credits to LLDCs, shall not be extended to public and private projects that normally should be *commercially viable* if financed on market or Arrangement terms' (OECD, 1991, pp. 2-3; emphasis added). The driving force behind this regulation is the desire to attract more commercial funds to environmentally-oriented projects and towards developing countries in general (Deutscher Bundestag, 1995). For example, the relevant procedure is obliged to view most industrial projects as being feasible in purely market terms, whereas infrastructure projects such as schools, hospitals, transport systems and environmental projects are likely to depend on additional resources from aid budgets. Once again, this is a very well-meaning guideline but the question is still how, in practice, the notion of the 'ability to attract commercial finance' can be implemented and enforced (Morrissey, 1993, p. 69).

In the opinion of the OECD (1991, p. 3), the implementation of the rule can be ensured by employing two key tests on aid eligibility: a project should be considered as non-viable, firstly, if it lacks the capacity to generate a cash flow sufficient to cover the project's operating costs and to service the capital employed (with prices in both respects being determined by the market); and, secondly, if after consultation with other participants, it seems reasonable to conclude that it is unlikely that the project can be financed either on market or Arrangement terms. In cases of disagreement, meetings are called in order to arrive at a decision on the basis of criteria such as cash flows, rates of return and feasibility studies. As is true for the Arrangement in general, the basic logic is to draw general conclusions from specific cases which can subsequently be put into the form of guidelines.

However, in a different attempt at reform the participants in the Arrangement have decided after two years of negotiation to prohibit entirely official interest subsidies in the case of commercial credits. As has been noted above, high interest countries have until now been able to continue subsidising their exports to developing countries down to the matrix floor rates, but after a brief transition period such practices will not longer conform to OECD rules with effect from the end of 1995. In addition, a new classification of the country categories will result in an extension of the permissible lengths of credits from 8 1/2 to 10 years for certain Central and East European countries, as well as South Africa. The consequences of this step are essentially twofold: on the one hand these measures should help bring Arrangement terms into greater conformity with the market, and on the other, it simultaneously strengthens the position of the official agencies.

In order to maintain their potential as political instruments, the agencies are forced to keep up with changes in the business environment. In the early 1990s, several official agencies noted an increasing competition from banks in the more profitable markets, because - like their governmental counterparts - commercial banks and other financial institutions involved in trade finance have also tended to become less risk-averse. In particular, private sector banking has recently become very active in supporting trade with the new independent states of the former Soviet Union (CIS). Moreover, for medium- and long-term business with Category I countries (where interest rate subsidies are not permissible), some banks are even prepared to offer longer repayment terms than those permitted under the present terms of the Arrangement. Therefore, there are sound reasons for believing that the most recent reforms are congruent with governmental concerns to build up their position in relation to the private market and to compete with the longer-term maturities now being offered by commercial lenders for similar projects.

In short, ideational factors, as manifested in the ongoing reform of regulations, have had a very uneven influence overall. At least when deriving from proposals by the Secretariat, they have always rapidly been connected with the specific interests of the member states. The above analysis has also raised some doubts as regards the status of the OECD as a forward-looking institution. Quite the opposite: negotiations in the export credit field and their manifestation in regulations seem to be much more the matter of an ex-post rationalisation of market reality rather than an anticipation of future trade relations. The translation of lofty ideas into workable mechanisms has proved to be extremely difficult, and to the extent that this enterprise has been successful, the participants have had to accept the bias in favour of a project specific approach which gives an advantage to those with access to more substantial official financing resources.

7.5   The External Dimension

As we have seen, along with the changes in the matrix system refinements and changes had to be made in the areas of mixed credits and sector agreements, because the participants displayed a tendency to discover new forms of subsidisation once the more traditional ones had been cut off. For their part, the developing countries rejected the whole concept of export credit 'rate fixing' on the understandable grounds that they would prefer to see competition in this area between the major lenders. If the US and the Europeans were actually forced to bid against each other in terms of subsidised export credits, then loan rates would undoubtedly drop, subsidy rates would increase and the LDCs would be the direct beneficiaries. In any case, they do not share the cosy assumption that over and above the political interests and competition between trading states a great deal of attention is given to humanitarian considerations or the development needs of the LDCs.

In particular, when the international credit trade declined during the debt crises some of the Consensus participants argued that the granting of official subsidies from industrialised countries was a reasonable means of maintaining a flow of resources to a wide range of LDCs, which could not otherwise afford to buy on strictly commercial terms. From the LDCs' point of view, the introduction of the matrix system was a step backwards when compared to its forerunner, since the possibility for attaining soft terms within the old Consensus system was reduced at precisely the time when they would have appeared most attractive in the short term and perhaps were most needed because of the heavy debt burden. The effect of the new matrix system has almost certainly contributed to the decrease in new projects in the developing world (Wallén, 1986, p. 272).

In historical terms, it has always been fairly self-evident that trade and aid policies have had to be dealt with in conjunction with each other (Aubrey, 1967, p. 62). Sooner or later, aid donors become faced with the contradiction of giving capital assistance to enable the poorer countries to import more, whilst simultaneously obstructing their exports by means of protective devices, thereby reducing the opportunities for developing countries to pay for more imports by greater export earnings. In the same way as the DAC had to confront the issue of the conditions of assistance, including the duration of trade credits, the Trade Committee has had to weigh up the questions of trade and export finance. Both contexts can be expected to produce the same dilemma: the fact that trade competition with longer-term credits is undesirable, though at the same time, if the terms are too short to match delays in output (from which credits can eventually be repaid), then the whole rhythm of development is potentially threatened. The timing of the two major elements involved - additional production from new facilities created with the help of export credit and the generation of additional foreign exchange through exports - does not necessarily coincide.

In the past, a donor country has quite often resented the fact that its aid has been used to bail out another creditor. The terms under which aid is given are therefore a crucial factor in such a potentially divisive situation, but quite apart from the consequences of competition, the underlying problem of growing indebtedness is a very serious one, because the debt servicing eats up virtually all the export earnings of developing countries. On any reasonable basis, the provision of more and lengthier credits on easier terms ought to be the outcome of the recognition of the problem by OECD members. Expanding credit terms is clearly desirable and would undoubtedly help mitigate these difficulties, albeit without resolving them or preventing the recurrence of crises while the total amount of indebtedness keeps on mounting.

However, it should also be recognised that conflicting objectives are involved here. Unfettered competition tends to make the credits lengthier and the terms softer, which eases the burden of indebtedness in the short run, but equally, it increases the friction between the competing industrial countries, thereby reducing the chances of reaching an overall agreement on the broader trade and aid problems facing the developing countries. Moreover, the extension of terms only provides a temporary relief, because the general 'overhang' of indebtedness increases and unless an effective use of capital resources during the extension period actually generates more foreign exchange for debt servicing, then the final reckoning is merely being postponed a little while longer.

When intergovernmental co-operation was actually put into effect within the OECD, the only facet of the multitude of problems the participants were really interested in was to limit competition between exporting nations in a cartel-like manner (Paul, 1983, p. 174). Whatever the type of agreement reached, supplier credits and buyer credits were and are treated synonymously (Hashek, 1986, p. 288), even though it makes a considerable difference to a project if it only constitutes a good deal for the exporter and the exporting country (regardless of the extent to which it is economically justified and can be eventually repaid from the cash flow it creates), or whether it is also a beneficial deal for the importer and the importing nation. The fact that most agencies lent through commercial banks made it difficult to introduce a realistic system of project evaluation and the supplier credit bias of the insurance agencies has only further exacerbated this deficiency. In OECD negotiations, very little attention has been paid to the implementation of criteria for project financing or to establishing distinctions within the bridge financing of serially produced goods and projects.

At the same time, the separation of concessionary from non-concessionary lending, which has been introduced into the Arrangement has had rather detrimental effects. One discussion of this issue tends to over-emphasise the role of competition in the credit field, seeming to argue that the total demand for investment goods to be bought on credit would be too low to be viable, which may well be the case for industrial countries, but is clearly not true of the Third World (Hashek, 1986, p. 291). Instead, a much closer co-operation between export credit and insurance agencies, and the international, interregional and commercial banks is needed in order to respond adequately to new lending requirements. In consequence, export credit insurance will have to accept project analysis and monitoring on the part of the international and interregional banks if they wish to avoid the same work being duplicated by others. Although risk and liquidity in lending are often dealt with separately by domestic institutions - risk being the domain of the insurer, liquidity that of the banks - both constitute inextricably linked aspects of any lending activity, so in practice close co-ordination between the two is extremely necessary.

Empirically, three broad trends were apparent in the years between 1986 and 1991 (Kuhn et al., 1994). Firstly, officially supported export credits to developing countries grew faster than non-guaranteed commercial bank credits; secondly, guaranteed bank credits were the fastest-growing component of all credits; lastly, the distribution of new credits differed among groups of debtor countries. In relation to the second aspect, it seems that banks were seeking official guarantees for a larger proportion of their trade-related lending to developing countries, most likely in response to a perceived increase in systemic risk. As regards the final point, officially supported credits to countries with debt-servicing difficulties (i.e. those that have rescheduled their debt to official creditors or have incurred external arrears) have outpaced non-guaranteed bank credits to these countries. Both types of credits grew considerably faster for other developing countries, but there the difference in growth rates between the two types was much less striking. In short, as one World Bank official has noted of the relationship between export credits and the debt crises (Xafa, 1987, p. 20):

> There has been a general tendency for the provision of export credit and cover to be out of phase with countries' adjustment efforts. ECA's have tended to carry on providing insurance cover for too long, insofar as it is difficult for them to reject credit applications exclusively on the strength of an unfavourable risk assessment. Competitive pressures have often prevented them from taking restrictive actions before substantial arrears emerge. In the debt rescheduling and recovery phase, the agencies until recently tended to wait too long before resuming insurance cover. Following a rescheduling, they often did not resume cover until well after the adoption of adjustment programs to restore credit-worthiness.

From the early 1980s until the beginning of the 1990s, the negotiations took place in a climate where the East-West divide and the experiences of the debt crises required a limitation in the scale of export finance (Brau and Puckahtikom, 1985). Nevertheless, as has already been pointed out above, the European trading states were able to bridge a slight shortage in finance through a more lax handling of their official insurance business. Together with the changes in Central and Eastern Europe after 1989, a more general upswing in the provision of official long-term finance has come about, though there are two good reasons for being less than optimistic about future prospects in this regard. Firstly, the majority of the new financing resources goes into the emerging markets of East Asia and, secondly, the subsidy issue (or better the national interest issue) has almost been forgotten beneath the welter of political stabilisation arguments. That this situation is undesirable is clear from the experiences to date with Western assistance for the transition of post-communist countries (Ners et al., 1992, p. 39):

> *To date, coordination has remained relatively ineffective* and has rarely strayed beyond the conference room, for three main reasons. First, the G-24

Coordination Unit does not possess resources of its own. Second a large proportion of assistance comes in the form of bilateral tied assistance, which is much more difficult to coordinate than multilateral. Third, the G-24 Coordination Unit has not been very successful in mobilizing joint-financing for projects

In order to improve on this situation, an appointed task force strongly recommended the introduction of complete and up-to-date data on aid assistance totals, because member states are at present reluctant to give such information either to the OECD or to the G-24 Co-ordination Unit. Usually, the data is not broken down into separate categories, which makes comparison virtually impossible, and it seems that national governments deliberately mix commitment with distribution figures in order to publish more impressive (albeit misleading) assistance figures. Indeed, as the task force has remarked, these practices have caused a large amount of disillusionment and have damaged relationships with both recipient governments and their publics. Furthermore, the group suggested banning the use of tied aid assistance to Central Europe, particularly in the form of export credits, and made specific reference to the reform efforts in the Arrangement with regard to Third World countries (Ners et al., 1992, p. 54).

Given all these external factors, it would appear to be a sensible solution to approach the export promotion issue through a forum which can attract greater participation. It can even be suggested that export credit regulations should be seen as a subtle form of non-tariff barriers and hence, as one of the many forms of subsidisation covered by the GATT code, Article 16 of which prohibits:

The provision by governments (or special institutions controlled by governments) of export credit guarantees or insurance programmes against increases in the costs of exported products or of exchange risk programmes, at premium rates, which are manifestly inadequate to cover the long-term operating costs and losses of the programmes.

The grant by governments (or special institutions controlled by and/or acting under authority of governments) of export credits at rates below those which they actually have to pay for the funds so employed (or would have to pay if they borrowed on international capital markets in order to obtain funds of the same maturity and denominated in the same currency as the export credit), or the payment by them of all or part of the costs incurred by exporters or financial institutions on obtaining credits in so far as they are used to secure a material advantage in the field of export credit terms.

While this provision at first sight appears to be fairly straightforward, it nevertheless contains several loopholes. Export credit subsidies are defined by reference to the difference between the level of interest charged by the government lending authority and that which the government would normally have to pay for such funds: no mention whatsoever is made to the ability of an exporter to secure funds at favourable rates. Governments are usually able to borrow at preferential rates that would be highly attractive to any commercial borrower, meaning that the real level of subsidy remains hidden. To determine the true rate of subsidisation, it is necessary to look at the rate offered by government lending institutions to the exporter and compare it to the rate which the exporter could expect to receive for export credits on the open market. In addition, in the case of official insurance agencies, it is not compulsory for additional business taxes to be included in the premium structure. Moreover, subsidisation is also clearly permissible insofar as it is not used to secure 'a material advantage in the field of export credit terms', i.e. if it is intended to match other countries' subsidies and is not attempting to gain any advantage, but is merely trying to maintain the existing market share. However, at no point does the code define the term 'material advantage' and the past history of GATT negotiations suggests that this diplomatic parlance is primarily designed to leave the issue open to further discussion (DeKieffer, 1985, p. 5).

According to the EC interpretation, as long as a subsidised export credit does not infringe the OECD guidelines, it does not constitute an export subsidy at all and cannot be denounced as such by any other country with contrary domestic tariff provisions. The US, Canada and Australia, on the other hand, argue that while subsidised export credits which are in conformity with OECD guidelines may indeed be unassailable in terms of the Subsidy Code itself, they can nevertheless be considered as constituting export subsidies and are fully recognisable in that form under the countervailing tariff laws of the signatory parties (Hufbauer and Shelton Erb, 1984, pp. 72-4). But because of the nature of the problem, this does not represent a solution: countervailing duty procedures are inadequate as a remedy for export subsidisation because the latter is basically project-specific and does not involve an ongoing flow of commerce in which the subsidy element on each item can be calculated upon its entry into the country. In most cases, the damage will already have been done earlier, i.e. with the winning of a contract. Similarly, any attempt at applying the GATT dispute settlement procedure is likely to prove illusionary because of a general unwillingness to allow any kind of effective retaliation. Once the dispute settlement panel reaches a conclusion, it is then referred to the GATT itself or to a relevant committee, at which point the issue is either resolved by consensus or, if one litigant raises objections, is simply blocked altogether.

In the final analysis, because of the comparatively unclear status of the export promotion issue, most participants have readily accepted the OECD regulation for practical reasons. A more rigorous treatment oriented primarily towards problem-solving would, however, redirect our interest back to the domestic context, firstly because a unilateral application of sanctions may ultimately be the only viable option, and secondly because if resources from the aid budget are used to promote exports, that implies that the democratic process is not working as expected.

PART IV
CONCLUSION

8 The Possibility of Reform

This concluding chapter brings together the recurring themes from each chapter in order to assess their importance from a comparative perspective. This book has employed a soft rational choice approach to the analysis of export promotion policies in Britain, France and Germany, making particular reference to the role of international institutions, and has essentially dealt with three interrelated themes: co-ordination, expertise and reform. By contrast, the conclusion is structured in such a way as to overcome that analytical distinction between the different levels. Section 8.1 discusses the concept of applied co-ordination, Section 8.2 the influence of expert knowledge, while Section 8.3 looks at the possibility of successful reform. Section 8.4 then puts forward some normative proposals.

8.1 Co-ordination

This book started off from the assumption that international institutions can have potentially detrimental effects, that is to say, that they are third parties with their own particular interests involved in how a dispute between their members is settled, contrary to the assumption of the majority of international relations research, which sees international institutions as facilitators of co-ordinated solutions. The argument of the book differed significantly from the bulk of regime-type analyses in that it took the role of institutions seriously, emphasising the number of ways in which they can complicate co-ordination problems, and describing their dependency on certain specific mechanisms in both the national and international contexts.

The concept of the third party and its logical implications has important consequences for the study of international relations, for at least two reasons. To begin with, this is a legitimate, coherent and complementary method for the study of institutions. Indeed, the study of politics, law and economics would be a fairly worthless undertaking if it were not directed towards the concrete improvement of policy-making (i.e. problem-solving through co-ordination). For any such improvement to become possible, however, it is obviously necessary to point out the existing deficiencies within individual institutions, to show where they go wrong and to analyse their failures. In this sense, it constitutes an integral part of critical social science and provides a genuine impulse for further interdisciplinary research.

The second and more important reason for the significance of the third party concept is that it brings out some serious omissions and errors in the reasoning behind international institutions. The normative notion of neutrality provided by the standard rational choice framework produces strong theoretical constraints, in which the form of the analysis is contradicted by the real world around us. For example, the well-known public relations activities which the European Community embarked upon during the single market project clearly manipulated both the style and the content of communication on this topic between the member states (Narr, 1989). Particularly with regard to the introduction of a common export promotion policy, official sources presented very one-sided and over-optimistic assessments of the problem. The various attempts to establish a monopoly and initiate internal competition, as predicted by some of the literature on political entrepreneurship, have shed new light on the Commission's activities in this policy-area, with the result that the interpretation of legal provisions, delegation to international institutions and ongoing coalition-building with national administrations are now investigated in new ways. The common denominator to all these potential lines of analysis is the belief that reasoning on the basis of transaction cost reduction alone is insufficient, and that a more realistic scenario demands international institutions be given an actor capacity.

From a policy-making perspective, it is possible to analyse the impact of international institutions by drawing on standard tools used for the study of comparative government, although a prerequisite for any such study is to decide on exactly what constitutes adequate empirical evidence. Instead of employing sophisticated statistical techniques or more formal methods, I have relied on raw data from official sources, which were then translated into uniform monetary units and linked to the institutional features of national export promotion systems (cf. Appendix). It is of course perfectly possible to correlate changes in export subsidies with purely domestic factors, but what these kinds of analysis omit is the interaction with international institutions, whose intervention in the form of regulations in domestic modes of resource transfers is a central factor. Instead, a process-oriented, retrospective analysis provides a sufficient means of reaching conclusions about departures from solutions appropriate to the problem in question.

The third party concept benefits immeasurably from incorporating contextual factors into the abstract reasoning of game theory (Rieger, 1986;

Kydd and Snidal, 1993, p. 114). Although there have been attempts to include institutional variation within the scope of formal models, these would have to be criticised as being too limited in terms of their practical applicability, and this book suggests two good reasons why such conclusions are justified. The first of these was presented in Chapter 2, where it was argued that institutions tend to follow a distinct organisational logic which prevents effective co-ordination between them. For example, whenever the European Community incorporates regulations from the OECD into its policy formation, it thereby gives American interests an even stronger legal backing then they originally had in the national systems of its members. The second stage in the reasoning was provided by the empirical chapters in the book (Chapters 3, 4, 5), which concretely demonstrated the explanatory power of the negative co-ordination hypothesis.

In the case of each national system, the output of the domestic co-ordination process displayed a remarkably similar pattern: while the costs of subsidy programmes are comparatively diffused, because of their financing through the state budget, the benefits accrue almost entirely to large-scale enterprises; on balance, more rather than less intervention takes place, differing only in respect of the amount of emphasis that is given to particular promotion instruments. Another similarity between the three countries has consisted in the arguments presented in defence of promotion policies namely that, 'we do it, because our competitors do it' - hence the argument in favour of mutually beneficial policy co-ordination through international institutions.

In Chapter 2, a special dilemma arose out of the assumption that international institutions perform the function of regulatory policy co-ordination because, in the examples of the European Community and the OECD, this involved the use of quite distinct mechanisms, which meant that it was the relevance of particular institutional choices that defined the agenda of the book.

In the case of the EC, the co-ordination mechanisms are based on legal provisions where the overriding goal of integration dictates following an approach that makes it possible to operate in the face of market reality. This strategy is reflected in a preference for the reorganisation of national economic system rather than a concern for the competitive position of firms. In the case of the OECD, co-ordination mechanisms are based on sanction-free value judgements. The maintenance of the existing trading system requires little more than voluntary agreements on national policy measures, which finds expression in a preference for economic relations between private enterprises competing on international markets. When such substantial differences exist between the two institutions, it can only be expected that they will also be translated into the type of policies enacted.

Chapter 6 investigated the restrictive interpretation of regulations concerning the use of export promotion instruments. Both the behaviour of the European Court and the Commission can be explained by use of the third party concept because neither of them has performed the role of a neutral arbiter. If co-ordination in the European Community is really intended to achieve the same results as in the OECD, then it would not be possible to maintain the claims to exclusive Community competencies. By the same token, the distinction between internal and external competition only makes sense if the interests of firms in foreign markets are ignored. Likewise, it might be the case that the interest constellation of the member states points to a co-ordinated, gradual reduction in state aids, but the Commission's rigorous approach to the question of state subsidies fits badly into an economic environment where the number of insolvent firms is constantly on the rise.

Chapter 7 then focused on the much less formal regulatory framework of the OECD. In most of the literature on international regimes, the guidelines for officially supported export credits are presented as having established an effective and stable form of policy co-ordination that has kept subsidies competitively neutral. If this description were accurate, we would expect that the respective rules avoided producing biases in favour of individual members, and similarly, that they excluded ways of circumventing their central objectives. However, an analysis of concrete co-ordination mechanisms indicates that this is not in fact the case. One central function that is usually ascribed to a regime is the formulation of common or shared principles, and if this was accepted into the analysis as an uncontested starting point, then there would be little difficulty in examining the content of international regulations: the incorporation of incompatible and contradictory aims would not become a matter of much concern.

The third party hypothesis and its contextual interpretation provided the principal instrument for understanding why previous research has had such difficulties in correctly evaluating the role of international institutions. Indeed, Chapter 6 demonstrated that it was the Commission's own interests that lay behind the repeated efforts to 'co-ordinate' the export promotion policies of the EC member states. The arguments presented in support of this hypothesis were based on various official documents submitted over the last thirty years. In general, the Commission, sometimes hampered by the Parliament, usually suggests the creation of new institutional structures with decision-making procedures that are apt to increase its own influence, but in view of the resistance of member states to the transfer of comprehensive policy-making powers, more strategic proposals have gradually begun to concentrate on small segments of export promotion policy. However, it was argued that this does not indicate either a fundamental break with, or a major re-interpretation of, functionalist logic, but in fact represents its confirmation. Instead of coming up with problem-solving responses, concrete institutional choices reflect the intention to create economic pressures which then justify imposing centralised solutions on the member states. Therefore, there are at least two substantial doubts surrounding co-ordination efforts at the European level that have yet to be dispelled: first of all, the legal architecture of the common commercial policy ultimately prevents the application of an international, rather than an internal market, solution; secondly, the likely outcome of the use of an independent spending budget is to reinforce the subsidy pattern of the national systems. Both factors illustrate the vertical and horizontal disintegration of the policies mentioned in Chapter 2.

The third party hypothesis and the corresponding analysis of co-ordination mechanisms also revealed one or two misleading arguments in the case of conventional international organisations. Chapter 7 discussed several different assessments of the OECD's role in limiting the use of export subsidies, all of which arrived at positive conclusions by arguing that competition had been stabilised and became fairer through the imposition of a strict regulatory framework. The chapter suggested that this description cannot possibly be correct for the whole policy space and supplied empirical evidence to demonstrate its invalidity over a longer period of time. The comparative analysis of the national promotion systems had already pointed to the widespread use of substitute measures for export credits and, in the case of Germany and France, even including their further extension. The reasons for the failure of welfare-improving policy co-ordination that were suggested in Chapter 7 were quite different to those found in the European context. For the OECD, the market remains the single most important co-ordination mechanism, which is then merely supplemented by administrative procedures. Hence, those states with the strongest economies will gain the most benefits from the system, and the introduction of decision-making on a case by case basis in the field of aid finance did indeed strengthen the bargaining position of the United States. Yet, in less competitive market sectors such as insurance and certain other fields, little or no institutional choice was available. This general finding can on the whole be reconciled with the organisational aim to 'contribute to the expansion of world trade', albeit with one qualification: the recorded import shares of developing countries prove that it is the United States, rather than the Europeans, who are the biggest beneficiaries.

The third party hypothesis in relation to co-ordination problems therefore encouraged the selection of national, supra- and international case studies, it helped test the theoretical arguments against the empirical material and was then responsible for some of the more important conclusions in this book.

8.2   Expertise

By combining the liberal, neo-realist and structuralist theories of international relations, it was possible to include expert knowledge as a variable in the international policy-making process, which represents a synthesis different from the application of any one theory in that it links institutional variation at the domestic and international level with the potential influence of ideational factors. Two of the theories examined in Chapter 1 (the liberal and neo-realist) implied following the same strategy, i.e. the use of incremental changes to improve policy co-ordination, whilst the third (structuralism) maintained that such changes only served the interests of established elites.

These theories are usually employed to try and comprehend or explain international phenomena; no attention is paid to their relevance for policy analysis. This book adopted a different perspective and was thus able to demonstrate that when the three paradigms are understood as being complementary to one another, the role of expertise becomes particularly problematic. Liberal institutionalists have identified international institutions as a classic location of epistemic communities, whereas realists have tended to trace the production of instrumental knowledge back to national interests, and structuralist to underline the ideological elements that are connected to the acquisition of new ideas. None of these approaches succeeds in giving an adequate description of policy formulation across various different levels, so Chapter 1 therefore developed two fundamental propositions, which were then used throughout the book. Following the line of argument taken by North (1990), the proposition of path dependence attempts to relate the institutional incentive structure to the direction taken by expert knowledge on specific policy issues. The second proposition, which refers to the policy space, deals with the substance of that knowledge: in order to make worthwhile recommendations, the analysis needs to focus on a whole range of closely connected policies.

By placing the analytical emphasis on regulatory policy co-ordination, both these propositions can be fully corroborated using concrete examples.

On the one hand, the recruitment of experts and their job definition is closely bound to the political purposes of international institutions because of the phenomenon known as 'bureaucratic capture', and on the other, the selective use of advice implies ignoring the possible repercussions of policy choices and often means reviving the process of bargaining on a case by case basis. Moreover, institutions at the international level merely pool the specialised knowledge available in national systems, which exacerbates the asymmetric power of particular groupings and in turn, conflicts occur within these groups since participants will tend to favour regulations that benefit their own industries.

In the British system of export promotion, policy formulation involves many government departments and - in the case of official guarantees - with an advisory council. If a realist approach were adopted, it would become very difficult to detect the interministerial conflicts and sectional interests behind the definition of 'national' interests. For example, the uneven influence of experts from the banking sector and export industries has been institutionalised to an extent that large firms have benefited most from subsidies, especially in the form of tied aid. Other expert opinions, as expressed in reports to Parliament and which challenge the dominant mode of public spending, have no immediate institutional impact and their views concerning the negative welfare effects of state intervention in the export sector were rejected in favour of arguments justified in terms of the imperatives of international competition.

Policy formulation in the French system is the task of interministerial committees, but without any direct advice from the finance or export sectors. Here, it is the occurrence of other institutional factors, both within the governmental hierarchy and the system of corporate management, responsible for policy outcomes favouring major industrial groups. In particular, export credit insurance became the target of criticism from non-governmental groups who were providing more information to the public about its political dimension. Several Members of Parliament demanded greater transparency, in order to allow for a full evaluation of the broader consequences deriving from the promotion system, but these efforts only resulted in a series of discussions about adequate means of control. The form and scope that the required expertise should take itself became a matter of dispute, while the definition of national interests still lies in the hands of the established committee structure.

German policy formulation in the case of export guarantees resides in an interministerial committee which also consults a group of external advisers, who are recruited from firms in the export sector and the major banks. In the recent post-unification phase, the increasing costs of official credit insurance has led to a reassessment of the overall role of export subsidies.

A study initiated by the Ministry of Economics questioned the use of the instrument for political ends, but nonetheless still considered it as necessary in order to compensate for the promotion activities of competitors. The discussion in Parliament focused on the introduction of additional criteria such as sustainable development and human rights into distribution procedures, which would require the institutionalisation of advice from non-governmental organisations through membership on the expert committee. These demands were rejected by the government, who argued that the current system of interministerial co-ordination already incorporates non-trade related factors into the decision-making process.

Despite their various differences, all three case studies share the same characteristic that the knowledge held by particular groupings has become an integral part of the decision-making process behind the distribution of subsidies. Again, in all three countries, a range of alternative expertise is available that is more critical of the dominant mode of government support for particular industries, with these counter-arguments paying greater attention to the broader political, economic and social repercussions of public intervention in the export sector. However, the confrontation between these different positions has not attained the level of institutionalisation, e.g. in the form of procedural modifications or access to advisory councils. The question therefore arises as to exactly how expert knowledge influences the international policy process. In other words, is the dominant pattern of interest group influence - as established in the domestic context - altered by delegation to non-national institutions?

Chapter 6 tried to answer this question by using a series of official expert reports undertaken by the Policy Co-ordination Group for Export Credits, a European interest group (UNICE) and an international non-governmental organisation (ICIA). The evidence supported the propositions concerning path dependence and bureaucratic capture, in contrast to the liberal and realist theories, which were unable to account for the role of expertise in policy formation. In reaction to criticism from outside the EC's institutional ensemble, the Commission made some adjustments to its general strategy, in the form of accepting legal differentiations in the treatment of the insurance of exports to non-OECD countries and of 'political risks'. This incremental change was introduced despite the fact that it was inconsistent with the Court's *Tubemeuse decision* concerning the relevance of third markets to internal competition. The documents used also suggest that other objections were ignored because they ran contrary to the political aims of the Commission. For example, the idea of an 'escape clause' was rejected since it would have protected the right to correct market failures at the national, rather than the European, level and by the same token, the *level playing field* concept was maintained in the area of political risk insurance, notwithstanding the inability of the private market to take on the resulting obligations. The consensus of opinion expressed by both UNICE and ICIA members lacked sufficient influence to encourage a move away from the harmonisation goal.

The decisive role played by the Community's internal expert reports indicate that the same dilemma as that occurring in the national context reappears at the European level. Policy recommendations which suggest problem-solving policies rarely survive beyond the agenda setting phase. In this respect, the findings of the *Stolzenburg report* were twofold: first, when trying to interpret obligations deriving from Community law, the Commission lacks an understanding of the complexity of national export promotion systems; second, the extension and improvement of pre-existing co-ordination techniques would be sufficient to deal with the growing number of export transactions. However, these conclusions were not embraced by the official discourse, which is much as to be expected from our theoretical hypothesis. Likewise, the *Tuffraut report* proved a similar point from a different direction by examining internal conflicts among experts and their procedural settlement through acceptance of the majority view. The results of the final report were in fact already predetermined in so far as the goal of harmonisation had to be accepted by all participants as the main focus of their discussions from the very beginning. Again, the path towards an integrated solution was reinforced by agreeing to the concept of the *level playing field* in connection with an enhanced status for the Policy Co-ordination Group. Thus, by replacing the heads of the respective expert groups and by making concessions to the French and British positions, the Commission's basic objective of harmonisation was able to prevail over institutionally less demanding proposals.

In Chapter 7, expert studies carried out within the institutional framework of the OECD were used to further substantiate the claim about path dependence. As before, policy recommendations directed towards practical problem-solving do actually exist, and these put forward arguments in favour of regulations dealing with the whole policy space of export promotion. On condition that mixed credits were prohibited, competition rules extended and new members admitted, most of the present deficiencies in the OECD Arrangement could be avoided. However, the most elementary requirements for the success of these proposals are lacking. For example, because the aggregate data provided by the member states are open to manipulation, their analytical value remains very limited, with the consequence that experts are obliged to concentrate their efforts on individual contracts in order to arrive at general guidelines. In practice, this found expression in the idea of 'commercial viability', which replaced the previous strategy of increasing 'concessionality levels' in aid finance, and thus confirmed our theoretical expectation that regulatory policy co-ordination tends to follow a specific path, at the same time as entailing additional negotiations. Indeed, case by case decision-making has a long-standing tradition within the OECD's Development Assistance Committee, and the new procedure necessitates dealing in precisely such a way with the question of the availability of finance at market conditions.

The expert reports initiated by the OECD helped contribute to incremental changes in the regulatory framework and a number of problem re-definitions and compromise solutions suggested by the organisation were successfully implemented, albeit only on issues of comparatively minor importance. As regards matters of greater significance, the influence of independent expertise is limited due to the divergence of interests among the member states and the attempts to develop new guidelines in the area of export credit insurance are a good case in point. Very much like the discussions in the European Community, the different characteristics of the national promotion systems determine attitudes towards policy recommendations, but in contrast to the EC experts, the OECD Secretariat invokes the *break-even principle* in order to regulate the use of state guarantees as a subsidy instrument. Aside from specific (national) interests, therefore, the production and influence of expertise is closely bound to concrete institutional contexts. The account presented here does not attempt to deny the general influence of ideas over time, though the constant emphasis on markets means that the OECD's advice inevitably gives an advantage to the United States, in its position as the strongest player in this arena.

All the results thus point to the same conclusion, namely that expertise matters in ways that are dependent upon the institutional structure, but its impact across different institutional settings will often be very similar, because of the focus on single policy issues, even if it differs according to the direction which individual policy recommendations take. When viewed in isolation, the case of the European Community provides some support for the structuralist theory of international relations, whereas in the case of the OECD, the realist approach looks more convincing. Yet, when studied in combination with the national level, both these rather one-dimensional interpretations are found wanting.

8.3   Reform

The literature on ideal-design usually proposes a set of distinct criteria as the basis for the institutional choices made by state actors for dealing with interdependence problems. Chapter 1 of this book investigated one of the logical repercussions of those problems, namely the possibility of successful reform, and here the most important aspect of this discussion was probably the inclusion of findings from policy-oriented research. In addition, Chapter 1 formulated a conceptual revision of the problem by incorporating the role of transaction benefits and redistributive institutions into the analysis, which constitutes a particularly important innovation because regime theory usually focuses on transaction costs and efficiency gains. For Tsebelis (1990), for example, institutions regularly produce particular policy outcomes and can be modified according to the information available about future events; for Sandler and Cauley (1977), efficient resource allocation can be ensured by adjusting institutional structures until the sum of marginal transaction benefits equals the sum of marginal transaction costs; Haas (1990) argues that institutional evolution becomes possible through learning processes which use several different time horizons simultaneously. I have argued that it is much more fruitful to recognise the existence of different kinds of institutions at the domestic and international levels, and when studying interaction between them strategic behaviour aimed at realising higher individual benefits must be considered. This leads to the conclusion that where conditions allow this kind of opportunism the attempts at reforms using the channels of international institutions will aggravate the original policy problem.

The empirical chapters on export promotion policies considered national system characteristics as exogenously given and studied the firm-government relationship within the existing institutional framework. Each chapter demonstrated how foreign policy interests intertwine with economic policy instruments in order to gain advantages in the international competition for market shares. However, some of the actors were not completely satisfied with the outcomes produced by existing institutions and pressed for reforms. The study of institutional change within national systems then showed how this provided the opportunity for a deliberate strategy of circumventing international regulations.

The argument can be made that domestic promotion systems are specifically designed to allow for the flexible use of promotion instruments, and institutional variation at the unit level can therefore be expected to have an independent impact on the direction that the respective reform measures take. In the case of Britain, for example, official export credit insurance and finance is provided by a government department with the financial subsidy coming exclusively in the form of an interest rate support scheme. Moreover, a significant proportion of aid finance is under the joint control of the Overseas Development Administration and the Department of Trade and Industry. In France official export credit insurance is instead the responsibility of a joint stock company in which state banks and insurance companies are the major shareholders. At the same time, the task of providing export and aid finance rests with a special export bank which is active both on its own account and on that of the Treasury. Finally, in the case of Germany, it is a private company that carries out export credit insurance on behalf of the state, while official export and aid finance is organised by a state bank, which is responsible to the Ministries of Economics and Economic Co-operation. Despite their formal diversity, all these systems have in common the fact that the distribution of resources can be officially linked to the provision of insurance cover by national agencies: hence the possibility of shifting subsidies from one promotion instrument to the other, depending upon the external restrictions imposed by international agreements.

In Chapters 3, 4 and 5, a range of examples relating to the political dimension of promotion policies demonstrated that - contrary to previous assumptions about domestic market failure - intervention by governments in fact favour the implementation of their own industrial and foreign policy goals. Each system allowed ad hoc modifications to procedural regulations if those were necessary for internal or external reasons, and various statements by leading politicians clearly suggest that support for domestic industries in the form of opening up markets abroad will continue to be a central concern of their activities in the foreseeable future. As a result, the interest constellation between the major European trading states is neither stable nor similar in terms of their relationships to importing countries and regions. In addition, the empirical evidence on country exposure and regional distribution - despite its limitations - further reinforced that conclusion.

In Britain, the government pushed for reform along the lines of the *level playing field* concept because official insurance services were not proving competitive. Equally, representatives of the banking sector, the private insurance market and major exporting firms were able to express their own preferences as to what institutional changes should be introduced. The outcome was that a part of the insurance guarantee department was privatised, at the same time as new procedural regulations were applied to the remainder. In so doing, the British system consolidated the interests of financial capital by means of establishing a redistributive institution, while the system characteristics enable the government to deal effectively with the resistance of industrial interests. Both the limited policy reversal in the shape of a reinsurance facility and the exclusion of aid finance from reform efforts can be interpreted in this way.

In the case of France, the Ministry of Economics and Finance argued for reform in terms of the concept of *libéralisme organisé* in order to compensate for the effects of its privatisation programme on the domestic support system. However, the failure of the reform measures initiated by the Bank of France indicated that government gives the expansion of trade priority over the conduct of monetary policy. On the other hand, when these two sets of interests converge with those of major French insurance companies and banks, the obstacles to institutional change disappear. In fact, the Ministry of Economics and Finance restructured the capital composition of the official insurance agency in order to ensure that export promotion remains entirely under national control. In the finance sector as well, the introduction of a new foreign exchange scheme managed to successfully accommodate the interests of exporting firms. Thus, the French institutions of export promotion can be considered to be efficient in so far as they cultivate the traditional relationship between financial and industrial capital.

Finally, the German Ministry of Economics urged for reform according to the idea of *Ordnungspolitik* in order to better adapt its official insurance system to those of its European competitors. A coalition of leading interest groups were unable to prevent changes in the premium system concerning the formation of new risk categories, but the introduction of an additional guarantee facility to mobilise finance from private capital markets successfully placated the demands from the banking and industrial sector. Furthermore, some modifications to the legal provisions relating to the tying of national exports and the selection of target countries produced a realignment between foreign policy interests and those of industry. Thus, the development financing infrastructure constitutes an example of a 'new deal' type redistributive institution because it was able to bring together parts of the previous winning actors (government) with the previous losers (banks and industry) in order to strengthen their joint position in external markets.

All three case studies dealt with national responses to increasing budget deficits resulting from the use of subsidy instruments in support of domestic industries, and showed the resilience of microeconomic systems of export promotion through their successful anticipation of reform attempts by international institutions. Since institutional change always depends on country-specific variables, even seemingly identical problem definitions can still lead to divergent policy outcomes, especially because states maintain their room for manoeuvre by giving different weight to each promotion instrument. Lastly, these findings raise serious doubts as to the capacity of international institutions to reduce state subsidies, and these can be summarised in the following paragraphs.

The general outline of the European Community's institutional development was described in Chapter 6, where it was shown how the attempted reforms reflected the organisational self-interest in a common trade policy, and this also helped explain why problem-solving reforms became impossible (because the proposed or implemented institutional changes contradicted the overall aim of co-ordination). All the historical examples mentioned - the setting up of the first working group, the passing of directives, the incorporation of OECD rules through Council decisions and the plans for the European Export Bank - point to this conclusion, and the impression is confirmed by the lack of attention paid to the potential repercussions for the competitive position of member states from the imposition of tighter institutional arrangements.

The institutional development of the OECD was the subject of Chapter 7, which demonstrated that the adopted reforms were essentially determined by American interests, parading under the guise of 'fair' rules of competition. Once again, therefore, real problem-solving was obstructed, that is to say that the institutional changes avoided adopting universal approaches to the reduction of export subsidies. The very foundation of the OECD had already implied that each promotion instrument would come under different jurisdictions, either of the Development Assistance Committee or of the GATT. Later on, when the first Consensus agreement between the major exporting countries was achieved, one of its main features proved to be the omission of previously regulated support measures. It is for this reason that the relationship between international organisations is so decisive to a proper understanding of institutional reform.

What is more, these kinds of organisational issues have to be viewed in conjunction with concrete policy problems: in this area international institutions are not merely incapable of dealing with interdependence problems, they actually create externalities themselves. Both Chapters 6 and 7 cited a number of instances where the political nature of export credits was paramount, and how, when dealing with third countries, the Community's as well as the OECD's organisational structure clearly favours business interests inside the member states. In the case of the former, the goal of a common trade policy offsets the subsidy issue; in the latter, state subsidies are justified on the basis that they help stabilise countries with economic adjustment problems.

The standard frameworks of ideal design theories thus lack the criteria for providing either accurate descriptions of, or practical solutions to, the problems caused by the reform process in different institutional settings. While the 'nested games' approach has the capacity to cope with institutional responses at the domestic level, the lack of information on the part of the EC as regards the outcome of a common trade policy has not lead to efficient institutional choices at the international level. Moreover, the structures that have gradually developed cannot really be considered to be the result of learning processes, because with the passing of time interorganisational co-ordination has actually become less likely due to parallel institutional changes. Finally, the reforms that have been implemented have ignored the need for simultaneous mutual adjustment in order to avoid negative cross-effects in relation to the entire control system of export subsidies.

8.4 Neutrality

Until now, the results of the empirical chapters have been used to underline the validity of our theoretical framework, and this final section, explores the broader implications of this approach and tries to move beyond its application to specific policy problems. In order to contribute more effectively to problem-solving, international institutions would have to reverse domestic distribution patterns, where the costs of government policies are widely diffused but the benefits tightly concentrated. However, from what has been argued above, it follows that the workings of their co-ordination mechanisms are unable to fulfil that task in certain issue-areas. Therefore, it can be suggested that the answer to deficiencies in international policy-making lies in the domestic sphere. In practical terms, this means allowing for symmetrical co-ordination by giving non-business interests an equal standing in governmental committees and advisory councils, and respecting the principle of neutrality by the establishment of rules which ensure that 'all interests are represented, fairly and effectively, in proportion to the strength of their legitimate claims' (Goodin and Reeve, 1989, p. 205).

A very similar conclusion can be found in recent proposals to try and deal with the lack of a problem-solving capacity at the European level, as presented by Scharpf (1996, p. 18). Because the drive towards economic liberalisation and regulations against distortion of competition could gain 'constitutional force' through the supremacy of Community law, the domestic balance among the competing policy objectives behind economic intervention has been off-set. Scharpf (1996, p. 35) suggests removing competition law from EC Treaty provisions in order to protect national freedom of action under globalised market conditions. Yet, as this book has shown, in terms of policy outcomes the member states would still be able to pursue their own policy preferences anyway. At the same time, the independent ability to continue with the use of subsidies was achieved by internal adjustments, so for both these reasons, the more realistic attempts at reform would have to focus on procedural modifications in the domestic decision-making centres. But what role does that leave for international institutions?

Ideally, it is possible to distinguish between the negative and positive neutrality of international institutions: where the former simply requires that a third party neither hinder nor help either side in a particular dispute, the latter is more demanding. Positive neutrality 'is a matter of ensuring that the rules of the game are observed in equal measure' by the parties with conflicting interests (Jones, 1989, p. 23). Which of the two conceptions should actually apply depends upon the institutional context and can only be answered with reference to the respective organisational goals. In the case of the European Community, for example, positive neutrality is inappropriate since the rules in themselves already constrain the member states to follow a specific path towards an ever closer union. Therefore, it seems to make sense for Community institutions to refrain completely from activities in the area of export promotion, and there are several good reasons why negative neutrality should prevail over some of the more ambitious, normative conceptions of neutrality.

In theory, neutrality can be achieved through the operation of perfectly competitive markets: according to O'Donnell (1989, p. 39), markets are neutral if 'the same prices, and other conditions are offered to all potential purchasers or suppliers of a particular good or service, subject only to differences in transaction or transport costs'. The general principles of the OECD, for example, could be understood as an attempt to avoid the preferential treatment of particular industries and countries. In the case of export subsidies, however, this intention has not been successfully translated into workable arrangements; even where competitive elements can be reintroduced into the markets for capital goods, they still 'tend to preserve the inequalities and biases inherited from earlier periods' (O'Donnell, 1989, p. 45). Consequently, Goodin and Reeves (1989, p. 8) have argued for solutions in the form of 'countervailing measures, which themselves are non-neutral' but which are nevertheless capable of achieving the desired result in the long run. Even so, the inherent risks in such a strategy are similar to the problems found in most models of strategic trade policy, and governments cannot be expected to intervene only when the specific assumptions of these models apply (Stegemann, 1989, p. 90).

International institutions with limited memberships cannot be reckoned to be well-qualified to address distributional asymmetries caused by the operation of markets: at best, they can only facilitate a convergence of interests among one group of states against the interests of another group of states. Whereas in private law contracts to the detriment of a third party are forbidden, institutional variation in international relations positively encourages this type of arrangement. Due to its organisational characteristics, the OECD merely exacerbates the problem of non-neutrality, a danger that was recognised by a number of oil exporting countries as early as the 1970s. They therefore demanded that the preferential treatment of developing countries as regards the question of the business environment should become part of a New Economic World Order, especially because the contract relations associated with the export of large-scale capital goods result in an unfair advantage to the supplier countries (Seidl-Hohenveldern, 1977, p. 171). At that particular point in time, however, the international codification of an *inegalité compensatrice* seemed much more attractive than the foundation of international courts or arbitration boards.

After the failure of global approaches to co-ordination, primarily because of the resistance of the United Nations system to institutional reform, regional organisations seemed to offer the most promising forum for meeting the demands of the developing countries. Again, the Community's own self-interest in the establishment of an independent European agency helps to explain the positive reaction to some of the proposals made in the area of export credit insurance (Seidl-Hohenveldern, 1977, p. 171). The basic idea was to allow state agencies or firms from the importing countries to insure their payments with the prospective European Export Bank. On the one hand, this system would have represented the interests of the developing countries in cases when claims have to be paid to European exporters, and on the other, it would also have increased the pressures on the member states to modify their premium rates and transfer additional resources to an independent Community fund. But national governments soon became aware of the threat such a compensatory mechanism would pose to their individual development co-operation policies: because of their connection with other policy areas, European solutions - even when operating within well-defined limits - were ultimately seen as creating too great a constraint on other instruments of domestic export promotion.

Moreover, in terms of their concrete results, the empirical data indicated that international institutions could not level out the existing asymmetries in the national provision of export subsidies. In other words, neither the co-ordination procedures of the EC nor those of the OECD were able to facilitate a pattern where the domestic distribution of costs and benefits was reversed. Though in theory neutrality could constitute 'an attribute of the system as a whole while not being an attribute of any of its components' (Goodin and Reeves, 1989, p. 203), the actual practice of export promotion suggests a somewhat different conclusion: namely that micro-level non-neutrality in the policy space of insurance, finance and aid has not been compensated for by intervention at a macro-level.

It should be noted, however, that this conclusion is context-specific and can be objected to for two reasons. Firstly, the delineation of the policy space is too imprecise and ignores other closely related policy areas; secondly, export promotion is only one comparatively small area of trade policy, which in turn is connected to more important policy-issues. Strictly speaking, it would then also be necessary to carry out a more detailed analysis in order to properly evaluate the overall performance of international institutions in the light of the neutrality requirement. Nevertheless, existing approaches to international policy-making (without the co-ordination framework) support the main findings of this book and such accounts present structural similarities with the analysis of the preceding chapters.

In the area of investment insurance, for example, Lipson (1978) claims that corporate preferences are crucial to the development of a programme that insures multinational corporations based in the United States against political risks. In his historical analysis of the question, Lipson found 'some independent scope for state policy', but explained key features of guarantee policy through the existence of 'private capital accumulation as the basic goal shared by private investors and the state' (Lipson, 1978, p. 375). At the international level, the World Bank attempts to 'improve the investment climate in developing countries' by means of agencies such as the International Centre for Settlement of Investment Disputes (ICSID) and the Multilateral Investment Guarantee Agency (MIGA). In both cases, 'the founders went to considerable lengths to ensure that the interests of both developed and developing countries were adequately represented, and thereby to create a ... fair and impartial decision-making body' (Rowat, 1992, p. 134). When seen in terms of 'co-ordination in context', the bias of domestic co-ordination mechanisms cannot be effectively corrected by the mechanisms available in these kinds of multilateral organisations, and the dominance of particular interests at the national level is likely to create co-ordination problems of the second and third order type.

An alternative perspective can be provided by changing the focus from the regulatory function of international institutions to their budget policies. Hauser (1986) has examined the impact of several factors that have determined the failure of United Nations' policy in the area of aid finance. Hauser argues that the external financing problems of developing countries could be solved by the provision of additional resources in a continuous and fairly structured way, and in particular, suggested that it is necessary to 'automate' the official development assistance given by the member states to UN organisations, thus increasing their financial steering capacity

(Hauser, 1986, p. 240). Here, one important factor complicating the co-ordination process between donor countries is the international bureaucracy itself: the UN Secretariats are tantamount to third parties with their own political interests involved as to how a dispute among their constituents might be solved.

Smith (1993) adopted a very similar approach when trying to analyse the appropriate scope of a European indirect tax policy. Here, like in the case of export promotion, differences in legal systems and corporate structures reduce the potential for efficiency gains from EC-wide regulation, even though the Commission has insisted for some time on the harmonisation of VAT systems and rates in the member states. In Smith's opinion, 'most of the progress towards harmonisation of the VAT base and other aspects of legislation in member states has been largely unnecessary', and is explained by 'the ultimate intention to turn VAT into a tax to be used to finance the EC's own budget' (Smith, 1993, p. 76). In the post-1992 phase, after Community institutions have had such a hard time trying to realise their far-reaching plans, incrementalism has become the preferred strategy for modifying the existing VAT system.

In the same study, Smith (1993, p. 87) noticed the existence of two different roles played by the Commission in the sub-field of environmental taxes. In the first place, legal action was taken against member states which introduced new tax incentives for reducing vehicle emissions, yet at the same time, a Community-wide carbon tax was proposed, the substance of which went way beyond any of the individual measures under consideration in the separate national systems. Harmonisation would thus limit the ability of national governments to make their own 'revenue choices', while handing over parts of their fiscal policy instruments to Community institutions. Problem-solving appeared not to be the prime motivating force behind this proposal, since 'the six most energy intensive industries would not be subject to the tax until other OECD countries adopted similar measures' (Smith, 1993, p. 91). Instead, the insertion of an exemption clause to be used selectively for particular industries indicated that the Commission's main interest was in creating an indirect subsidy instrument at the European level. In effect, therefore, the attempts to introduce environmental concerns into indirect tax policy only contributed to furthering the diversity between the national systems. Again, the institutional self-interest of a third party serves to complicate the original co-ordination problem among governments.

Several other studies dealing with broader policy issues in various contexts revolve around the same theme: the viability of domestic solutions is negatively influenced by the intra- and interorganisational co-ordination problems of international institutions. For this reason, for example, the IMF and GATT were considered as viable rivals to the European integration model during earlier bouts of 'Euro-pessimism' (Hager, 1982). In the area of social policy, Kaufmann (1986) proposes that the Council of Europe should initiate changes in national legislation, because that would allow for a more flexible approach than that provided by Community institutions. In general, the multitude of 'international dilemmas' - development, the environment, human rights, security - do indeed demand complementary co-ordination mechanisms (Senghaas, 1991), but their actual design frequently prevents the implementation of adequate responses to policy problems.

Prittwitz (1984) has examined the activities of the international institutions that attempt to control transboundary air pollution, by using what he calls 'aptitude profiles' and focusing on the organisational features of the United Nations' Economic Commission for Europe (ECE), the OECD and the European Community. Each institution has a distinctive way of approaching this particular interdependence problem, suggesting the potential need for co-ordinated action between them. Over time, however, the Community has become the most influential arena in this field, despite its limits in terms of membership and evaluation standards (Zürn, 1996, p. 26). Schneider (1986, pp. 233-7) has observed a similar development in the regulation of chemical substances, where national administrations initially tried to achieve co-ordination within the framework of the OECD.

The 'techniques and tactics' of the European Court of Justice offer yet another example of institutional self-interest and 'opportunistic' behaviour, this time in relation to the field of human rights (O'Neill and Coppel, 1992). In their interpretation of the Community's implementation of the European Convention on Human Rights, O'Neill and Coppel stress the importance of the strategic use of fundamental principles developed in the Council of Europe, to expand the Court's influence over national jurisdictions. Though case law indicates that human rights are treated as being superior to the specific acts of the member states, the Court 'clearly subordinates human rights to the end of closer economic integration in the Community' (O'Neill and Coppel, 1992, p. 49). In other words, the transfer of a general agreement from one institutional setting to another once more ends up subverting the original intention of co-ordination.

In the area of security policy, statements by former American Secretary of State Warren Christopher have indicated similar potential pitfalls: 'We can promote more durable European security through interlocking structures, each with complementary roles and strengths' (Mearsheimer, 1995, p. 6), but in practice, as the prominent example of the war in the former Yugoslavia shows, co-ordination mechanisms between the United Nations (UN) and the North Atlantic Treaty Organisation (NATO), or between NATO and the Western European Union (WEU) do not function very well at all. In particular, the UN 'possesses inherent characteristics' that made it impossible to perform the role of an effective mediator in this complex international dispute (Touval, 1994, p. 45). Moreover, the most recent attempts to create a 'collective security system' reflect a trend towards less demanding institutional solutions that have already appeared in other contexts. In reviewing the poor record of various security arrangements, Mearsheimer (1995, p. 35) traced the reasons for this back to their 'different and ultimately incompatible logics'. Thus, as before, the problem of second and third order co-ordination is crucial to an overall understanding of policy failure.

All these examples illustrate the broader implications of the arguments put forward in this book, both in specific and more general policy areas. In the European context, the result-oriented analysis of co-ordination problems contrasts sharply with the standard 'liberal intergovernmentalist approach'. In the absence of other detailed empirical research, the claim that neutrality constitutes a 'central feature' of the Treaty of Rome in cases of external representation, agenda setting and enforcement can only be considered to be, at best, problematic (Moravcsik, 1993a, p. 511; Ehlermann, 1995, pp. 1224-5), especially since the European bureaucracy, which represents the central mechanism for ensuring such neutrality, does not appear to be open to impartial advice (Ellis, 1989, p. 84).

Two additional factors - also deriving from the third party hypothesis - point in the same direction. Firstly, if expert committees and new institutional structures at the Community level permit the participation of Commission officials on the same terms as representatives from the member states, the former cannot be considered as neutral because they 'take part in the contest in the same way and on the same terms' as the parties who have delegated some of their powers (Waldron, 1989, p. 63). Secondly, path dependent institutional development at the European level is not reconcilable with the notion of neutrality. For such a system to become truly neutral, it would require that the aggregate result of gains and losses across the different levels even out in the long run. Yet, the institutional reform envisaged in the Draft Constitution of the European Union merely reinforces already existing doubts concerning this kind of calculation. Symptomatic of the whole problem is the new draft Article 41, concerning the co-ordination of Member States' policies, in which the Commission and the European Parliament are said to *participate* in the co-ordination of these policies by the Council (Snyder, 1995, p. 70), but given that it is never specified exactly what is meant by this type of involvement, the co-ordination concept still remains extremely indeterminate in terms of actual substance.

It would be wrong to see these factors as being confined to supranational institutions, seeing as recent reform discussions have indicated the existence of similar problems in the context of the OECD, where the United States has been trying to cope with threats to cartel stability by an increasing politicisation of the organisation's function (Braunberger, 1994, p. 11; Bayne, 1997, pp. 370-1). These threats mainly come from the actual or prospective competition of rival institutions such as the IMF, the World Bank, the European Commission and the Bank for International Settlements, all of whom also provide economic advice to governments. With the rapid growth of new economies in Asia, Latin America and Eastern Europe, the setting up of one or more identical institutions has became a real possibility, so the gradual extension of membership has therefore been reluctantly accepted, at the cost of destroying the internal (asymmetrical) balance between the OECD's original member states. At the same time, the debate about the selection of a new General Secretary and a further tightening of the organisation's mission proves illustrative of the aim to maintain the inherent bias in the present system.

To sum up, the core of this book has verified a relatively straightforward hypothesis: international institutions complicate co-ordination problems. The concentration on the policy space of export promotion certainly does not imply that the range of applications is limited to areas of economic policy, and in fact, the general nature of the analysis leaves room for the investigation of many other policy issues. Indeed, a comprehensive assessment of the neutrality principle could only be based on more extensive studies of this kind. At the theoretical level, it is tempting to suggest that it would be worth pursuing optimal solutions, e.g. international institutions only intervene in cases where governments cannot guarantee that all legitimate interests are equally represented in the domestic policy-making process. However, this book has demonstrated that even the second-best solution is not a realistic alternative: institutional self-interest is incompatible with the proper conduct of mediation and neutral arbitration in cases of conflicts between member states. By contrast, the third-best solution, that of negative neutrality, would appear to be a less demanding and much more promising alternative, and at least leaves the state with the opportunity to organise a genuinely liberal political system.

Appendix

Table: **National currency per SDR**[a]

	German mark	French franc	Pound sterling	US dollar
1980	2.4985	5.7598	1.8700	1.2754
1981	2.6245	6.6904	1.6392	1.1639
1982	2.6215	7.4184	1.4636	1.1031
1983	2.8517	8.7394	1.3855	1.0469
1984	3.0857	9.4022	1.1798	0.9802
1985	2.7035	8.3052	1.3151	1.0984
1986	2.3740	7.8957	1.2055	1.2231
1987	2.2436	7.5756	1.3192	1.4187
1988	2.3957	8.1536	1.3447	1.3457
1989	2.2312	7.6064	1.2217	1.3142
1990	2.1255	7.2968	1.3552	1.4227
1991	2.1685	7.4096	1.3078	1.4304
1992	2.2193	7.5714	1.0996	1.3750
1993	2.3712	8.0978	1.0784	1.3736

[a] end of period
Source: International Monetary Fund (1985-1994).

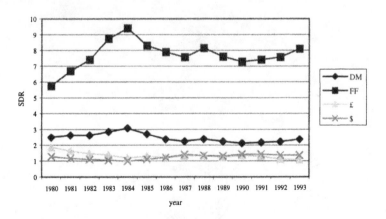

Figure: **National currency per SDR**
Source: International Monetary Fund (1985-1994).

Bibliography

Abraham, F. (1990), *The Effects on Intra-Community Competition of Export Subsidies to Third Countries,* Commission of the European Communities, Brussels.

Abraham, F., Couwenberg, I. and Dewit, G. (1993), 'Towards an EC Policy on Export Financing Subsidies: Lessons from the 1980s and Prospects for Future Reform', *The World Economy,* vol. 15, pp. 389-405.

Adams, W.J. (1995), 'France and Global Competition', in G. Flynn (ed.), *Remaking the Hexagon,* Westview Press, Boulder and Oxford, pp. 87-115.

Agir Ici (1991a), *Un Système d'Assurance d'Exportation à Reformer,* Manuscript, Paris.

Agir Ici (1991b), *Réformer la Coface,* Manuscript, Paris.

Albert, M. (1993), *Capitalism versus Capitalism,* Whurr, London.

Ansari, J.A. (1986), *The Political Economy of International Economic Organization,* Wheatsheaf, Brighton.

Aubrey, H.G. (1967), *Atlantic Economic Cooperation,* Praeger, New York.

Ausfuhrkredit-Gesellschaft (1991), *Bericht über das 39. Geschäftsjahr,* AKA, Frankfurt am Main.

Bayne, N. (1987), 'Making Sense of Western Economic Policies: the Role of the OECD', *The World Today,* vol. 43, pp. 27-30.

Bayne, N. (1997), 'What Governments Want from International Economic Institutions and How they Get It', *Government and Opposition,* vol. 32, pp. 361-79.

Bellers, J. (1990), *Außenwirtschaftspolitik der Bundesrepublik Deutschland 1949-1989,* Lit, Münster.

Biersteker, T.J. (1993), 'Constructing Historical Counterfactuals to Assess the Consequences of International Regimes: The Global Debt Regime and the Course of the Debt Crisis of the 1980s', in V. Rittberger (ed.), *Regime Theory and International Relations,* Clarendon Press, Oxford.

Blair, D.J. (1992), *Trade Negotiations in the OECD,* Kegan Paul International, London and New York.

Boulouis, J. (1988), 'Sur la Notion de Politique Commune et ses Implications Juridiques', in J. Schwarze and H.G. Schermers (eds), *Structure and Dimensions of European Community Policy,* Nomos, Baden-Baden, pp. 55-9.

Bourgeois, J. (1991), 'Handelspolitik', in H. von der Groeben et al. (eds), *Kommentar zum EWG-Vertrag,* 4th edn., vol. 3, Nomos, Baden-Baden, pp. 3121-267.

Bowler, S. (1988), 'Government-Business Bargaining and the Impact of EC Institutions: the Lindblom Problem', *Political Studies*, vol. 36, pp. 524-32.

Brau, E.H. and Puckahticom, C. (1985), 'Export Credit Cover Policies and Payments Difficulties', *Occasional Paper*, no. 37, International Monetary Fund, Washington, DC.

Braunberger, G. (1994), 'Die OECD in einer neuen Welt', *Frankfurter Allgemeine Zeitung*, 11 June 1994, no. 133, p. 11.

Brown, M.L. and O'Connor, J.M. (1996), 'Cross-Pressures in Western European Foreign Aid', in S.W. Hook (ed.), *Foreign Aid toward the Millennium*, Lynne Rienner, Boulder and London, pp. 91-107.

Breach, G. (1990), 'The Role of Export Credit Insurance', *IDS Bulletin*, vol. 21, pp. 67-70.

Bressand, A. (1982), 'Rich Country Interests and Third World Development: France', in R. Cassen et al. (eds), *Rich Country Interests and Third World Development*, Croom Helm, London and Canberra, pp. 307-32.

Bryant, R.C. (1995), *International Coordination of National Stabilization Policies*, The Brookings Institution, Washington, DC.

Bundesverband der Deutschen Industrie (1992a), *Harmonisierung der staatlichen Exportkreditversicherungen in den EG-Mitgliedsländern - Kurzfristdeckungen*, Manuscript, BDI, Köln.

Bundesverband der Deutschen Industrie (1992b), 'EG-Harmonisierung der Kreditversicherung kommt', *BDI Informationen und Meinungen*, no. 8.

Byatt, I.C.R. (1984), 'Byatt Report on Subsidies to British Export Credits', *The World Economy*, vol. 7, pp. 163-78.

Cable, V. (1982), 'British Interests in Third World Development', in R. Cassen et al. (eds), *Rich Country Interests and Third World Development*, Croom Helm, London and Canberra, pp. 182-214.

Cafruny, A.W. (1987), *Ruling the Waves: the Political Economy of International Shipping*, The University of California Press, Berkeley.

Callut, P. (1991), *Die Kreditversicherung und der einheitliche Binnenmarkt 1992 (kurzfristige Geschäfte)*, Manuscript, Brüssel.

Calvert, R.L. (1992), 'Leadership and its Basis in Problems of Social Coordination', *International Political Science Review*, vol. 13, pp. 7-24.

Camps, M. (1975), *'First World' Relationships: the Role of the OECD*, Atlantic Institute for International Affairs and Council on Foreign Relations, Paris and New York.

Carmichael, W.B. (1986), 'National Interest and International Trade Negotiations', *The World Economy*, vol. 9, pp. 341-57.

Carruth, R.A. (1989), *Industrial Policy Coordination in International Organizations*, Peter Lang, Frankfurt am Main.

Cassen, R. et al. (eds) (1982), *Rich Country Interests and Third World Development*, Croom Helm, London and Canberra.

Cassen, R. et al. (1994), Does Aid Work?, 2nd edn., Clarendon Press, Oxford.

Cheney, D.M. (1985), 'The OECD Export Credits Agreement', *Finance and Development*, vol. 22, pp. 35-7.

Chisholm, D. (1989), *Coordination without Hierarchy*, University of California Press, Berkeley and Los Angeles.

Cizauskas, A.C. (1983), 'Export Credit Financing', *Development Forum Business Edition*, vol. 127, pp. 1-2.

Cohen, S.S., Galbraith, J. and Zysman, J. (1982), 'Rehabbing the Labyrinth: the Financial System and Industrial Policy in France', in S.S. Cohen and P.A. Gourevitch (eds), *France in the Troubled World Economy*, Butterworths, London, pp. 49-75.

Coleman, W.C. (1997), 'The French State, Dirigisme, and the Changing Global Financial Environment', in G.R.D. Underhill (ed.), *The New World Order in International Finance*, Macmillan, London, pp. 274-93.

Commission of the European Communities (1984), 'Commission Decision concerning the French Government's Intention to accord special Exchange Risk Cover to French Exporters in respect of a Tender for the Construction of a Power Station in Greece (84/416 EEC)', *Official Journal*, vol. 27, no. L 230, pp. 25-7.

Commission of the European Communities (1987), 'Proposal for a Council Regulation concerning the Establishment of a European Export Credit Insurance Facility to provide Export Credit Insurance for Export Contracts to Third Countries sourced in more than one Member State (COM 87/251 final)', *Official Journal*, vol. 30, no. C 230, pp. 4-5.

Commission of the European Communities (1989), *Relations between the European Community and International Organisations*, Brussels.

Commission of the European Communities (1990), 'Proposal for a Council Regulation concerning the Establishment of a Reinsurance Pool for Export Credits to Central and Eastern European Countries (SEC 90/2123 final)', *Official Journal*, vol. 33, no. C 302, pp. 6-8.

Commission of the European Communities (1991a), 'Commission Regulation concerning the Conditions under which a Credit Guarantee Agreement, introducing a Credit Guarantee for Exports of Agricultural Products and Foodstuffs to the Soviet Union, shall be concluded with a Pool of Commercial Banks (EEC 2150/91)', *Official Journal*, vol. 34, no. L 200, pp. 12-3.

Commission of the European Communities (1991b), 'Commission Regulation on Amendment of Regulation EEC 2150/91 concerning the Conditions under which a Credit Guarantee Agreement, introducing a Credit Guarantee for Exports of Agricultural Products and Foodstuffs to the Soviet Union, shall be concluded with a Pool of Commercial Banks (EEC 3363/91)', *Official Journal*, vol. 34, no. L 318, pp. 31-2.

Commission of the European Communities (1991c), Proposal for a Council Decision on the Application of certain Guidelines in the Field of Officially Supported Export Credits, COM 91/217 final.

Commission of the European Communities (1991d), *Application of Article 92 and 93 EEC Treaty concerning Export Credit Insurance Agencies competing with Private Insurance Companies*, Manuscript, Brussels.

Commission of the European Communities (1992), *The Principle of Subsidiarity*, SEC 92/1990 final.

Commission of the European Communities (1993), *Application of Article 92 and 93 EEC Treaty in the Field of Export Credit Insurance*, Manuscript, Brussels.

Compagnie Française d'Assurance du Commerce Extérieur (1980-1992), *Rapport d'Activité*, Coface, Paris.

Confederation of British Industry (1982), *UK Export Credit Insurance and Finance*, Manuscript, CBI, London.

Cooper, R.N. (1976), 'Worldwide versus Regional Integration: is there an Optimum Size of the Integrated Area?', in F. Machlup (ed.), *Economic Integration*, Macmillan, London, pp. 41-53.

Cooper, R.N. (1983), 'Managing Risks to the International Economic System', in R.J. Herring (ed.), *Managing International Risk*, Cambridge University Press, Cambridge, pp. 23-53.

Council of the European Communities (1960), 'Decision setting up a Policy-Co-ordination Group on Credit Indurance, Credit Guarantees and Financial Credits', *Official Journal*, vol. 3, no. 66, pp. 1339-40.

Council of the European Communities (1970a), 'Council Directive on the Adoption of a Common Credit Insurance Policy for Medium- and Long-Term Transactions with Public Buyers (70/509/EEC)', *Official Journal*, vol. 13, no. L 254, pp. 1-25.

Council of the European Communities (1970b), 'Council Directive on the Adoption of a Common Credit Insurance Policy for Medium- and Long-Term Transactions with Public Buyers (70/510/EEC)', *Official Journal*, vol. 13, no. L 254, pp. 26-51.

Council of the European Communities (1971), 'Council Directive on Harmonisation of the basis Provisions in respect of Guarantees for Short-Term Transactions (Political Risks) with Public Buyers or with Private Buyers (71/86/EEC)', *Official Journal*, vol. 14, no. L 36, pp. 14-6.

Council of the European Communities (1973), 'Council Decision on Consultation and Information Procedures in matters of Credit Insurance, Credit Guarantees and Financial Credits (73/391/EEC)', *Official Journal*, vol. 16, no. L 346, pp. 1-6.

Council of the European Communities (1976), 'Council Decision on Amendment of Decision 73/391/EEC on Consultation and Information Procedures in matters of Credit Insurance, Credit Guarantees and Financial Credits (76/641/EEC)', *Official Journal*, vol. 19, no. L 223, pp. 25-6.

Council of the European Communities (1982), 'Council Decision on the Rules applicable, in the Fields of Export Guarantees and Finance for Export, to certain Subcontracts with Parties in other Member States in the European Communities or in Non-Member Countries (82/854/EEC)', *Official Journal*, vol. 25, no. L 357, pp. 20-2.

Council of the European Communities (1984), 'Council Directive concerning the reciprocal Obligations of Export Credit Insurance Organizations of the Member States acting on behalf of the State or with its Support, or of Public Departments acting in place of such Organizations, in the Case of Joint Guarantees for a Contract involving one or more Subcontracts in one or more Member States of the European Communities (84/568/EEC)', *Official Journal*, vol. 27, no. L 314, pp. 24-7.

Council of the European Comunities (1991a), 'Council Decision on the conclusion by the European Economic Comunity of an Agreement in the Form of an Exchange of Letters between the European Economic Community and the Union of Soviet Socialist Republics on a Credit Guarantee for Exports of Agricultural Products and Foodstuffs from the Community to the Soviet Union (91/373/EEC)', *Official Journal*, vol. 34, no. L 202, pp. 39-45.

Council of the European Communities (1991b), 'Council Regulation introducing a Credit Guarantee for Exports of Agricultural Products and Foodstuffs from the Community to the Soviet Union (EEC 599/91)', *Official Journal*, vol. 34, no. L 67, pp. 21-2.

Court of Justice of the European Communities (1975), 'Opinion given pursuant to the Second Subparagraph of Article 228 (1) of the EEC Treaty', *Official Journal*, vol. 18, no. C 268, pp. 18-23.

Court of Justice of the European Communities (1990), 'Case C-142/87, Kingdom of Belgium v Commission of the European Communities', *European Court Reports*, vol. 2, pp. 959-1021.

Court of Justice of the European Communities (1991), 'Case C-63/89, Les Assurances du Crédit and Compagnie Belge d'Assurance Crédit SA v Council and Commission of the European Communities', *European Court Reports*, vol. 3, pp. 1799-851.

Cox, R.W. (1981), 'Social Forces, States and World Orders: Beyond International Relations Theory', *Millenium*, vol. 10, pp. 126-55.

Crawford, B. (1987), 'How Regimes Matter: Western Control of East-West Trade Finance', *Millenium*, vol. 16, pp. 431-52.

Czada, R. (1996), 'The Treuhandanstalt and the Transition from Socialism to Capitalism', in A. Benz and K.H. Goetz (eds), *A new German Public Sector?*, Dartmouth, Aldershot.

Dahl, R.A. and Lindblom, C.E. (1976), *Politics, Economics and Welfare*, 2nd edn., The University of Chicago Press, Chicago.

Davis, P. and Dombrowski, P. (1997), 'Appetite of the Wolf: German Foreign Assistance for Central and Eastern Europe', *German Politics*, vol. 6, pp. 1-22.

Dean, R.W. (1974), *West German Trade with the East: the Political Dimension*, Praeger, New York.

Dehousse, R. (1992), 'Does Subsidiarity Really Matter?', *LAW Working Paper*, no. 92/32, European University Institute, Florence.

Dehousse, R. and Majone, G. (1993), 'The Dynamics of European Integration: The Role of Supranational Institutions', Paper presented at the European Community Studies Association Third Biennial International Conference, 27-29 May 1993, Washington, DC.

Dehousse, R. and Weiler, J.H.H. (1990a), 'The Legal Dimension', in W. Wallace (ed.), *The Dynamics of European Integration*, Pinter, London and New York, pp. 242-60.

Dehousse, R. and Weiler, J.H.H. (1990b), 'EPC and the Single Act: From Soft Law to Hard Law?', *EPU Working Paper*, no. 90/1, European University Institute, Florence.

DeKieffer, D.E. (1985), 'The Role of Export Credits in International Trade', in J.H. Jackson, R.O. Cunningham and C.G.B. Fontheim (eds), *International Trade Policy: The Lawyer's Perspective*, Chapter 17, Matthew Bender, New York, pp. 1-17.

Deutsch, K.W. et al. (1957), *Political Community in the North Atlantic Area*, Princeton University Press, Princeton.

Deutscher Bundestag (1994), 'Die demokratische, ökologische und entwicklungspolitische Gestaltung der Vergabe von Hermes-Bürgschaften', *Drucksache*, no. 12/5949, pp. 1-7.

Deutscher Bundestag (1995), 'Einführung von Umwelrichtlinien für Ausfuhrbürgschaften durch die Organisation for Economic Co-operation and Development (OECD)', *Drucksache*, no. 13/383.

Deutsches Institut für Wirtschaftsforschung (1987), 'Deutsche Entwicklungshilfe: Mehr Lieferbindung durch Mischfinanzierung', *Wochenbericht*, no. 10, pp. 121-8.

Dieckmann, N. (1985), *Das Britische Exportfinanzierungssystem: eine landeskundliche Untersuchung*, Hamburger Buchagentur, Hamburg.

Dixit, A.K. (1996), *The Making of Economic Policy: a Transaction-Cost Politics Perspective*, MIT Press, Cambridge and London.

Doig, A. (1997), 'Truth-Telling and Power', *Parliamentary Affairs*, vol. 50, pp. 143-65.

Dörr, C. (1993), 'Auswirkungen des EG-Binnenmarktes auf die staatlichen Exportkreditversicherungen', in Bundesverband der Deutschen Industrie (ed.),

Exportkreditversicherung und Exportfinanzierung vor neuen Herausforderungen, Dokumentation, BDI, Köln, pp. 32-40.

Duff, J.M. (1981), 'The Outlook for Official Export Credits', *Law and Policy in International Business*, vol. 13, pp. 891-959.

Dutet, J.-P. (1982), 'La Compagnie Française d'Assurance pour le Commerce Extérieur', in G. Défosse (ed.), *Les Exportations Françaises et leur Financement*, Presses Universitaires de France, Paris.

Economist, The (1983), 'ECGD: The three Privateers?', 20 August 1983, vol. 288, p. 80.

Economist, The (1997), 'Governments and Exports', 1 February 1997, vol. 342, pp. 21-3.

Eeckhout, P. (1994), *The European Internal Market and International Trade*, Clarendon Press, Oxford.

Ehlermann, C.-D. (1995),'State Aid Control in the European Union: Success or Failure?', *Fordham International Law Journal*, vol. 18, pp. 1212-29.

Ellis, M.(1989), 'The Neutrality of the Civil Service', in R.E. Goodin and A. Reeves (eds), *Liberal Neutrality*, Routledge, London and New York, pp. 84-105.

Ernst, W. and Beseler, H.-F. (1983), 'Handelspolitik', in H. von der Groeben et al. (eds), *Kommentar zum EWG-Vertrag*, 3rd edn., vol. 1, Nomos, Baden-Baden, pp. 1881-963.

European Parliament (1977a), 'Report on the Proposal from the Commission of the European Communities to the Council for a Regulation setting up a European Export Bank (Nyborg Report)', *Working Document* , no. 66/77, PE 42.970/fin.

European Parliament (1977b), 'Report on the Harmonization of Export Aid Systems (Cousté Report)', *Working Document*, no. 129/77, PE 47.346/fin.

European Parliament (1984a), 'Report on Export Credit Subsidies (Delorozoy Report)', *Working Document*, no. 1-1482/83, PE 87.680/fin.

European Parliament (1984b), 'Resolution on Export Credit Subsidies', *Official Journal*, vol. 27, no. C 104, pp. 132-3.

European Parliament (1991), 'Report on the Commission Proposal for a Council Regulation concerning the Establishment of a Reinsurance Pool for Export Credits to Central and Eastern European Countries (Lemmer Report)', *Session Document*, no. A3-0222/91, PE 150.319/fin.

European Parliament (1993), 'Consequences for Development Policy of the Entry into Force of the Maastricht Treaty (Oral Question)', *Session Document*, no. B3-1642/93, PE 164.816.

Everling, U. (1964), 'Die Koordinierung der Wirtschaftspolitik in der Europäischen Gemeinschaft als Rechtsproblem', *Recht und Staat*, vol. 296-7, pp. 1-39.

Export Credits Guarantee Department (1992-1994), *Annual Report and Trading Accounts*, HMSO, London.

Export-Import Bank of the United States (1993), *Report to the U.S. Congress on Export Credit Competition and the Export-Import Bank of the United States*, Washington, DC.

Ferretti, R. (1984), *La Coordination de l'Action des Organisations Internationales au Niveau Européen*, Bruylant, Bruxelles.

Fleisig, H. and Hill, C. (1984), 'The Benefits and Costs of Official Export Credit Programs', in R.E. Baldwin and A.O. Krueger (eds), *The Structure and Evolution of recent US Trade Policy*, The University of Chicago Press, Chicago and London, pp. 321-58.

Foreign Affairs Committee (1994), *Public Expenditure: Pergau Hydro-Electric Project, Malaysia, The Aid and Trade Provision and Related Matters*, vol. 1-2, HMSO, London.

Frankfurter Allgemeine Zeitung (1993a), 'Antragsflut statt Hilfe für Osteuropa', 26 July 1993, no. 170, p. 12.

Frankfurter Allgemeine Zeitung (1993b), 'Entäuschung in Deutschland - der ICE unterliegt', 21 August 1993, no. 193, p. 11.

Frankfurter Allgemeine Zeitung (1994), 'Kritik am OECD-Schiffsbauabkommen', 21 July 1994, no. 167, p. 11.

Franko, L.G. and Stephenson, S. (1980), *French Export Behavior in Third World Markets*, Center for Strategic and International Studies, Washington, DC.

Fratianni, M. and Pattison, J. (1982), 'The Economics of International Organizations', *Kyklos*, vol. 35, pp. 244-62.

Frohlich, N. and Oppenheimer, J.A. (1978), *Modern Political Economy*, Prentice-Hall, Englewood Cliffs.

Frohlich, N., Oppenheimer, J.A. and Young, O.R. (1971), *Political Leadership and Collective Goods*, Princeton University Press, Princeton.

Fues, T. (1993), 'Ökologische und entwicklungspolitische Kritik der Hermes-Bürgschaften', *WEED Arbeitspapier*, no. 1/93, Weltwirtschaft, Ökologie & Entwicklung e.V., Bonn.

Fues, T. (1994), *Reforming Export Guarantee Systems: Challenges ahead for Northern NGOs*, Manuscript, Eurodad, Brussels.

Galtung, J. (1968), 'A Structural Theory of Integration', *Journal of Peace Research*, vol. 5, pp. 375-95.

Garrett, G. (1992), 'International Cooperation and Institutional Choice: The European Community's Internal Market', *International Organization*, vol. 46, pp. 533-60.

Garrett, G. and Weingast B.R. (1993), 'Ideas, Interests, and Institutions: Constructing the European Community's Internal Market', in J. Goldstein and R.O. Keohane (eds), *Ideas and Foreign Policy*, Cornell University Press, Ithaca, pp. 173-206.

Gatsios, K. and Seabright, P. (1989), 'Regulation in the European Community', *Oxford Review of Economic Policy*, vol. 5, pp. 37-60.

Gehring, H.-P. (1993), 'Zukunft des Hermes-Instrumentariums: Möglichkeiten und Grenzen', in Bundesverband der Deutschen Industrie (ed.), *Exportkreditversicherung und Exportfinanzierung vor neuen Herausforderungen*, Dokumentation, BDI, Köln, pp. 15-31.

Gill, J. (1986), 'Export Credit Insurance - Why Government?', *The Geneva Papers on Risk and Insurance*, vol. 11, pp. 265-68.

Glibert, F. (1983), 'Réassurance et Coassurance des Risques politiques', *Tome*, vol. 9, pp. 261-76.

Glotzbach, M. (1973), *Die staatliche Ausfuhrkreditversicherung in Frankreich und Deutschland*, Duncker & Humblot, Berlin.

Goodin, R.E. (1976), *The Politics of Rational Man*, Wiley & Sons, London.

Goodin, R.E. (1980), *Manipulatory Politics*, Yale University Press, New Haven and London.

Goodin, R.E. (1982), *Political Theory and Public Policy*, The University of Chicago Press, Chicago and London.

Goodin, R.E. (1988), *Reasons for Welfare*, Princeton University Press, Princeton.

Goodin, R.E. and Reeves A. (1989a), 'Liberalism and Neutrality', in R.E. Goodin and A. Reeves (eds), *Liberal Neutrality*, Routledge, London and New York, pp. 1-8.

Goodin, R.E. and Reeves A. (1989b), 'Do Neutral Institutions add up to a Neutral State?', in R.E. Goodin and A. Reeves (eds), *Liberal Neutrality*, Routledge, London and New York, pp. 193-210.

Grieco, J.M. (1990), *Cooperation among Nations*, Cornell University Press, Ithaca.

Gygi, B. (1991), *Internationale Organisationen aus der Sicht der neuen politischen Ökonomie*, Physica-Verlag, Heidelberg.

Haas, E.B. (1990), *When Knowledge is Power*, University of California Press, Berkeley.

Haas, E.B., Williams, M.P. and Babai, D. (1977), *Scientists and World Order*, University of California Press, Berkeley and Los Angeles.

Haas, P.M. (1992), 'Introduction: Epistemic Communities and International Policy Coordination', *International Organization*, vol. 46, pp. 1-35.

Haas, P.M. (1993), 'Epistemic Communities and the Dynamics of International Environmental Co-operation', in V. Rittberger (ed.), *Regime Theory and International Relations*, Clarendon Press, Oxford, pp. 168-201.

Hager, W. (1982), 'Little Europe, Wider Europe and Western Economic Cooperation', *Journal of Common Market Studies*, vol. 21, pp. 171-97.

Hahn, H.J. and Weber, A. (1976), *Die OECD - Organisation für Wirtschaftliche Zusammenarbeit*, Nomos, Baden-Baden.

Halfen, B. (1991), *Gesamtwirtschaftliche Wirkungen staatlicher Ausfuhrgewährleistungen*, Dissertation, Gutenberg-Universität, Mainz.

Hall, P.A. (1986), *Governing the Economy*, Polity Press, Cambridge.

Hall, P.A. (1994), 'The State and the Market', in P.A. Hall, J. Hayward and H. Machin (eds), *Developments in French Politics*, revised edn., Macmillan, London, pp. 171-87.

Handelsblatt (1991), 'Paris sucht nach einer neuen Formel für die defizitäre Exportkreditversicherung', 13 May 1991, no. 90, p. 8.

Harrison, R.J. and Mungall, S. (1990), 'Harmonization', in A.J.R. Groom and P. Taylor (eds), *Frameworks for International Co-operation*, Pinter, London, pp. 56-68.

Hashek, H.H. (1986), 'Export Credit Insurance and the Debt Crisis', *The Geneva Papers on Risk and Insurance*, vol. 11, pp. 285-91.

Haufler, V. (1997), 'Financial Deregulation and the Transformation of International Risk Insurance', in G.R.D. Underhill (ed.), *The New World Order in International Finance*, Macmillan, London, pp. 76-100.

Hauser, H.-M. (1986), *Reform der Entwicklungsfinanzierung durch Automatisierung*, Nomos, Baden-Baden.

Hayward, J. (1986), *The State and the Market Economy*, Wheatsheaf, Brighton.

Henderson, D. (1988), 'The State of International Economic Co-operation', *The World Today*, vol. 44, pp. 213-5.

Henderson, D. (1993), 'International Economic Co-operation Revisited', *Government and Opposition*, vol. 28, pp. 11-35.

Hermes Kreditversicherungs-AG (1993a), *Ausfuhrgarantien und Ausfuhr-bürgschaften der Bundesrepublik Deutschland*, Hermes, Hamburg.

Hermes Kreditversicherungs-AG (1993b), *Geschäftsbericht 1992*, Hermes, Hamburg.

Hermes Kreditversicherungs-AG (1994), 'Entgeltreform - Neues Entgeltsystem ab 1. Juli 1994', *AGA-Report*, no. 49, pp. 1-9.

Hessel, S. (1987), 'Mitterand's France and the Third World', in G. Ross, S. Hoffmann and S. Malzacher (eds), *The Mitterand Experiment*, Polity Press, Cambridge, pp. 324-37.

Heymann, P.B. (1973), 'The Problem of Coordination: Bargaining and Rules', *Harvard Law Review*, vol. 86, pp. 797-877.

Hichert, I. (1986), *Staatliche Exportabsicherung*, Deutscher Instituts-Verlag, Köln.

Hill, C. (1994), 'The Capability-Expectations Gap, or Conceptualizing Europe's International Role', in S. Bulmer and A. Scott (eds), *Economic and Political Integration in Europe*, Blackwell, Oxford and Cambridge, pp. 103-26.

Hirschmann, A.O. (1969), *National Power and the Structure of Foreign Trade*, University of California Press, Berkeley and Los Angeles.

Hoffmann, S. (1987), 'Mitterand's Foreign Policy, or Gaullism by any other Name', in G. Ross, S. Hoffmann and S. Malzacher (eds), *The Mitterand Experiment*, Polity Press, Cambridge, pp. 294-305.

Hollenbach, B. (1992), 'Multi-Sourcing', Paper presented at the Annual Conference of the Institute of International Research on Optimal Risk Insurance and Financing of Exports, 19-20 October 1992, Düssseldorf.

Hook, S.W. (1995), *National Interest and Foreign Aid*, Lynne Rienner, Boulder and London.

Houbé-Masse, M.-L. (1992), *La CEE et les Crédits à l'Exportation*, Édition Apogée, Rennes.

Hufbauer, G.C. and Shelton Erb, J. (1984), *Subsidies in International Trade*, MIT Press, Cambridge and London.

Hurrell, A. (1995), 'Regionalism in Theoretical Perspective', in L. Fawcett and A. Hurrell (eds), *Regionalism in World Politics*, Oxford University Press, Oxford, pp. 37-73.

Hveem, H. (1992), 'Hegemonic Rivalry and Antagonistic Interdependence: Bilateralism and the Management of International Trade', Paper presented at the First Pan-European Conference in International Relations, 16-19 September 1992, Heidelberg.

International Monetary Fund (1985-94), *International Financial Statistics Yearbook*, Vol. 38-47, IMF, Washington, DC.

Irish Times, The (1994), 'The Beef Tribunal Report', 3 August 1994, no. 43,973, pp. 5-9.

Jepma, C.J. (1991), *The Tying of Aid*, OECD, Paris.

Jepma, C.J. (1994), *Inter-nation Policy Co-ordination and Untying of Aid*, Avebury, Aldershot.

Joerges, C. (1994), 'European Economic Law, the Nation-State and the Maastricht Treaty' in R. Dehousse (ed.), *Europe after Maastricht: an Ever Closer Union?*, C.H. Beck, München, pp. 29-62.

Johnson, G.G. (1991), 'Comment', in I. Husain and J. Underwood (eds), *African External Finance in the 1990s*, The World Bank, Washington, DC., pp. 135-7.

Johnson, G.G., Fisher M. and Harris, E. (1990), *Officially Supported Export Credits*, International Monetary Fund, Washington, DC.

Jones, P. (1989), 'The Ideal of the Neutral State' in R.E. Goodin and A. Reeves (eds), *Liberal Neutrality*, Routledge, London and New York, pp. 9-38.

Kageneck, W. Graf von (1990), *Hermes-Deckungen*, Recht und Wirtschaft, Heidelberg.

Kahler, M. (1982), 'International Response to Economic Crises: France and the Third World in the 1970s', in S.S. Cohen and P.A. Gourevitch (eds), *France in the Troubled World Economy*, Butterworths, London, pp. 76-96.

Kahler, M. (1989), 'Organization and Cooperation: International Institutions and Policy Coordination', *Journal of Public Policy*, vol. 8, pp. 375-401.

Kahler, M. (1995), *International Institutions and the Political Economy of Integration*, The Brookings Institution, Washington, DC.

Karl, W.-D. (1980), 'Unkontrollierte Außenwirtschaftspolitik der Bundesrepublik? Zu Problemen der parlamentarischen Legitimation außenwirtschaftspolitischer Entscheidungen', *Zeitschrift für Parlamentsfragen*, vol. 3, pp. 404-22.

Katzenstein, P.J. (1978a), 'Introduction: Domestic and International Forces and Strategies of Foreign Economic Policy', in P.J. Katzenstein (ed.), *Between Power and Plenty*, University of Wisconsin Press, Madison, pp. 3-22.

Katzenstein, P.J. (1978b), 'Conclusion: Domestic Structures and Strategies of Foreign Economic Policy', in P.J. Katzenstein (ed.), *Between Power and Plenty*, University of Wisconsin Press, Madison, pp. 295-336.

Katzenstein, P.J. (1990), 'Analyzing Change in International Politics: The New Institutionalism and the Interpretative Approach', *MPIFG Discussion Paper*, no. 90/10, Max-Planck-Institut für Gesellschaftsforschung, Köln.

Kaufmann, F.-X. (1986), 'Nationale Traditionen der Sozialpolitik und europäische Integration', in L. Albertin (ed.), *Probleme und Perspektiven europäischer Einigung*, Landeszentrale für Politische Bildung, Düsseldorf, pp. 69-82.

Keohane, R.O. (1984), *After Hegemony*, Princeton University Press, Princeton.

Keohane, R.O. (1988), 'Bargaining Perversities, Institutions, and International Economic Relations', in P. Guerrieri and P.C. Padoan (eds), *The Political Economy of International Co-operation*, Croom Helm, London, pp. 28-50.

Keohane, R.O. (1993), 'The Analysis of International Regimes: Towards a European-American Research Programme', in V. Rittberger (ed.), *Regime Theory and International Relations*, Clarendon Press, Oxford, pp. 23-45.

Kessler, M. (1996), 'Geschäft mit dem Risiko', *Wirtschaftswoche*, 4 April 1996, no. 15, pp. 33-6.

Klenk, J. (1994), 'Organization for Economic Co-operation and Development - OECD', in A. Boeckh (ed.), *Internationale Beziehungen*, Lexikon der Politik, vol. 6, C.H. Beck, München, pp. 355-61.

Kloten, N. (1985), 'Die Koordinierung westlicher Wirtschaftspolitik', in K. Kaiser and H.-P. Schwarz (eds), *Weltpolitik*, Bundeszentrale für Politische Bildung, Bonn, pp. 378-97.

Kohler-Koch, B. (1989), 'Zur Empirie und Theorie internationaler Regime', in B. Kohler-Koch (ed.), *Regime in den internationalen Beziehungen*, Nomos, Baden-Baden, pp. 17-85.

Kohler, D.F. (1984), *Economic Cost and Benefits of Subsidizing Western Credits to the East*, The Rand Corporation, Santa Monica.

Kreditanstalt für Wiederaufbau (1994), *Annual Report 1993*, KfW, Frankfurt am Main.

Kreile, M. (1978), 'West Germany: the Dynamics of Expansion', in P.J. Katzenstein (ed.), *Between Power and Plenty*, University of Wisconsin Press, Madison, pp. 191-224.

Kuhn, M.G. et al. (1994), *Official Financing for Developing Countries*, International Monetary Fund, Washington, DC.

Kulke-Fiedler, C. (1989), 'Trends of State Export Credit Policy of Industrialised Nations', *IPW Berichte*, vol. 18, pp. 8-12.

Kunreuther, H. and Kleindorfer, P. (1983), 'Insuring against Country Risks: descriptive and prescriptive Aspects', in R.J. Herring (ed.), *Managing International Risk*, Cambridge University Press, Cambridge, pp. 223-55.

Kydd, A. and Snidal, D. (1993), 'Progress in Game-Theoretical Analysis of International Regimes', in V. Rittberger (ed.), *Regime Theory and International Relations*, Clarendon Press, Oxford, pp. 112-35.

Lainé, C. (1982), 'Les Tentatives d'Entente Internationale pour limiter la Surenchère des Aides publiques', in G. Défosse (ed.), *Les Exportations Françaises et leur Financement*, Presses Universitaires de France, Paris.

Laver, M. (1997), *Private Desires, Political Actions*, Sage, London.

Le Prestre, P.G. (1986), 'A Problématique for International Organizations', *International Social Science Journal*, vol. 107, pp. 127-38.

Lessard, D.R. (1986), 'The Management of International Trade Risk', *The Geneva Papers on Risk and Insurance*, vol. 41, pp. 255-64.

Letovsky, R. (1990), 'The Export Finance Wars', *Columbia Journal of World Business*, vol. 25, pp. 25-35.

Lindblom, C.E. (1977), *Politics and Markets*, Basic Books, New York.

Lipson, C. (1978), 'The Development of Expropriation Insurance: the Role of Corporate Preferences and State Initiatives', *International Organization*, vol. 32, pp. 351-75.

Little, I.M.D. and Clifford, J.M. (1965), *International Aid*, Allen and Unwin, London.

Lochner, N. (1962), 'Was bedeuten die Begriffe Harmonisierung, Koordinierung und Gemeinsame Politik in den Europäischen Verträgen?', *Zeitschrift für die gesamte Staatswissenschaft*, vol. 118, pp. 35-61.

Loriaux, M. (1991), *France after Hegemony*, Cornell University Press, Ithaca and London.

Lowet, G. (1984), 'The European Umbrella in the Pipeline Conflict: A new Coverage Function', *The International Spectator*, vol. 19, pp. 137-48.

Machin, H. and Wright, V. (1985), 'Economic Policy under the Mitterand Presidency 1981-1984: an introduction', in H. Machin and V. Wright (eds), *Economic Policy and Policy-Making under the Mitterand Presidency 1981-1984*, Pinter, London, pp. 1-43.

Majnoni, G. (1981), *Euromercati e Finanziamento dello Esportazioni*, Il Mulino, Bologna.

Majone, G. (1989), *Evidence, Argument and Persuasion in the Policy Process*, Yale University Press, New Haven.

Majone, G. (1991), 'Market Integration and Regulation: Europe after 1992', Paper presented at the Conference on Production Organization, Dynamic Efficiency and Social Norms, 4-6 April 1991, Rome.

Majone, G. (1992), 'Ideas, Interests and Policy Change', *SPS Working Paper*, no. 92/21, European University Institute, Florence.

Majone, G. (1994), 'Comparing Strategies of Regulatory Rapprochement', in Organisation for Economic Co-operation and Development (ed.), *Regulatory Co-operation for an Interdependent World*, OECD, Paris, pp. 155-77.

Majone, G. (ed.) (1996), *Regulating Europe*, Routledge, London.

March, J.G. and Olsen, J.P. (1989), *Rediscovering Institutions*, The Free Press, New York.

Marer, P. (ed.) (1975), *US Financing of East-West Trade*, International Development Research Center, Bloomington.

Marks, J. (1991), 'The United Kingdom back at Centre Stage', *Middle East Economic Digest*, vol. 35, pp. 7-14.

Martin, L.L. (1992), 'Interests, Power and Multilateralism', *International Organization* 46, pp. 765-92.

Maule, D. (1992), 'Der englische Versicherungsmarkt für die Absicherung politischer Risiken', Paper presented at the Annual Conference of the Institute of International Research on Optimal Risk Insurance and Financing of Exports, 19-20 October 1992, Düssseldorf.

Mayntz, R. and Scharpf, F.W. (1975), *Policy-Making in the German Federal Bureaucracy*, Elsevier, Amsterdam, Oxford and New York.

Mearsheimer, J.J. (1995), 'The False Promise of International Institutions', *International Security*, vol. 19, pp. 5-49.

Melitz, J. and Messerlin, P. (1987), 'Export Credit Subsidies', *Economic Policy*, vol. 4, pp. 150-75.

Messerlin, P. (1986), 'Export-credit Mercantilism à la Française', *The World Economy*, vol. 9, pp. 385-408.

Metcalfe, L. (1994), 'The weakest Links: Building Organisational Networks', in Organisation for Economic Co-operation and Development (ed.), *Regulatory Co-operation for an Interdependent World*, Paris, OECD, pp. 49-71.

Meyer, B.H. (1993), 'Ausfuhrrisikoabdeckung privater Kreditversicherer', in Bundesverband der Deutschen Industrie (ed.), *Exportkreditversicherung und Exportfinanzierung vor neuen Herausforderungen*, Dokumentation, BDI, Köln, pp. 41-55.

Mitrany, D. (1994) [1966], 'A Working Peace System', in B.F. Nelsen and A. C.-G. Stubb (eds), *The European Union*, Lynne Rienner, Boulder, pp. 77-97.

Moravcsik, A. (1989), 'Disciplining Trade Finance: the OECD Export Credit Arrangement', *International Organization*, vol. 43, pp. 173-204.

Moravcsik, A. (1993a), 'Preferences and Power in the European Community: A Liberal Intergovernmentalist Approach', *Journal of Common Market Studies*, vol. 31, pp. 473-524.

Moravcsik, A. (1993b), 'Introduction: Integrating International and Domestic Theories of International Bargaining', in P.B. Evans, H.K Jacobson and R.D.

Putnam (eds), *Double-Edged Diplomacy*, University of California Press, Berkeley, Los Angeles and London, pp. 3-42.

Morris, J. (1984), 'Reflections on the Byatt-Report', *The World Economy*, vol. 7, pp. 341-4.

Morrissey, O., Smith, B. and Horesh, E. (1992), *British Aid and International Trade*, Open University Press, Buckingham.

Morrissey, O. (1993), 'The Mixing of Aid and Trade Policies', *The World Economy*, vol. 16, pp. 69-84.

Nahrendorf, R. (1995), 'Deutschland braucht eine effiziente Außenwirtschafts- politik', *Internationale Politik*, vol. 1, pp. 46-54.

Narr, W.-D. (1989), 'Von den kommenden Segnungen der europäischen Gemeinschaft - Ansichten eines provinziellen Weltbürgers', *Leviathan*, vol. 17, pp. 574-95.

Neary, P. (1991), 'Export Subsidies and Price Competition', in E. Helpman and A. Razin (ed.), *International Trade and Trade Policy*, MIT Press, Cambridge, pp. 80-95.

Nello, S.M.S. (1985), 'EC - East European Economic Relations', *Working Paper*, no. 85/183, European University Institute, Florence.

Nello, S.M.S. (1991), *The New Europe*, Wheatsheaf, New York.

Ners, K. et al. (1992), *Moving Beyond Assistance*, Institute for EastWest Studies, New York.

North, D.C. (1990), *Institutions, Institutional Change and Economic Performance*, Cambridge University Press, Cambridge.

O'Donnell, A.T. (1989), 'The Neutrality of the Market', in R.E. Goodin and A. Reeves (eds), *Liberal Neutrality*, Routledge, London and New York, pp. 39-60.

O'Neill, A. and Coppel, J. (1992), 'The European Court of Justice Taking Rights Seriously?', *LAW Working Paper*, no. 92/21, European University Institute, Florence.

Onida, F. (1993), 'L' Intervento di Sace - Mediocredito a Sostegno delle Esportazioni Italiane nel Contesto Internazionale: Tendenze, Prospettive, Critiche, Proposte', *CESPRI Working Paper*, no. 63, Università Bocconi, Milano.

Ordeshook, P.C. (1992), *A Political Theory Primer*, Routledge, New York and London.

Organisation for Economic Co-operation and Development (1985), *Twenty Five Years of Development Cooperation*, Development Assistance Committee, Paris.

Organisation for Economic Co-operation and Development (1990), *The Export Credit Financing Systems in OECD Member Countries*, 4th edn., OECD, Paris.

Organisation for Economic Co-operation and Development (1991a), *Helsinki Package*, Manuscript, OECD, Paris.

Organisation for Economic Co-operation and Development (1991b), 'Kommuniqué der Ministertagung der Organisation für Wirtschaftliche

Zusammenarbeit und Entwicklung vom 4. und 5. Juni 1991 in Paris', *Europa-Archiv*, vol. 17, pp. 444-62.

Organisation for Economic Co-operation and Development (1992), *Arrangement on Guidelines for Officially Supported Export Credits*, OECD, Paris.

Paul, W. (1983), 'Internationale Abkommen über Mindestzinsen und Höchstlaufzeiten in der staatlich unterstützten Exportfinanzierung', in M. Feldsieper und R. Groß (eds), *Wirtschaftspolitik in weltoffener Wirtschaft*, Festschrift, Duncker & Humblot, Berlin, pp. 165-77.

Pearce, J. (1980), *Subsidized Export Credit*, Chatham House Papers, Royal Institute of International Affairs, London.

Peipers, H. (1993), 'Einführung', in Bundesverband der Deutschen Industrie (ed.), *Exportkreditversicherung und Exportfinanzierung vor neuen Herausforderungen*, Dokumentation, BDI, Köln, pp. 9-14.

Phythian, M. and Little, W. (1993), 'Administering Britain's Arms Trade', *Public Administration*, vol. 71, pp. 259-77.

Pijl, K. van der (1984), *The Making of an Atlantic Ruling Class*, Verso, London.

Pollmann, U. (1993), 'Sorglos rundum', *Die Zeit*, 12 March 1993, no. 11, p. 23.

Presse- und Informationsamt der Bundesregierung (1990), 'Erklärungen der Staats- und Regierungschefs sowie Vertretern der Europäischen Gemeinschaften zum Weltwirtschaftsgipfel in Houston', *Europa-Archiv*, vol. 16, pp. 422-38.

Prior, H. (1968), *Die Interministeriellen Ausschüsse der Bundesministerien*, Gustav Fischer, Stuttgart.

Prittwitz, V. (1984), *Umweltaußenpolitik - Grenzüberschreitende Luftverschmutzung in Europa*, Campus, Frankfurt und New York.

Project and Trade Finance (1993a), 'France - Coface', *World Export Credit Guide*, pp. 31-4.

Project and Trade Finance (1993b), 'United Kingdom - ECGD', *World Export Credit Guide*, pp. 110-5.

Prout, C. (1976), 'Finance for Developing Countries: An Essay', in A. Shonfield (ed.), *International Economic Relations of the Western World 1959-1971*, vol. 2, Oxford University Press, London, pp. 360-404.

Putnam, R. (1988), 'Diplomacy and Domestic Politics: The Logic of Two-Level Games', *International Organization*, vol. 42, pp. 427-60.

Rallo, J. (1983), 'The European Community and the Multinational Enterprise', in L. Hurwitz (ed.), *The Harmonization of European Public Policy*, Greenwood Press, Westport and London, pp. 159-82.

Rambousek, W.H. and Siegrist, M. (1993), 'Silberstreifen am düsteren Horizont', *Der Monat*, no. 11, Bankverein, Basel.

Randel, J. and German T. (eds) (1993), *The Reality of Aid*, Actionaid, London.

Rawls, J. (1972), *A Theory of Justice*, Oxford University Press, Oxford.

Ray, J.E. (1986), 'The OECD "Consensus" on Export Credits', *The World Economy,* vol. 9, pp. 295-309.

Raynauld, A. (1992), *Financing Exports to Developing Countries,* OECD, Paris.

Rieger, H.C. (1986), 'Game Theory and the Analysis of Protectionist Trends', *The World Economy,* vol. 9, pp. 171-92.

Robson, J. (1986), 'Can America win la Guerre?', *Euromoney (March),* pp. 135-41.

Rose, R. (1991), 'Comparing Forms of Comparative Analysis', *Political Studies,* vol. 39, pp. 446-62.

Rosecrance, R. (1986), *The Rise of the Trading State,* Basic Books, New York.

Rowat, M.D. (1992), 'Multilateral Approaches to Improving the Investment Climate of Developing Countries: The Cases of ICSID and MIGA', *Harvard International Law Journal,* vol. 33, pp. 103-44.

Ruberti, R. (1992), 'Export Credit Insurance under Present World Conditions with Special Reference to the Countries of East Europe', *Review of Economic Conditions in Italy,* vol. 1, pp. 53-74.

Ruggie, J.G. (1972), 'Collective Goods and Future International Collaboration', *American Political Science Review,* vol. 66, pp. 874-93.

Ruloff, D. (1987), 'Politische Risiko-Analyse und Dritte Welt: zu Begriff, Methoden, Theorien und empirischen Resultaten', *Politische Vierteljahresschrift,* vol. 28, pp. 259-79.

Sandler, T. and Cauley, J. (1977), 'The Design of Supranational Structures', *International Studies Quarterly,* vol. 21, pp. 251-76.

Scharpf, F.W. (1986), 'Policy Failure and Institutional Reform: Why should Form follow Function?', *International Social Science Journal,* vol. 108, pp. 179-89.

Scharpf, F.W. (1988), 'The Joint-Decision Trap: Lessons from German Federalism and European Integration', *Public Administration,* vol. 66, pp. 239-78.

Scharpf, F.W. (1991), 'Die Handlungsfähigkeit des Staates am Ende des zwanzigsten Jahrhunderts', *Politische Vierteljahresschrift,* vol. 32, pp. 621-34.

Scharpf, F.W. (1992), 'Can there be a stable Federal Balance in Europe?', *CES Discussion Paper,* no. 15, Nuffield College, Oxford.

Scharpf, F.W. (1994a), 'Games Real Actors Could Play: Positive and Negative Coordination in Embedded Negotiations', *Journal of Theoretical Politics,* vol. 6, pp. 27-53.

Scharpf, F.W. (1994b), 'Community and Autonomy: Multi-level Policy-making in the European Union', *Journal of European Public Policy,* vol. 1, pp. 219-42.

Scharpf, F.W. (1996), 'Negative and Positive Integration in the Political Economy of European Welfare States', in G. Marks et al. (eds), *Governance in the European Union,* Sage, London, pp. 15-39.

Schelling, T. (1980), *The Strategy of Conflict,* 2nd edn., Oxford University Press, New York.

Schmidt, V.A. (1995), 'The New World Order, Incorporated: The Rise of Business and the Decline of the Nation-State', *RSC Working Paper*, no. 5, European University Institute, Florence.

Schneider, V. (1986), *Politiknetzwerke der Chemikalienkontrolle*, de Gruyter, Berlin und New York.

Schricke, C. (1989), 'La CEE et l'OCDE à l'heure de l'Acte unique', *Revue Générale de Droit International Public*, vol. 93, pp. 797-829.

Schulte, S.,Volz, J. and Weise, C. (1991), *Die Außenwirtschaftsförderung der wichtigsten Konkurrenzländer Deutschlands*, Duncker & Humblot, Berlin.

Schulz, B. (1994), 'Das Embargo macht den Briten Sorgen', *Frankfurter Allgemeine Zeitung*, 22 March 1994, no. 68, p. 17.

Schumann, H. (1994), 'Wirtschaftliche Dimensionen der Außenpolitik', *Zeitschrift für Politik*, vol. 41, pp. 146-61.

Schwab, S. (1989), *Risiko-Management durch staatliche Exportkreditversicherung*, Peter Lang, Frankfurt am Main.

Schwartz, M. (1993), 'La Coface - Missions et Restructuration du Capital', *Les Notes Bleues de Bercy*, no. 18, pp. 1-8.

Seidl-Hohenveldern, I. (1977), *Versicherung nichtkommerzieller Risiken und die Europäische Gemeinschaft*, Heymann, Köln.

Selznick, P. (1985), 'Focusing Organizational Research on Regulation', in R.G. Noll (ed.), *Regulatory Policy and the Social Sciences*, University of California Press, Berkeley, pp. 362-7.

Senghaas, D. (1991), 'Internationale Politik jenseits des Ost-West-Konflikts', *Leviathan*, vol. 4, pp. 491-520.

Shutt, H.D. (1985), *The Myth of Free Trade*, Blackwell, Oxford.

Sickenberger, P. (1992), 'Formen staatlicher Exportförderung', in E. Dichtl and O. Issing (eds), *Exportnation Deutschland*, 2nd edn., C.H. Beck, München, pp. 101-20.

Sie Dhian Ho, M. and Werkhorst, K. (1995), 'Regional and Global Disciplining of Officially Supported Export Credit Insurance', *Journal of European Public Policy*, vol. 2, pp. 447-64.

Smith, S. (1993), 'Subsidiarity and the Co-ordination of Indirect Taxes in the European Community', *Oxford Review of Economic Policy*, vol. 9, pp. 67-94.

Snidal, D. (1985), 'Coordination versus Prisoners' Dilemma: Implications for International Cooperation and Regimes', *American Political Science Review*, vol. 79, pp. 923-42.

Snyder, F. (1993), 'The Effectiveness of European Community Law: Institutions, Processes, Tools and Techniques', *The Modern Law Review*, vol. 56, pp. 19-54.

Snyder, F. (1995), 'The Draft Constitution of the European Union: Comments on the Institutional Aspects', *RSC Working Paper*, no. 95/9, European University Institute, Florence.

Spaulding, R.M. (1991), 'German Trade Policy in Eastern Europe, 1890-1990: Preconditions for Applying International Trade Leverage', *International Organization*, vol. 45, pp. 343-68.

Spindler, J.A. (1984), *The Politics of International Credit*, The Brookings Institution, Washington, DC.

Stegemann, K. (1989), 'Policy Rivalry among Industrial States: What can we learn from Models of Strategic Trade Policy', *International Organization*, vol. 43, pp. 73-100.

Stein, A.A. (1983), 'Coordination and Collaboration: Regimes in an Anarchic World', in S.D. Krasner (ed.), *International Regimes*, Cornell University Press, Ithaca, pp. 115-40.

Stein, E. (1990), 'External Relations of the European Community: Structure and Process', in A. Clapham (ed.), *Collected Courses of the Academy of European Law*, vol. I-1, Martinus Nijhoff, Dordrecht, Boston and London, pp. 117-88.

Steinherr, A. (1985), 'Policy Coordination in the European Community', *Recherches Economiques de Louvain*, vol. 51, pp. 285-99.

Stolzenburg, G. (1992), *Schlußbericht über Exportkredite/Kreditversicherung und gemeinsamer Markt*, Manuscript, Hamburg.

Stolzenburg, G. and Moltrecht, E. (1991), 'Sicherungsmöglichkeit durch staatliche Exportkreditversicherung', *Export*, no. 3, pp. 1-34.

Stopford, J. and Strange, S. (1991), *Rival States, Rival Firms*, Cambridge University Press, Cambridge.

Strange, S. (1971), *Sterling and British Policy*, Oxford University Press, London.

Strange, S. (1986), *Casino Capitalism*, Blackwell, Oxford.

Strange, S. (1992), 'States, Firms and Diplomacy', *International Affairs*, vol. 68, pp. 1-15.

Strange, S. (1996), *The Retreat of the State*, Cambridge University Press, Cambridge.

Streit, M.E. (1993), 'European Industrial Policy: An Economic and Constitutional Challenge', *Staatswissenschaften und Staatspraxis*, vol. 4, pp. 388-416.

Taylor, K. (1984), 'A Case for Export Credit Subsidies', *The Banker*, pp. 29-37.

Taylor, P. (1983), *The Limits of European Integration*, Croom Helm, London and Sydney.

Taylor, P. (1987), 'Prescribing for the Reform of International Organization: the Logic of Arguments for Change', *Review of International Studies*, vol. 13, pp. 19-38.

Taylor, P. (1990), 'Co-ordination in International Organization', in A.J.R. Groom and P. Taylor (eds), *Frameworks for International Co-operation*, Pinter, London, pp. 29-43.

Thomas, G. (1982), 'Les Opérations concernant les Biens d'Équipement et leur Financement par des Crédits Fournisseurs à Moyen et Long Terme', in G.

Défosse (ed.), *Les Exportations Françaises et leur Financement*, Presses Universitaires de France, Paris, pp. 125-49.

Tomkins, A. (1997), 'Intelligence and Government', *Parliamentary Affairs*, vol. 50, pp. 109-29.

Touval, S. (1994), 'Why the U.N. Fails', *Foreign Affairs*, vol. 73, pp. 44-57.

Toye, J. and Clark, G. (1986), 'The Aid and Trade Provision: Origins, Dimensions and Possible Reforms', *Development Policy Review*, vol. 4, pp. 291-313.

Tsebelis, G. (1990), *Nested Games*, University of California Press, Berkeley.

Tudyka, K. (1990), 'Politische Ökonomie der internationalen Beziehungen' in V. Rittberger (ed.), *Theorien der Internationalen Beziehungen*, Westdeutscher Verlag, Opladen, pp. 130-50.

Tuffraut-Barriant, D. (1993), *Second and Final Report to the Policy Coordination Group for Export Credits and the Formulation of Common Principles for Premium Systems and Cover Policy*, Manuscript, Brussels.

Tversky, A. and Kahneman, D. (1986), 'The Framing of Decisions and the Psychology of Choice', in J. Elster (ed.), *Rational Choice*, Blackwell, Oxford, pp. 123-41.

Underdal, A. (1991), 'International Cooperation and Political Engineering', in S.S. Nagel (ed.), *Global Policy Studies*, Macmillan, London, pp. 98-120.

Union des Confédérations de l'Industries et des Employeurs d'Europe (1992a), *Credit Insurance in the Context of the Single Market*, Manuscript, UNICE, Brussels.

Union des Confédérations de l'Industries et des Employeurs d'Europe (1992b), *UNICE preliminary Comments on future Community Rules applying to Short-Term Export Credit Insurance*, Manucript, UNICE, Brussels.

Uvin, P. (1993), 'Do as I Say, Not as I Do: The Limits of Political Conditionality', *European Journal of Development Research*, vol. 5, pp. 63-83.

Vaubel, R. (1986), 'A Public Choice Approach to International Organization', *Public Choice*, vol. 51, pp. 39-57.

Waldron, J. (1989), 'Legislation and Moral Neutrality', in R.E. Goodin and A. Reeves (eds), *Liberal Neutrality*, Routledge, London and New York, pp. 61-83.

Wallén, A. (1984), 'Export Credit Subsidization and the Consensus Arrangement', *Aussenwirtschaft*, vol. 39, pp. 261-9.

Wallén, A. (1986), 'Some Comments on the Present Consensus Arrangement and its Implications to World Trade', *The Geneva Papers on Risk and Insurance*, vol. 11, pp. 269-73.

Wallén, A. (1987), 'The OECD Arrangement on Guidelines for Officially Supported Export Credit: Past and Future', in R. M. Rodriguez (ed.), *The Export-Import Bank at Fifty: The International Environment and the Institution's Role*, Lexington Books, Lexington, pp. 97-104.

Waltz, K. (1979), *Theory of International Politics*, Addison-Wesley, Reading, MA.

Walzenbach, G.P.E. (1994), 'Policy Co-ordination and Institutional Choice in the Case of Export Credit', Paper presented at the 22nd Annual Joint Sessions of the European Consortium for Political Research, 17-22 April 1994, Madrid.

Wassenberg, A.F.P. (1990), 'Games within Games: On the Politics of Association and Dissociation in European Industrial Policy-Making', in B. Marin (ed.), *Governance and Generalized Exchange: Self-Organizing Policy Networks in Action*, Campus and Westview, Frankfurt am Main and Boulder, pp. 255-88.

Weis, W. (1990), *Hermesbürgschaften: ein Instrument deutscher Außenpolitik?*, Tuduv, München.

Wielemans, R. (1985), 'Les Assureurs-Crédit Publics face à la Crise Internationale', *Tome*, vol. 24, pp. 25-41.

Williamson, O. (1975), *Markets and Hierarchies*, The Free Press, New York.

Wilson, J.Q. (1973), *Political Organizations*, Basic Books, New York.

Windhoff-Héritier, A. (1985), 'Politikarena und Policy Netz - Zum analytischen Nutzen zweier Begriffe', *Discussion Paper*, Internationales Institut für Vergleichende Gesellschaftsforschung, Berlin.

Xafa, M. (1987), 'Export Credits and the Debt Crisis', *Finance and Development*, vol. 24, pp. 19-22.

Yarbrough, B.V. and Yarbrough, R.M. (1992), *Cooperation and Governance in International Trade*, Princeton University Press, Princeton.

Young, O.R. (1989), *International Cooperation*, Cornell University Press, Ithaca and London.

Young, O.R. (1994), *International Governance*, Cornell University Press, Ithaca and London.

Zürn, M. (1996), 'Die Implementation internationaler Umweltregime und "positive Integration"', *MPIFG Discussion Paper*, no. 96/3, Max-Planck-Institut für Gesellschaftsforschung, Köln.

Zysman, J. (1978), 'The French State in the International Economy', in P.J. Katzenstein (ed.), *Between Power and Plenty*, University of Wisconsin Press, Madison, pp. 255-93.

Zysman, J. (1983), *Governments, Markets, and Growth*, Cornell University Press, Ithaca and London.

Index